'The origins of football's many codes and their complex relationship to each other has been one of sporting history's great grey areas, dominated by hearsay and invention. No longer. Tony Collins' cool and illuminating *How Football Began* brings range, precision and sources to bear on the matter. As is often the case, the truths that emerge are infinitely more interesting than the myths they dispel.'

David Goldblatt, Author of *The Ball is Round: A Global History of Football* and *The Game of Our Lives*

HOW FOOTBALL BEGAN

This ambitious and fascinating history considers why, in the space of sixty years between 1850 and 1910, football grew from a marginal and unorganised activity to become the dominant winter entertainment for millions of people around the world.

The book explores how the world's football codes – soccer, rugby league, rugby union, American, Australian, Canadian and Gaelic – developed as part of the commercialised leisure industry in the nineteenth century. Football, however and wherever it was played, was a product of the second industrial revolution, the rise of the mass media, and the spirit of the age of the masses.

Important reading for students of sports studies, history, sociology, development and management, this book is also a valuable resource for scholars and academics involved in the study of football in all its forms, as well as an engrossing read for anyone interested in the early history of football.

Tony Collins is Emeritus Professor of History in the International Centre for Sports History and Culture at De Montfort University, UK. His previous books include *Rugby's Great Split*, *Rugby League in Twentieth Century Britain*, *A Social History of English Rugby Union* and *The Oval World* – each of which won the Lord Aberdare prize for sports history book of the year – as well as his global history *Sport in Capitalist Society*.

HOW FOOTBALL BEGAN

A Global History of How the World's Football Codes Were Born

Tony Collins

Routledge
Taylor & Francis Group

LONDON AND NEW YORK

First published 2019
by Routledge
2 Park Square, Milton Park, Abingdon, Oxon OX14 4RN

and by Routledge
711 Third Avenue, New York, NY 10017

Routledge is an imprint of the Taylor & Francis Group, an informa business

British Library Cataloguing-in-Publication Data
A catalogue record for this book is available from the British Library

Library of Congress Cataloging-in-Publication Data
A catalog record for this book has been requested

ISBN: 978-1-138-03874-5 (hbk)
ISBN: 978-1-138-03875-2 (pbk)
ISBN: 978-1-315-17721-2 (ebk)

Typeset in Bembo
by Apex CoVantage, LLC

The cover of the paperback version of this book is based on the cover of
the 1867 *Routledge Handbook of Football*.

CONTENTS

PLATES

INTRODUCTION

Football has got to do with everything.

Arnold Bennett, 1911[1]

How did football start? Why did the modern codes of football – Association, American, Australian, Canadian, Gaelic, Rugby League and Rugby Union – all emerge within barely a generation during the nineteenth century? And why did association football eclipse all of them to become a truly global game?

These questions are the starting point for *How Football Began*. It charts the rise of football from its origins, through the creation of the first clubs, its emergence as a mass spectator sport to it becoming a world game on the eve of World War One. It explains why football divided into Association and rugby codes, and how the rugby code itself split into league and union, Australian, American, Canadian and Gaelic. It discusses the false starts of women's football and the obstacles women faced to play the game. And it examines the ways in which soccer spread across Europe and Latin America before World War One.

As the different varieties of the game expanded across the world they were shaped by the same fault-lines. Wherever it was played, football was haunted by divisions over amateurism and professionalism, and how to respond to the challenge of becoming a mass spectator sport. Nationalism, whether the unacknowledged everyday British nationalism of much of the game or the explicit nationalism of Gaelic football, was etched into DNA of the sport. Myth-making and invented traditions were common to all forms of football, as the game developed a narrative that would give it legitimacy and a role in the cultural life of its nation.

Moreover, the book aims to emphasise the incredible speed at which football emerged and became part of everyday life. In the space of two generations at the end of the Victorian era the sport went from a handful of clubs to become part of the lifeblood of millions of people around the world. No form of entertainment had ever risen so rapidly in such a short space of time. Football's 'shock of the new' prefigured that of the cinema and pop music in the twentieth century. The sport had become an integral part of capitalism's second industrial revolution, a mass entertainment spectacle that seemed to replicate the competition and vicissitudes of everyday life in the great industrial cities.

How Football Began also takes a different perspective to most histories of the football codes, because it looks at football as the Victorians did: as a single game that was played under different rules. The huge differences we see today in the various types of football did not exist in Victorian times. Until around 1880 it was common for players and teams to switch between one set of rules and another, sometimes on a weekly basis. As a new social phenomenon that transformed the leisure lives of millions of men and women, football had the same cultural and economic impact on society regardless of the shape of the ball or the number of players in a team.

It also offers a new approach by treating football as a transnational phenomenon, and in particular as a product of the British Empire and the wider Anglophone world. From its inception, football in the nineteenth century was part of an English-speaking world that was shrinking due to the invention of the telegraph, the steam ship and the mass-circulation press. Discussions, reports and news about football circulated across national boundaries. In America, Walter Camp studied the rulebooks of the different codes of football around the world. Melbourne's William Hammersley visited the Football Association in the 1880s to persuade them to try Australian Rules. Albert Baskerville corresponded with American football administrators before leading his pioneering New Zealand rugby league team to Britain in 1907. During World War One female Australian Rules players in Perth could read about women soccer players in Preston. From its inception in the mid-nineteenth century, football saw itself as part of the transnational culture of the British Empire, and from the early twentieth century its footprint quickly became global.

Most of all, the book will unravel the social and economic reasons for the game's rise throughout the world and to seek to explain why the game came to mean so much to so many people, how it could bring people together and tear them apart, make women sing for joy and make grown men weep openly on the streets.

It is not just about football. It is about the society that created it and which football in turn helped to fashion.

Note

1 Arnold Bennett, *The Card* (London: Methuen, 1911), p. 134.

1

THE FAILURE OF THE FOOTBALL ASSOCIATION

It has been proposed to hold a sort of 'Football Congress' consisting of representatives from the public schools and clubs, who should be empowered to draw up an equitable body of rules adapted for universal use. . . . Until we have a universally acknowledged and accepted code of rules for the regulation of both public and private matches, football can never attain the proud position among the national sports of England [as] the 'cricket of the winter months'.

—Sporting Gazette, 1863[1]

In the history of sport, few organisations have begun so unsuccessfully as the Football Association (FA). Its original goal of uniting all football clubs under one code of rules was a complete failure. Just four years after its formation, even its own members considered winding it up. And for the first decade and a half of its existence, it played second fiddle to rugby football. This was not an auspicious start for what would become the world game.

The FA was founded on 26 October 1863, when representatives of eleven clubs and schools in London answered an advertisement in the weekly *Bell's Life in London* for a meeting 'for the purpose of promoting the adoption of a general code of rules for football'.[2] Held at the Freemason's Tavern in central London's Great Queen Street, the meeting was intended to be the culmination of a discussion that started in the letters page of *The Times* at the beginning of October, when a pupil of Eton College called for 'the framing of set rules for the game of football to be played everywhere' and that the captains of the football teams of the public schools, universities and 'one or two London clubs' should 'frame rules for one universal game'.[3] An animated discussion ensued, with letters from current and former pupils of Harrow, Charterhouse, Winchester and Rugby schools, each largely agreeing with the sentiment but emphasising the superiority of their own school's code of rules.[4] Joining the debate, the *Sporting Gazette* backed the call for a single set of rules, arguing:

> where would be the interest in the [cricket] contests between the elevens of Surrey, Sussex, Kent, Yorkshire, Nottingham and Cambridgeshire if the representatives of these counties has their own private opinion respecting the laws of the game and the duties of umpires?[5]

Despite this animated debate, when the meeting finally convened at the Freemason's Tavern none of the public schools were represented, with the exception of Charterhouse, whose football captain Benjamin Hartshorne told the delegates that his school wouldn't join the new organisation until the other public schools did. This boycott did not merely deprive the new association of prestige. It also made the framing of a set of commonly accepted rules almost impossible. Each of the leading English public schools – Eton, Harrow, Charterhouse, Rugby, Winchester, Westminster and St Paul's – played football according to its own unique set of rules. Eton even had two codes. One for its 'Wall Game' played against a wall in a narrow strip of land five metres wide and 110 metres long, and another for the Field Game, played on a more familiar open pitch. Each school differed in its concept of offside, the extent to which the ball could be handled, the method of scoring, the shape and size of the ball, and much else besides. A school's method of playing football was a matter of intense pride to past and present pupils, and ideas about the rules of the game were a symbol of each school's sense of superiority.

The formation of the FA was not the first attempt to design a single code of rules for football. In 1856 the Cambridge University Foot Ball Club, which appears to have been set up in 1846 by former pupils of Eton, Harrow, Rugby and Shrewsbury, had printed a set of rules based on the principle of taking the best of each school's rules.[6] These eleven rules allowed any player to catch the ball and prescribed a liberal offside rule that put a player onside if there were three defenders between him and the goal. These rules gained no support outside of the university and did not deter students from forming separate university clubs devoted to Eton (in 1856), Harrow (1863) and Rugby (1857) football rules. In 1859 the editor of *Bell's Life* suggested adopting a single code of rules for football (he proposed those of the Eton field game) but quickly abandoned the suggestion after receiving 'many other letters on this subject by public schoolmen, but they are so mixed up with abuse of each other that we consider them better unpublished, and the correspondence closed'.[7] Other writers, such as the Uppingham School headmaster J.C. Thring, the journalist John Dyer Cartwright and a number of pseudonymous authors also campaigned for football to be played under a universal set of rules.[8]

All of the men who gathered at the Freemason's Tavern had been educated in the traditions of public school football.[9] Their aim was to find a way of framing the schoolboy rules that would allow them to play as adults and popularise the sport among like-minded young middle-class men, thus ensuring that football became part of the social and business networks of the growing professional classes. But now it came to deciding on a universal code the delegates were hamstrung. Not only did they know that their decisions would be ignored by the public schools, but they themselves were no less divided about how to codify a commonly accepted set of rules.

At least three of the ten clubs in attendance, Blackheath Football Club (FC), Blackheath Proprietary School and the Blackheath-based Perceval House, were well-known adherents of Rugby's School's football rules. Barnes FC, the club of the FA's founding secretary, Hull-born solicitor Ebenezer Cobb Morley, regularly played under rugby rules, as did the Civil Service club. Indeed, it was not unusual for adult clubs to play under different rules from week to week in order to have regular matches. Moreover, each delegate was committed to his own ideas about the best way to play football. So when they re-convened in November to discuss the rules they became embroiled in discussions about the efficacy of crossbars, the desirability of 'fair catching' and the dangers of unrestrained deliberate kicking of shins, otherwise known as hacking. Such was the intensity of the discussion that it was decided to hold a further, third meeting the following week to arrive at the 'final settlement of the laws'.[10]

But the next meeting settled nothing. The draft set of rules presented to that third meeting by Ebenezer Morley was something of a football Frankenstein's monster, hurriedly bolting together various features of the different public school codes. Rule 9 allowed players 'to run with the ball towards his adversaries' goal if he makes a fair catch or catches the ball on the first bound', while Rule 13 permitted a player catching the ball directly from a kick or on its first bounce to pass it by hand to another player. These were two of the key elements of football as played at Rugby School, as was Rule 10, which allowed defenders to 'be at liberty to charge, hold, trip or hack' the ball-carrier. Yet the very next rule stated that 'neither tripping nor hacking shall be allowed'.[11]

If this wasn't baffling enough, the meeting then plunged into further confusion when Morley, supported by John Alcock, whose education at Harrow School made him no friend of Rugby School football rules, informed the delegates that he had decided to repudiate his own draft rules. Instead, he proposed that the FA should adopt a new code that had recently been drawn up by students at Cambridge University, which Alcock had only just seen before the meeting.[12] These rules made no mention of carrying the ball but did forbid tripping and hacking. In a state of bewilderment, the delegates voted both for Morley's original draft and the Cambridge rules.[13] No satisfactory explanation was ever given by Morley and Alcock for their unexpected volte face but it is possible that they felt that the social cachet of aligning the FA with Cambridge University might compensate for their failure to persuade the public schools to join the FA.

A few days later the meeting re-convened yet again and amidst considerable acrimony voted to adopt a revised version of the Cambridge rules that removed any ambiguity about hacking or carrying the ball. Blackheath's F.M. Campbell appealed for the decision to be delayed until further discussions could take place but was slapped down by Alcock and Arthur Pember, the FA president. Realising that it had been the victim of a coup, Blackheath resigned from the FA, little more than five weeks after being a founding member.[14] Eight years later, the club would become one of the founders of the Rugby Football Union (RFU).

Despite getting their own way, Morley and Alcock's rules were something of a dead letter. Indeed, when 'first match under the rules of the Football Association' took place on 19 December 1863, Barnes FC won it by scoring six tries to Richmond's nil.[15] As with Blackheath, Richmond would also abandon the FA and become a founding member of the RFU. As the Barnes' result shows, the FA's initial rules bore little resemblance to modern soccer. Their six tries were a consequence of FA Rule 7, which allowed the attacking team to touch down the ball behind their opponents' goal line for the right for a free kick at goal, just as in rugby. The FA's 1866 rules even allowed matches to be decided on the number of touchdowns scored if the goal score was equal (rugby did not allow tries to be counted in the score until 1886). Rule 8 legislated for a 'fair catch' where a player could catch the ball in the air before it had bounced and, again as in rugby, make a 'mark' to gain a free kick. Rule 6 also bore a strong resemblance to rugby in that any player in front of the ball was offside. Throw-ins had to be taken at right angles to the pitch as in rugby's line-out, and there were no cross bar on the goals.[16] Even the Royal Engineers' club, which would appear in four of the first seven FA Cup finals, played under their own rules that allowed running with the ball. Handling the ball by outfield players was not completely outlawed by the FA until 1870. It would only be through a long process of trial and error that association football, as the FA's version of football was called, came to resemble modern soccer.

Having failed in its mission to unite all football clubs under one set of rules, the FA's fortunes plummeted. At its first anniversary, the FA minute book noted that 'no business was conducted' and its committee did not meet again until February 1866. By 1867 membership numbered just ten clubs, barely half the nineteen that were members in December 1863.[17] When John Alcock's younger brother Charles published the first edition of his *Football Annual* in 1868 he recorded thirty clubs using the FA's rules but forty-five playing Rugby School rules, despite the fact that no governing body yet existed for rugby-playing clubs. To no-one's great surprise, or interest, at the FA's 1867 annual meeting Morley suggested that they 'should seriously consider that night whether it were worthwhile to continue the association or dissolve it'.[18] However, the other five delegates at the meeting were not quite as pessimistic as Morley and concluded that it would be worthwhile for the association to continue.

Their optimism was vindicated. Within a generation, the FA's brand of football would become a social, cultural and commercial juggernaut, the most popular sport the world had ever known. But it would also be almost unrecognisable to that small group of men who had met at the Freemason's Tavern.

Notes

1 *Sporting Gazette*, 10 October 1863.
2 Attendees listed in *Bell's Life in London*, 31 October 1863. The advertisement appears in the 17 October issue. For the documentary record of the FA's rules and committee minutes, see Tony Brown, *The Football Association 1863–83: A Source Book* (Nottingham: Soccerdata, 2011).
3 'Etonensis', *The Times*, 5 October 1863.
4 *The Times*, 6, 7, 9 and 10 October 1863.
5 *Sporting Gazette*, 10 October 1863.
6 The flimsy history of early football at Cambridge can be found in Graham Curry, 'The Trinity Connection: An Analysis of the Role of Members of Cambridge University in the Development of Football in the Mid-Nineteenth Century', *The Sports Historian*, vol. 22 (November 2002), 46–74.
7 *Bell's Life*, 2 and 16 January 1859.
8 See, for example, Graham Curry, 'The Contribution of John Dyer Cartwright to the Football Rules Debate', *Soccer and Society*, vol. 4, no.1 (Spring 2003), 71–86. Thring and other pseudonymous authors can be found in the *Sporting Gazette*, October to December 1863, *passim*.
9 For biographical details of the founders, see Any Mitchell, *The Men Who Wrote the Laws of Association Football* at www.scottishsporthistory.com/sports-history-news-and-blog/the-men-who-wrote-the-laws-of-association-football, accessed 21 December 2017.

10 *Bell's Life*, 21 November 1863.
11 *Bell's Life*, 28 November 1863.
12 *Bell's Life*, 5 December 1863.
13 The 1863 Cambridge football rules are in the *Sporting Gazette*, 21 November 1863.
14 *Bell's Life*, 5 December 1863.
15 *Sporting Gazette*, 26 December 1863.
16 The rules are in *Bell's Life*, 5 December 1863.
17 Adrian Harvey, *Football: The First Hundred Years* (Abingdon: Routledge, 2006), p. 159. *Bell's Life*, 12 December 1863.
18 Quoted in Harvey, *Football: The First Hundred Years,* p. 162.

2

BEFORE THE BEGINNING

Folk football

> Then strip lads, and to it, though sharp be the weather,
> And if, by mischance, you should happen to fall,
> There are worse things in life than a rumble on heather,
> And life is itself but a game at football.
>
> —Sir Walter Scott, 1815[1]

The high social status of the men who formed the FA in 1863 would have come as a surprise to most of those who had played the game in previous centuries. Before the industrial revolution football was largely seen as plebeian entertainment, a folk practice that was played regularly on religious holidays and rural festivals. The first written reference to it in Britain appears to be William Fitzstephen's preface to his 1174 biography of Thomas à Becket, which describes a Shrovetide game of ball between London apprentices. In the first decade of the fourteenth century Nicholas Farndon, the lord mayor of London, banned football because it caused 'certain tumults', and in 1365 Edward III declared a national ban on football and handball because they distracted the population from archery practice.[2] Richard II re-imposed the ban in 1388, stating that 'servants and laboured shall have bows and arrows, and use the same on Sundays and holidays, and leave all playing at ball whether handball or football'. It was the same in Scotland, where the first four King Jameses all banned the sport. Yet by Shakespeare's time, football had become such a part of national culture that references to it in literature were not uncommon, perhaps most notably in *King Lear* when the Earl of Kent taunts a servant as a 'base football player'.

PLATE 1   Folk football at Kingston–upon–Thames, Shrove Tuesday 1846 (*Illustrated London News*, 28 February 1846)

Britain was just one of many countries around the world that throughout history have played games we today would call football. In France, 'soule' occupied much the same place in popular culture as football did in Britain, while in Italy 'Calcio Fiorentino' became a major feature of life in Florence as part of the celebrations of Epiphany and Lent in the fifteenth and sixteenth centuries. But these were merely the most well-known European versions of the game. The simple truth is that most cultures in most regions of the world have played games with a ball that is propelled by hand and foot towards some form of goal. From the Americas to Aboriginal Australia, humans have found limitless pleasure, unbounded fascination and deep satisfaction in playing and watching these games, which they may or may not have called football. In China, Cuju, or Ts'u Chu, emerged from a form of military training as a ceremonial game of the royal court under the Han Dynasty and survived in various forms for 1,500 years. Women occasionally played and apparently in its later years professionals were engaged to play the game. But as with many ancient sports, Cuju was a largely ceremonial game, played at the gatherings of the elite. Others, like Ulama and the various ball games of Mesoamerica, had a religious or ritual significance. But none of these games were either a direct ancestor or an inspiration for the modern games of football; humanity's endless desire to play with a ball has always been shaped by the social and economic characteristics of the society it created.

In Britain, traditional football was a product of the rhythm and structures of life in a rural society. Matches were staged as local customs during the ebbs and flows of an agricultural economy. Festival games held across Britain and Ireland at Christmas or Shrovetide were often occasions for teams of hundreds to attempt to carry, kick and throw a ball to goals at either end of a village or town. The Derby Shrovetide game reputedly involved 1,000 men, the Sedgefield game 800, Diss Common in Norfolk 600, while at Alnwick in Northumberland 200 men lined up for the annual match. With such numbers, the playing was similarly large. Goals were three miles apart for the Ashbourne game in Derbyshire, at Workington they were set at Curwen's Hall at one end of the town and the harbour at the other, while Whitehaven's goals were set at the docks and a wall outside of the town. With local pride at stake, few rules and often challenging terrain to navigate, including rivers and streams, the risks of physical injury were considerable, further contributing to football's reputation for violence and disorder.[3]

But this was not the only type of football to be played. Some were far more organised and based on clearly defined rules. In 1729 Derbyshire played Gloucestershire in Islington for five guineas; sixty years later the stakes had increased somewhat when Cumberland played Westmoreland in a twenty-two-a-side match at London's Kennington Common for a thousand guineas.[4] In East Anglia from the fifteenth to the eighteenth century 'camp-ball' was played on dedicated pitches, known as 'camping closes' where ten- or fifteen-a-side teams fought to carry the ball to their opponents' goal.[5] 'Hurling to goals' was played in Cornwall between teams of fifteen to thirty players and, like camp-ball, allowed forms of blocking (not unlike modern American football) and required a player to throw the ball to a teammate when tackled.[6] Nor was traditional football always entirely restricted to men. In October 1726 women played a six-a-side match on Bath's bowling green, married women played unmarried in Inveresk in Midlothian in the late 1700s, and as late as 1866 and 1888 women took part in the annual Uppies versus Doonies match at Kirkwall in Orkney Islands.[7]

Although many of the larger matches required the support of the local landowners, the large numbers who gathered to play or watch often aroused suspicion or concern in the authorities. As early as 1480 villagers protested against the enclosure of land in Bethersden in Kent by occupying it and playing with 'foteballes'.[8] In 1649 fears that a royalist revolt lay behind 'a great Foot-ball play near Norwich, where the people were very tumultuous and disorderly' proved well founded when part of the crowd declared for Charles I.[9] And as the enclosure of common lands intensified in the eighteenth century, football again became a pretext for crowds to gather in protest, such as at White Roding, Essex, in 1724, or at Kettering in 1740 when a match served as a pretext for the attempted destruction of a local mill.[10] From its earliest times in Britain, football was always, as noted by the early chronicler of sport Joseph Strutt, 'much in vogue among the common people of England'.[11]

By the time that Strutt wrote this in 1801 football was increasingly under attack from the economic and social forces that were transforming Britain from a rural agricultural society into an urban industrial power. Enclosures of common lands led to more than 6 million acres of land taken into private ownership between 1750 and 1830, sweeping away many of the traditional customs and leisure activities of village life. As a Suffolk vicar explained in 1844, his parishioners now had

> no village green or common for active sports. Some thirty years ago, I am told, they had a right to a playground in a particular field, at certain seasons of the year, and were then celebrated for their football; but somehow or other this right has been lost and the field is now under the plough.[12]

In countless other towns and villages strenuous efforts were made by businessmen, religious evangelicals and moral reformers to stamp out football games that caused town centres to close or violated the Sabbatarian's sense of good order. This was formalised in 1835 when the Highways Act banned football being played on roads.

Not all footballers went quietly. Attempts to stop Derby's Shrovetide football match being played were regularly frustrated by determined opposition before it was finally repressed in the 1850s. Football games continued to be played informally in streets, at festivals and during holiday times such as wakes. The 1842 Royal Commission on Children in Mines and Manufactories noted that football was played widely in the West Riding coal fields. These types of football were essentially traditional rural recreations, which persisted in a similar way to quoits, cudgels and Maypole dancing. Occasionally organised football matches did take place in the first half of the nineteenth century. In 1829 a fifteen-a-side match was played for prize money of £6 between the Leicestershire villages of Wigston and Blaby. Rochdale staged games between teams dubbed the 'Body Guards' and the 'Fear Noughts' in the 1840s. On Good Friday 1852 a match between Enderby in Leicestershire and Holmfirth in West Yorkshire was played for £20 at Sheffield's Hyde Park.[13] But these were one-off

events arranged for specific occasions – there were no organised competitions or nationally agreed rules other than what had been decided for that
particular match.

Organised football matches were few and far between during the first
half of the nineteenth century. Even the most assiduous researchers have
been able to locate only fifty-eight organised matches played between 1830
and 1859.[11] We have no way of measuring the extent to which the playing
of football declined during the industrial revolution, because no records
were kept and newspaper reports are too fragmentary, but the sheer weight
of anecdotal evidence confirms the 1842 judgement of the *Nottingham
Review* that 'the field games of old England have almost entirely passed away.
Football, throwing the quoit, spell and knur, archery have become obso-
lete and forgotten, like an old fashion in apparel, or a custom known only
by a name'.[15] The game's decline was recognised by footballers themselves.
When the landlord of the Hare and Hounds Inn at Bolton offered a forty-
pound cheese to the winners of a match in January 1847, it was intended 'to
revive the old sport of foot ball'.[16] The short-lived gentleman's club Surrey
FC in 1849 was created partly in recognition of the atrophy of football (and
wrestling) over the previous decades:

> wrestling and football play continued to dwindle, until at length
> Good Friday became the only day upon which they were brought
> into operation. . . . its practice had been discontinued in the neigh-
> bourhood of the metropolis. The only locality where the game
> could now be said to exist near to London was that of Kingston

reported *Bell's Life*, which went to say that the aim of the club 'was to restore
the equally healthful game of football to that district'.[17]

The position of football before the 1850s can best be gauged by the
fact that sports weeklies such as *Bell's Life*, *The Field* and dozens of local
daily newspapers carried regular reports of cricket, boxing, horse racing and
many other sports – but almost nothing on football. Newspaper coverage
of the game was confined to short and highly irregular reports or advertisements. But that should not be surprising. Outside of the public schools,
football was essentially an informal leisure practice or folk custom that had
no connection to the highly organised sport of the late Victorian era.[18]
Insofar as we know anything about the games that were played then, there
is nothing to suggest any connection between them and modern football's
rules, playing styles, organisation or cultural meaning. When football did
emerge as a mass spectator sport in the last third of the nineteenth century
it had been reinvented. Outward appearances can often lead to continuities

being imagined where none exist. The fact that a penguin walks upright on its hind legs does not make it an ancestor of humans.

How could football fail to become a major spectator sport before 1860? Why was it that when cricket, boxing and horse racing codified their rules and became commercial spectator attractions in the eighteenth century, football remained a marginal sport? Unlike these sports, football lacked the aristocratic patronage of the 'Fancy' – the leisured rich who provided the financial backing to sport in the Georgian era – and was not viewed as a sport that could be commercially exploited through gambling. Its lowly social status and reputation for violence precluded its developing like cricket because young aristocrats would simply not play alongside the common people. Its ephemeral nature made it unsuitable for gambling, the engine that drove the transformation of cricket, boxing and other eighteenth-century sports. And in striking contrast to the Victorian era, there were no clubs formed to play football, underlining its lack of appeal to the emerging associational culture of the urban middle classes. Without aristocratic patronage or middle-class social networks, there was no force that could standardise the rules of football or impose a governing structure, as the Marylebone Cricket Club (MCC) had done in cricket or the Jockey Club in horse racing.

Moreover, the most popular and therefore the most commercialised sports of the Georgian era were based on individual professionals: the boxer, the jockey, the pedestrian walker or runner and the cricket professional. With the exception of cricket, eighteenth- and early nineteenth-century sport was based on individuals competing against each other. And even though cricket is a team game, its dominance by aristocratic amateurs on and off the field, together with the fact that no more than a handful of professionals were employed by teams, meant that it did not need a large market of regular paying spectators to financially sustain its teams. The economic basis for the development of the modern football codes – a large population with significant leisure time and disposable income, plus a national transport and communication network to facilitate playing and promoting the game – would not emerge in Britain until the last three decades of the nineteenth century.

Notes

1 Sir Walter Scott, *The Lifting of the Banner*, written in 1815 for a football match between Ettrick and Yarrow.

2 The best summary of the early history of football games remains Francis P. Magoun's 'Football in Medieval England and in Middle-English Literature', *American Historical Review*, vol. 35, no. 1 (October 1929), pp. 33–45, from which this paragraph's references are taken.

3 Hugh Hornby, *Uppies and Downies: The Extraordinary Football Games of Britain* (London: English Heritage, 2008).

4 *Daily Journal*, 13 September 1729; Issue 2710. The Cumberland match is recalled in *Bell's Life*, 7 October 1849.

5 Edward Moor, *Suffolk Words and Phrases: or, An Attempt to Collect the Lingual Localisms of that County* (London: Woodbridge, 1823), pp. 63–6. David Dymond, 'A Lost Social Institution: The Camping Close', *Rural History*, vol. 1, no. 2 (October 1990), pp. 165–92.

6 Richard Carew, *Survey of Cornwall* (1710) (London: Faulder edition, 1811), p. 197.

7 *Mist's Weekly Journal*, 8 October 1726. *Bolton Chronicle*, 28 February 1846. John D.M. Robertson, *The Kirkwall Ba'. Between the Water and the Wall* (Edinburgh: Dunedin Academic Press, 2005), pp. 115–21.

8 Heather Falvey, *Custom, Resistance and Politics: Local Experiences of Improvement in Early Modern England* (unpublished PhD thesis, University of Warwick 2007), p. 360.

9 *Severall Proceedings in Parliament*, 28 November 1650–5 December 1650.

10 Derek Birley, *Sport and the Making of Britain* (Manchester: Manchester University Press, 1993), p. 115. E.P. Thompson, 'The Moral Economy of the English Crowd in the Eighteenth Century', *Past & Present*, vol. 50, no. 1 (1971), p. 116.

11 Joseph Strutt, *The Sports and Pastimes of the People of England* (1801) (London: Methuen edition, 1903), p. 93.

12 Quoted in Eric Hobsbawm, *Industry and Empire* (London: Weidenfeld & Nicolson, 1968), p. 79.

13 *Leicester Chronicle*, 14 February 1829. *Bell's Life*, 26 December 1841, 2 January 1842 and 28 March 1852.

14 Adrian Harvey, *Football: The First Hundred Years* (Abingdon: Routledge, 2005), pp. 60–1 and 64. Graham Curry has made similar observations in 'The Origins of Football Debate: Comments on Adrian Harvey's Historiography', *International Journal of the History of Sport*, vol. 31, no. 17 (2014), p. 2160.

15 *Nottingham Review*, 14 October 1842. The best account of this decline remains Robert Malcolmson, *Popular Recreations in English Society 1700–1850* (Oxford: Oxford University Press, 1973), pp. 138–45.

16 *Bell's Life*, 26 December 1847.

17 *Bell's Life*, 7 October 1849.

18 For a contrary view see Peter Swain, 'The Origins of Football Debate: Football and Cultural Continuity, 1857–1859', *International Journal of the History of Sport*, vol. 35, no. 5, pp. 631–49.

3

THE GENTLEMAN'S GAME

If cricket on an Eton Field trained up our youth for Waterloo,
Sure Rugby's noble game has sealed the fate of many a battle too.
"Sunk in ease" cry croaking ravens, England's nodding to her fall,
Know 'tis false, ye tim'rous cravens, For her sons still love football.
—*The Goal*, 1873[1]

There was, however, one section of British society where football had become hugely popular during the first half of the nineteenth century: its elite private schools. By the time of the Great Reform Act of 1832, which gave the vote to the middle classes, football was on its way to becoming an essential part of the education of young men educated at Britain's public schools, as the elite private schools were known. Eton, Charterhouse, Harrow, Rugby, Westminster and Winchester each developed their own distinctive versions of the game. The undermining of football's plebeian traditions by the industrial revolution allowed the public schools and the middle classes to embrace football as a symbol of the new ideology of Muscular Christianity.

Freed from the physical and social dangers of playing football against those they saw as their social inferiors, these upper-middle class school-boys took up the game with gusto. This should not be surprising. Public schools were often located in places where folk football had a long history. In the town of Rugby in the English midlands, for example, football had been played every New Year's Day since the early 1700s and as late as 1845 'six tailors of Rugby' challenged teams in the area to a match for a prize of £5.[2] For school authorities, football was welcomed as an outlet for the excess physical energies of adolescent youths. For the boys, the violence with which they played was a source of pride: 'the savage "rouge" or the wild broken bully, would cause a vast sensation amongst our agricultural friends', an Old Etonian remembered in the 1860s.[3]

By the middle of the nineteenth century, the public schools had imbued football, and also cricket, with a moral purpose and educational role that would have been unthinkable in the gambling-obsessed Georgian era. The ethos that underpinned Britain's elite schools was Muscular Christianity, which placed vigorous and masculine physical activity at the centre of its character-building outlook. At root it was an expression of British nationalism, rendering the teachings of the Church of England into a credo that both justified and maintained the principles of the British Empire. Thomas Arnold, the headmaster of Rugby School from 1828 to 1841, had popularised a Muscular Christian educational philosophy that sought to create 'healthy minds in healthy bodies' which, although he personally had no interest in sport, valued games as importantly as academic studies. Healthy minds were those seen as free of sin and moral weakness, and vigorous football was promoted as a reliable antidote to the great triangular fear of the Victorian public schools: masturbation, effeminacy and homosexuality. 'Every school ought to regard it as part of its duty to and mission to rid itself almost entirely of delicate complexions, narrow chests and feeble limbs', declared Loretto headmaster and prominent Scottish rugby official H.H. Almond.[4] Football therefore came to be seen as a vital part of the training of the boys and young men who would grow up to lead the government, industry and empire.

Other than two teams, two goals and a ball, every school's football rules were unique. Even the ball was not uniform: Eton's ball was round but much smaller than a modern soccer ball, Harrow's resembled a large cushion and Rugby's was an irregular ovoid. Offside differed, in that Harrow and Rugby deemed any attacking player in front of the ball to be offside, whereas the Eton game deemed a player to be onside if there were at least three defenders between him and the goal. Almost all schools allowed a ball in the air to be caught with the hands but Eton only allowed the hands to be used to knock the ball down. When the ball went over the touchline, play at Eton and Winchester was restarted with a form of scrum, known as a 'bully' and a 'hot', respectively, at Harrow and Winchester by kick-in and at Rugby by a right-angled throw-in. A ball that went behind the goal line resulted in a bully in front of goal at Eton, a kick for goal at Rugby or a kick-out by the defending side at Harrow and Charterhouse. To complicate matters, the 'Wall Game' version of Eton football consisted of little more than endless scrummaging as the ball was slowly propelled back and forth against a wall towards rarely reached goals. All schools decided matches solely by goals, except for the Eton field game, which also counted 'rouges', the equivalent of a try in the Rugby game.[5]

The rules of the Rugby School version of football were printed for the first time in 1845, and those for the Eton field game appeared in print in 1847. But these circulated only among boys of the two schools and had little influence on the spread of public school football into the wider population. The book that played a major role in expanding the popularity of football was not a rulebook but a novel, *Tom Brown's Schooldays*. Written by Thomas Hughes, an old boy of Rugby School, it was published in 1857. Based on his own experiences of life at Rugby, Hughes' book depicted the values of Muscular Christianity as a boy's adventure yarn, replete with trials of courage and tests of character, a portrait of a saintly Thomas Arnold, and stern warnings against bullying, effeminacy and 'funk', as cowardice was known. Hughes' book portrayed football as a school for moral education and character building through the simple technique of writing the most thrilling descriptions of a football match yet committed to print.

It was a runaway best-seller. A guide for boys about to be packed off to boarding school, a yardstick by which parents could judge a school and a handbook for aspirational private schools, *Tom Brown* made football not only morally respectable but also fashionable. It brought Rugby School and its version of football to a new, national audience. This prestige was enhanced several-fold in 1864 when the Clarendon Commission published the report of its inquiry into the state of England's leading public schools. It lauded Rugby above all other schools, declaring it as 'a national institution, as being a place of education and a source of influence for the whole Kingdom'.[6] Thanks to a best-selling novel and a Royal Commission seal of approval, the Rugby version of football was now identified in the public mind with morality, education and excitement.

This was the reason why Rugby School's football survived and flourished as an adult sport. None of the other public school codes of football survived outside of their native environments, despite the social prestige of the institutions that produced them. Although elements of Eton and Harrow's rules were incorporated into the rules of the FA, the FA's game was very different to that seen on any public school playing field. Rugby's sense of separateness from other schools' football was heightened by the crusading moral certitude that the school imbued in its pupils, causing 'Old Rugbeians', as its former pupils were known, to disdain those who did not share its traditions. This was a not unimportant factor when it came to understanding the opposition to its style of football. Antipathy to Rugby School football rules often reflected public hostility to the widely perceived arrogance of its alumni.

The enthusiasm for football among public schoolboys often did not diminish as they began their adult lives. The game that had meant so much to them at school now became the focus of their adult recreation. The mid-1800s were a period of widespread concern about the health hazards of living in the rapidly growing but dirty and polluted industrial cities. The sedentary lifestyles of the new legions of office-bound lawyers, accountants, clerks and other administrators of the burgeoning capitalist economy spurred the formation of gymnasia, athletic clubs and football teams. And, as with the other male clubs, these new football clubs constituted an entirely masculine kingdom. They provided a respite from the new world of Victorian middle-class domesticity, offering young men a haven from women, children and family duty, while giving them the opportunity to display an overtly masculine physicality in defiance of contemporary fears of softness and effeminacy. Football was not only fashionable, it had also become, perhaps more importantly, respectable. Between the publication of *Tom Brown's Schooldays* in 1857 and the formation of the FA at the end of 1863, numerous football clubs would be formed by privately educated young men, including Edinburgh Academicals (1857), Sheffield (1857), Liverpool (1857), Blackheath (1858), Richmond (1861), Wanderers (1859), Manchester (1860), Crystal Palace (1861), Lincoln (1862), Bradford (1863), Royal Engineers (1863) and the Civil Service (1863).

Although football supporters have long debated which was the 'first' adult club to be formed, the reality was that the sudden creation of clubs to play football in the 1850s and 1860s was part of a burgeoning new associational world of social and business networks of the Victorian middle classes. Between 1830 and 1870, fifteen of what would become seen as the most prestigious elite gentleman's clubs were formed in London, such as the Garrick Club (1831), East India Club (1849) and the Hurlingham Club (1869). In the provinces, the same social clustering took place, and as can be seen from the previously mentioned roll-call of football clubs formed in industrial cities, the game was one of its most conspicuous beneficiaries. Perhaps the earliest example of these new middle-class football clubs was that formed in Edinburgh by John Hope in 1824. He had played football at Edinburgh's High School and, on moving to what is now Edinburgh University and discovering that the game wasn't played there, formed his own 'football' club. Composed largely of young Edinburgh solicitors, Hope's club lasted for seventeen years playing internal matches against each other.[7]

This would be the initial pattern for all clubs of the mid-Victorian era. Liverpool members would divide into Rugby and Cheltenham old boys versus the rest, Bradford played captain's side versus secretary's side, and many clubs played fair versus dark, married against single, and when all else failed, A–M versus N–Z or some other alphabetical adversarial arrangement. Clubs made no effort to attract spectators and paid little attention to those who did watch. None of the twenty-one provincial football clubs listed in the 1868 Football Annual charged an entrance fee to watch a match. Indeed, admission to some of Sheffield FC's early matches was by invitation only. The first football clubs were precisely that: associations of young men organised solely for the enjoyment of their members.

The football played by these clubs was neither soccer nor rugby as we know them today. The obvious modern differentiation between the two football codes – that football is a kicking game and rugby is largely a handling game – cannot be extended back to the 1850s or 1860s.[8] Clear differentiation between the association and rugby codes did not emerge until the 1870s. So, for example, handling the ball and passing it by hand were a minor part of the Rugby School version of football. Even when the Rugby Football Union was formed in 1871, the use of hands was subordinate to dribbling and kicking the ball. Play revolved around scrummaging and kicking to set up scrummages. Forwards, who would usually comprise fifteen of what were twenty-a-side adult teams until 1877, aimed to break through their opponents by dribbling the ball with their feet through the scrum. Until 1886 a rugby match could only by won by the side scoring the most goals. Conversely, scrum-type struggles for the ball were common in Eton and Winchester schools' football games, and references to 'scrimmages' are not uncommon in reports of matches played under Sheffield Association rules.[9]

Far from being a 'handling code' at this time, Rugby School's football rules severely limited handling the ball. If the ball was caught on the full from a kick – a 'fair catch' – the catcher was allowed to kick the ball unhindered by the opposing side, as was the case in the early rules of both the FA and the Sheffield FA. But if the ball was on the ground, it could not be picked up unless it was bouncing. A rolling or stationary ball could not be touched with the hand. Using the feet to propel the ball was a major feature of the football games that emerged from Rugby School, and, conversely, catching and handling the ball was also common among those games that would later become associated with soccer. In fact, all forms of football that were played in the 1850s and 1860s had far more in common than that which set them apart. Kicking and handling the ball differed only by degree. Rather than being two distinct codes, there was one football with a spectrum of views about how it could be played.

Outside of a few public school partisans, rules were a matter of pragmatism and subordinate to the desire to play the game. The view of one of the founders of the Hull club (today's Hull FC rugby league side), William Hutchinson, that 'we played any mortal code possible with other clubs away from home so long as we could get a game of some sort', would have been widely endorsed. Hull's first away match was under FA rules at Lincoln in 1866 and, despite being known as a rugby club, they regularly played against FA sides, so much that when the *Nottinghamshire Guardian* called for the formation of a Midlands football association, it included Hull alongside Nottingham, Lincoln and Newark as one of the leading clubs of the region.[10] Stoke Ramblers, the forerunner of Stoke City, played Sheffield rules against clubs in Derbyshire and South Yorkshire, and rugby matches against the Congleton and Leek clubs in their first season. Sale FC committed themselves in 1870 to play association and rugby on alternate Saturdays.[11] Even rugby-playing Bradford still set aside two Saturdays a season on their fixture list for 'association practice' as late as 1873. Like Blackheath, London's Civil Service FC was a founder member of both the FA and the RFU. Manchester FC, arguably Lancashire's most socially prestigious rugby club, entered the FA Cup in 1877. Clapham Rovers were so successful at both rugby and association that they were not only a founding member of the RFU in 1871 but also won the FA Cup in 1880. The fluid nature of the rules of the game at this time and the lack of what might be termed 'code-patriotism' is exemplified by Bramham College, a small private school in West Yorkshire. It played its own code of rules (which had soccer-style goals, rugby's offside and 'fair catch' rules, and allowed the ball to be propelled forward by the runner bouncing the ball in front of him, as in Australian Rules) and was an early member of the FA, but its old boys were founders of Bradford, Huddersfield and Hull rugby clubs.[12]

Ultimately, the vast majority of footballers just wanted to play a game – and codes of rules were merely a means to this end.

Notes

1 Anonymous poem, 'The Rugby Union Game', *The Goal*, 27 December 1873.
2 Jennifer Macrory, *Running with the Ball: The Birth of Rugby Football* (London: Collins, 1991), p. 14, and *Bell's Life*, 21 December, 1845.
3 Quoted in Richard Sanders, *Beastly Fury: The Strange Birth of British Football* (London: Bantam, 2009), p. 75.
4 H.H. Almond, 'Athletics and Education', *Macmillan's Magazine*, vol. 43 (November 1880–April 1881), p. 292.
5 C.W. Alcock (ed.), *The Football Annual 1870* (London: Lilywhite, 1870), pp. 73–5. Steven Bailey, 'Living Sports History: Football at Winchester, Eton and Harrow', *The Sports Historian*, 15 (May 1995), pp. 2–31.
6 *Report of the Commissioners on the Revenues and Management of Certain Colleges and Schools*, British Parliamentary Papers. Public Schools and Colleges, Volume XX, Education, General 9. 1864, p. 266.

7 John Hutchinson, 'Sport, Education and Philanthropy in Nineteenth-Century Edinburgh: The Emergence of Modern Forms of Football', *Sport in History*, vol. 28, no. 4 (2008), pp. 547–65, and John Hutchinson and Andy Mitchell, 'John Hope, the Foot-Ball Club of 1824 and Its Sporting Legacy', *Soccer & Society*, vol. 19, no. 1, pp. 75–88.

8 For examples of this approach, see Adrian Harvey, 'Football's Missing Link: The Real Story of the Evolution of Modern Football', *The European Sports History Review*, vol. 1 (1999), pp. 90–116, and Graham Curry and Eric Dunning, *Association Football: A Study in Figurational Sociology* (Abingdon: Routledge, 2015).

9 *Sheffield & Rotherham Independent*, 27 March 1876. For a broader discussion of the evolution of rugby rules, see Tony Collins, *A Social History of English Rugby Union* (Abingdon: Routledge, 2009), ch. 6.

10 William Hutchinson in *Yorkshire Evening Post*, 1 December 1900. Bradford FC 1873/74 Fixture Card, reprinted in *Yorkshire Evening Post*, 5 January 1901. *Nottinghamshire Guardian*, 28 January 1870.

11 Graham Williams, *The Code War* (Harefield: Yore, 1994), pp. 32–4.

12 *The Bramham College Magazine*, November 1864, p. 182, and Tony Collins, *Rugby's Great Split* (London: Frank Cass, 1998), pp. 10–11.

4

SHEFFIELD

Football beyond the metropolis

> It may not be generally known that Sheffield holds, or ought to hold, a very prominent position in the football world. Perhaps in no other town in the kingdom (London, of course, excepted) is the game played to anything like the extent to which it is in Sheffield. There are now fourteen clubs in the town, almost every cricket club having a football club connected with it.
>
> —*Sporting Life*, 1867[1]

It was this enthusiasm to play football that animated Nathaniel Creswick and William Prest when they founded Sheffield FC in 1857. As with the founders of all the other clubs formed at this time, both were members of their local middle class. Creswick was a solicitor whose father owned a silver-plating business and Prest was a wine merchant. Both were members of Sheffield Cricket Club who thought that football would be a good way of keeping fit during the winter. Sheffield, like its rival and near-neighbour Nottingham, had developed a vibrant cricketing culture, and Creswick and Prest soon found that their new football club did not lack for members. It quickly outgrew informal agreements about how to play football and decided to design its own set of rules.

Although none of its leading members had attended a public school, they had been educated in local private schools and the club saw itself as a socially elite institution. Emulation of their social superiors has long been a defining characteristic of the British middle classes and the Sheffield footballers were no exception. So, to inform their discussions about football rules, they wrote to all of the public schools asking for a copy of their football rulebooks.[2] Having compared the rules of each school, the club picked out those elements it liked, combined them with its own ideas and in October 1858 voted to adopt what would become known as the Sheffield rules of football.

Over the past two decades or so, these rules have become soccer's version of the William Webb Ellis myth. Just as rugby union promoted the myth of Ellis picking up the ball and running with it during a game of football at Rugby School in 1823 – without a shred of evidence – to explain the birth of rugby, so too have soccer fans pointed to the Sheffield football rules as being the true origins of the modern game.[3] Uncomfortable with the fact that what is often called the 'people's game' was founded by the upper-middle class administrators of the Football Association, many soccer supporters have looked to Sheffield rules as a pure kicking and non-handling form of football untouched by the public schools. But such a belief, like the Webb Ellis myth, has no foundation in reality. This can be seen when the wording of the 1858 Sheffield rules is compared to those of a leading English public school [in brackets]:

1   Kick off from the middle must be a place kick. [vi. Kick off from middle must be a place.]
2   Kick-out must not be from more than twenty-five yards out of goal. [vii. Kick out must not be from more than ten yards of our goal if a place-kick, not more than twenty-five yards if a punt, drop or knock on.]
3   Fair catch is a catch direct from the foot of the opposite side and entitles a free kick. [i. Fair catch is a catch direct from the foot.]
4   Charging is fair in case of a place kick, with the exception of kick off, as soon as a player offers to kick, but may always draw back unless he has actually touched the ball with his foot. [ix. Charging is fair in case of a place kick, as soon as the ball has touched the ground.]

Far from Sheffield rules being free of public school influence, the rules in brackets are direct quotations from the *1845 Laws of Football Played at Rugby School.*

The links between Sheffield and Rugby School rules go even deeper. Sheffield's Rule 8, forbidding the ball from being picked up from the ground, was common among rugby clubs and appears in the 1862 Rugby School rules. Moreover, Sheffield rules did allow the ball to be handled by outfield players. Rule 3 allowed catching with hands if the ball was caught on the full in what was known as a 'fair catch', a term still in use in American football and which became known as a 'mark' in rugby and Australian

Rules. Rule 9 allowed a bouncing ball to be stopped by the hand, is a variation on the Rugby School rule of allowing a bouncing ball to be caught. Rule 10, 'No goal may be kicked from touch, nor by free kick from a fair catch', is also based on Rule 5 of the 1845 Rugby School rules, which also allow a goal to be scored from a fair catch. The eleventh of the Sheffield rules, defining when a ball is in touch and how it should be returned to play, uses the same wording as Rugby's 1862 rules, with the exception that a Rugby player was also allowed to throw the ball in to himself. Even Sheffield's Rule 6, prohibiting the ball being 'knocked on' with the hand and penalising it with a free kick, appears with slightly different wording in Rule 11 of the 1862 rugby rules. Only Sheffield's Rules 5 and 7, forbidding pushing, hacking, tripping, holding or pulling a player over, have no link with Rugby School rules.[4] This may possibly suggest that they objected to the roughness of the rugby game, but this was also true of some adult rugby clubs, many of whom banned hacking and tripping, as did the Rugby Football Union when it was formed in 1871.

This is not to suggest that Sheffield football was a version of the Rugby School game. Like trying to appreciate the taste of food simply by reading a recipe book, it is impossible to understand how a game was played merely from its written rules. But the similarity of Sheffield and Rugby School rules does highlight the fact that differences taken for granted today did not exist in the 1850s and 1860s. Far from being committed exclusively to a kicking game, Sheffield FC had no objections to playing Rugby-style matches until at least the late 1860s. In 1863 they played Garrison FC under rules that allowed 'striking and throwing the ball'. The following year they played home and away matches against Leeds Rugby Club using 'rules [that] were of a mongrel type, neither rugby nor association', according to Leeds' founder J.G Hudson. In 1868 they played against Manchester FC, then as now a rugby club, losing the rugby match by one goal and eight touchdowns to nil in Manchester but winning the home game by two rouges to nil. It was not until 1876 that Sheffield FC played its last rugby match, against Hull FC.[5]

For almost ten years from 1859 to 1868, the Sheffield game allowed players to score a 'rouge', a rule taken directly from Eton's field football game. A rouge was scored 'by the player who first touches the ball after it has been kicked between the rouge flags [which were placed twelve feet away at the side of each goalpost]'. Touching the ball down with the hand clearly has nothing in common with modern soccer, although Australian Rules football still has extra posts called 'behind posts' and Canadian football retains the term rouge for a ball kicked into the end zone and not returned. The similarity of this rule to rugby can be seen quite clearly in the match report

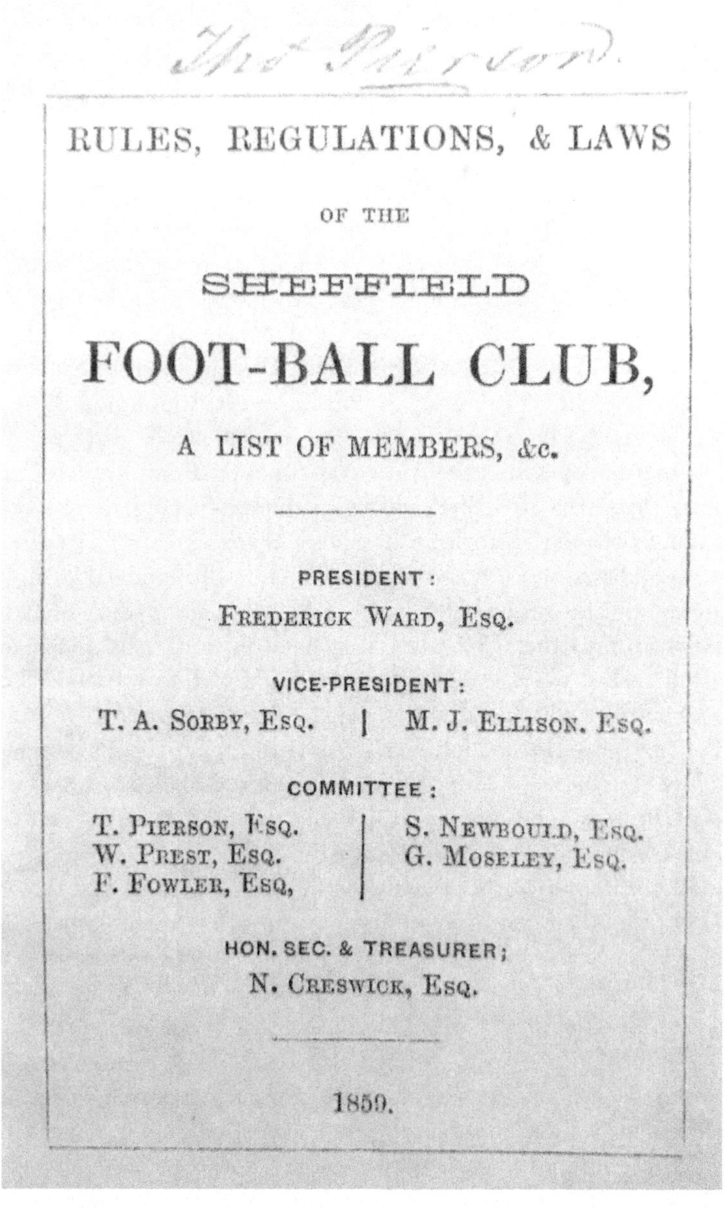

Thos Pierson.

RULES, REGULATIONS, & LAWS

OF THE

SHEFFIELD

FOOT-BALL CLUB,

A LIST OF MEMBERS, &c.

PRESIDENT :

FREDERICK WARD, ESQ.

VICE-PRESIDENT :

T. A. SORBY, ESQ. | M. J. ELLISON. ESQ.

COMMITTEE :

T. PIERSON, ESQ.   S. NEWBOULD, ESQ.
W. PREST, ESQ.   G. MOSELEY, ESQ.
F. FOWLER, ESQ,

HON. SEC. & TREASURER ;

N. CRESWICK, ESQ.

1859.

PLATE 2   Sheffield F.C.'s rulebook, 1859

of the 1867 Youdan Cup final, which was won by Hallam FC, who scored two rouges to Norfolk FC's nil. *Bell's Life* described Hallam's first rouge:

> After half an hour's play the ball was kicked by Elliott, not through the goal, but just over it, and was touched down by Ash in splendid style, after running round two opponents before getting to the ball, thus securing a rouge.

The touchdown became such an important part of Sheffield football during this period that it often became the most important way of scoring, as in 1860 when Sheffield FC defeated the 58th Regiment club by a goal and ten rouges to a goal and five rouges.[6] In some games, the rule was varied to allow the player who touched down the ball to take an unimpeded kick at goal, just as was the case at Rugby School.[7] The fair catch remained a feature of the Sheffield FA's rules even after the FA had abolished it.

But, as would become the case wherever people played any type of football, the rules under which the game was conducted did not determine its popularity. Five years after Sheffield FC had been formed, there were over a dozen clubs playing football in the Sheffield area. In 1867 twelve clubs – most of them based in local communities such as Broomhall, Hallam, Heeley, Norton and Pitsmoor – formed the Sheffield Football Association to organise regular fixtures. That same year its teams took part in the Youdan Cup, a knock-out tournament sponsored by local theatre owner Thomas Youdan. The final, which was won by Hallam's two touchdowns, attracted a crowd of 3,000 people. The following year another knock-out competition, the Cromwell Cup, was played for by four sides and once again sponsored by a local theatrical entrepreneur, the incongruously named Oliver Cromwell. This combination of regular competition between clubs representing their local communities, the crowds that matches attracted and the regular discussion of football matters in the press meant that Sheffield was the first city to develop something resembling a modern football culture, which within a generation was replicated in almost every town and city in Britain.

Why was Sheffield the first to develop a football culture? Partly because the economy of the city in the first half of the nineteenth century was based on small-scale, highly skilled metal manufacturing, which meant that the working classes had more leisure time and disposable income to watch and, albeit in a limited fashion at first, take part in sport. The city was also one where 'Saint Monday', the tradition of workers not going to work on Monday, lasted into the late nineteenth century.[8] Perhaps because of this, Sheffield already had a vibrant, pre-existing sporting culture based on cricket. Since the 1820s, it had been the stronghold of cricket in Yorkshire and second only to Nottingham as the most important cricketing centre outside of London. In 1821 George Steer and son-in-law cricketer William Woolhouse built and opened a cricket ground to the east of the city, which by August 1824 was reportedly attracting crowds of between 15,000 and 20,000 for major matches. The enthusiasm for organised sport and the desire of local businessmen to profit from it saw new cricket grounds being opened at Hyde Park and Cross Scythes by the end of the decade. Sheffield cricket was resolutely commercial, matches being played for stake money with sums of £100 being common and even £1,000 not being unknown.[9] It was also a game for all the classes, as demonstrated by the Darnall club's attempts to attract the working classes in 1829 by charging tradesmen sixpence and 'working people', by which they meant labourers, just threepence. And, as would be the case with soccer and rugby in the last decades of the nineteenth century, professional cricketers become local heroes, none more notably than the Sheffield-born all-rounder Tom Marsden, one of the first local professionals and one of the finest exponents of single-wicket cricket of his age, regularly attracting five-figure crowds to his matches.[10]

Many of Sheffield's early footballers were also cricketers and its clubs were also cricket clubs, such as Hallam FC, or closely associated with them, and Sheffield's football culture was built on this pre-existing sporting tradition. Youdan and Cromwell's sponsorship of cup competitions was simply a continuation of the long relationship between local cricket and the entertainment industries. Even the formation of the Sheffield FA had a commercial impetus, as its clubs sought to come together to buy cheaper advertising space from local newspapers and provide a cost-effective insurance scheme for its players. The same point can be made about Nottingham, where the strength of local cricket culture provided an infrastructure for the development of football in the early 1860s. When the newly formed Nottingham FC hosted Sheffield FC at the start of 1865 its side included Richard Daft and George Parr, two of the greatest cricketers of the Victorian era and experienced sporting entrepreneurs.[11] The fact that the football club became known as the Nottinghamshire County FC underlines the extent to which it sought to follow the pattern of cricket.[12] As the new-found enthusiasm for football slowly began to blossom from the late 1850s, Sheffield and Nottingham already had in place the customs and structures that would nourish this new sporting phenomenon.

Notes

1 *Sporting Life*, 30 January 1867.
2 Adrian Harvey, *Football: The First Hundred Years* (Abingdon: Routledge, 2006), p. 95.

3 For example, John Goulstone claims that 'one could quite convincingly trace soccer's main ancestral line before 1867 back to Sheffield in 1857' in his *Football's Secret History* (Catford: 3–2 Books, 2001), p. 50, while Adrian Harvey and Peter Swain believe that Sheffield 'both saved and created the rules of the [association] game' in 'On Bosworth Field or the Playing Fields of Eton and Rugby? Who Really Invented Modern Football?' *International Journal of the History of Sport*, vol. 29, no. 10 (2012), p. 1427.

4 The Sheffield rules can be found in Harvey, *Football, The First Hundred Years*, pp. 97–8. The 1845 Rugby School rules are in Jennifer Macrory, *Running with the Ball: The Birth of Rugby Football* (London: Collins, 1991), on pages 86–9 and subsequent rule amendments on pages 96–101.

5 Sheffield FC, Notebook of Match Reports mss, entry for 9 May 1863. *Yorkshire Evening Post*, 8 December 1900. C.W. Alcock (ed.), *John Lilywhite's Football Annual* (Lilywhite: London, 1868). *Sheffield & Rotherham Independent*, 6 March 1876.

6 Sheffield Rules reprinted in Harvey, *Football, The First Hundred Years*, p. 117. Youdan Cup report in *Bell's Life*, 9 March 1867. Match report in *Bell's Life*, 23 December 1860. The rouge was also used a method of scoring in Nottingham football as late as the 1869–70 season; see match reports in the *Nottingham Daily Express*, 15 January 1869 and 7 March 1870.

7 See for example the report on the Nottingham versus Sheffield match in *Nottinghamshire Guardian*, 2 February 1866.

8 Dennis Smith, *Conflict and Compromise: Class Formation in English Society 1830–1914* (London: RKP, 1982), pp. 51–5. E.P. Thompson, 'Time, Work-Discipline and Industrial Capitalism', in *Customs in Common* (Harmondsworth: Penguin, 1993), pp. 374–5. D.A. Reid, 'The Decline of Saint Monday 1766–1876', *Past & Present*, vol. 71, no. 1 (1976), pp. 76–101.

9 Rob Light, *Cricket's Forgotten Past: A Social and Cultural History of the Game in the West Riding, 1820–70* (Unpublished PhD thesis, De Montfort University, 2008), pp. 40–3.

10 Light, *Cricket's Forgotten Past*, p. 93 and pp. 61–2.

11 *Nottinghamshire Guardian,* 6 January 1865.

12 See Andrew Dawes, *The Development of Football in Nottinghamshire c. 1860–1915* (Unpublished PhD thesis, De Montfort University, 2017) and Graham Curry and Eric Dunning, 'The "origins of football debate" and the Early Development of the Game in Nottinghamshire', *Soccer and Society*, vol. 18, no. 7 (2015), pp. 866–79.

5

THE END OF THE UNIVERSAL GAME

> In the year 1871, eight years after the formation of the Association, the Football Rugby Union [sic] came into existence on the lines of the FA. These two institutions soon embraced all the football players of the United Kingdom. Thus, though one general code of rules for universal adoption was not realised, two codes were . . . brought into existence and universally adopted.
>
> —R.G. Graham, FA secretary, 1899[1]

Sheffield may have been the first city to develop a recognisably modern football culture, but it was merely the first cuckoo of a football spring that would soon blossom across all industrial towns and cities in Britain. A few miles north of Sheffield, football clubs were formed by privately educated young men in Bradford, Leeds, Hull and Huddersfield, and the popularity of the game among the middle classes became such that the first representative football match of any type was played in Leeds in 1870 when Yorkshire played Lancashire. Although played under rugby rules, the Yorkshire team included five players from Sheffield FC. The social tenor was indicated by the advertisement for the match that appeared in the *Yorkshire Post*: 'Lancashire will be represented by Gentlemen from Manchester, Rochdale, Preston, Burnley and other towns. Yorkshire by Gentlemen from Bradford, Huddersfield, Hull, Sheffield and Leeds'. In Lancashire, former pupils of Eton and Rugby schools formed the first clubs in Liverpool and Manchester, followed by Sale (1861), Swinton (1866) and Rochdale (1867), each one established by young business and professional men who were also members of existing cricket or athletics clubs. Slightly to their south, Stoke Ramblers were formed in 1868 by old boys of Charterhouse school who brought together the town's young accountants, solicitors and civil engineers to play football with their local peers.[2] Football, regardless of its rules, was becoming a social and cultural phenomenon across the industrial north of England.

The clubs formed in the north invariably had a geographic name and quickly came to be seen as representatives of their locality. This was in contrast to many of the clubs formed at the same time in London which had no geographic connection at all, as can be seen in the names of many of the founder members of the FA and RFU, such as Wanderers, Crusaders, Harlequins, Flamingoes, Gipsies, Mohicans and even the No Names. This difference was not merely one of nomenclature. The mid-nineteenth century was the era of Victorian municipalism, where provincial civic pride and local rivalry inspired the erection of ever-more ornate and elaborate town halls and other municipal buildings. Leeds opened its huge neo-classical town hall in 1858, while Manchester began the nine-year construction of its own neo-Gothic town hall in 1868; almost every other town across the north sought to emulate them. This competitiveness reflected local trade rivalries between the cotton and woollen manufacturing towns on both sides of the Pennines. Football clubs in Bradford, Huddersfield, Leeds, Liverpool and Manchester were all led by scions of textile manufacturers and merchants, and the game itself soon became a vehicle of municipal pride and civic rivalry.

Almost all of these northern clubs initially identified with the Rugby School tradition of football. Of the thirty clubs that were members of the FA in 1868, only three were from the north: Sheffield, Bramham College (both of whom played under their own rules) and Hull College, who do not appear to have played any competitive fixtures.[3] Lincoln, which joined the FA in 1864, only to resign and then rejoin, allowed running with the ball in hand.[4] Even Adrian Harvey's survey of thirty-seven southern clubs playing football between 1868 and 1873 shows twenty-four of them playing rugby rules, and the *Nottinghamshire Guardian*, in a region where rugby rules were rarely played, conceded at the start of 1870 that 'the Rugby rules, which allow carrying the ball, are the most commonly practised'.[5] The popularity of Rugby School football was partly due to the kudos that *Tom Brown* had given the game, but it was also a consequence of the desire of young men to play football of whatever code was available locally. Sam Duckitt recalled that when he and his friends set up the Halifax FC in 1873, 'we were absolutely unacquainted with the rules of either Rugby or Association. Of course, when we did commence to play, we fell in at once with the prevailing

Rugby rules', because those were the rules played by all of the local sides.[6] In much of the north, not to play rugby rules would mean not to play football.

Football's growth in popularity among the provincial middle classes in the 1860s largely passed the FA by. In contrast, the number of clubs playing Rugby School rules, or a modified version of them, continued to rise. The FA's existential crisis of 1867 stimulated it to seek new members and it wrote to all football clubs, including those at public schools, appealing for them to 'aid' – not even join – it in establishing 'a universal code according to which all matches may be played'.[7] The rule changes of 1867, which brought the FA closer to the Eton and Harrow games, were motivated by Charles Alcock as being 'the only step to inducing the public schools to join them'.[8] The fluidity of football rules at the time can be seen by the letter's reference to 'a universal code' and by the fact it was also sent to Rugby School. The school declined to join but replied asking if the FA was also interested in establishing a common set of rules for clubs following Rugby's football traditions. This was not a mistake on their part. Even as late as 1870 FA secretary Charles Alcock appealed 'to all footballers alike, whether they be of the hacking or non-hacking persuasion' to join the FA to 'effect a code of rules that shall unite all the various differences under one recognised head' and create 'one universal game'.[9] Rugby School's request does not appear to have been followed up, but Alcock's letter more than fulfilled its purpose when Westminster and Charterhouse schools both joined the FA, two of twelve schools which affiliated in response to the letter.

Was the revival of the FA due to 'the successful nature of football activity in Sheffield [that] encouraged the FA to continue at a time when its officials were considering disbanding the organisation', as some historians have argued?[10] In reality the FA's leaders paid little heed to their northern compatriots. When a London FA team played Sheffield FC in 1866 the match was played under the FA's rules. Sheffield FC delegate William Chesterman attended the FA's 1867 annual general meeting and proposed three amendments to the FA rules, one of which was in support of the rugby-style rouge, all of which were decisively voted down. Instead, the FA went in precisely the opposite direction and sought to bring their game more in line with those public schools that played 'non-handling' football. It was E.C. Morley's Barnes FC, not the Sheffield club, that proposed banning the use of hands to knock down the ball, a significant step towards a 'hands-free' version of football.[11] The reality was that Sheffield had very little influence over the FA. Over the next decade the Sheffield clubs were forced to accept its leadership and abandon almost all of their unique rules before being absorbed by the FA in 1878.

The FA underwent further changes in 1868, when its committee was enlarged from four to ten members. This was not merely a numerical increase but significantly altered the social status of the FA by bringing in former pupils of Eton, Harrow, Charterhouse and Westminster. This considerably raised the FA's credibility with public school and gentleman's club football-ers, especially in London, and went some way to countering the authority of the rugby game. Just as significantly, the late 1860s also saw the rise to prominence within the FA of Charles Alcock. Alcock, who combined the patrician authority of his Harrow education with the organisational drive of a Victorian sporting entrepreneur, was appointed secretary and treasurer of the FA in February 1870. He was a talented footballer and cricketer, as well as secretary of Surrey County Cricket Club between 1872 and 1907, editor of the monthly *Cricket* magazine and *Lilywhite's Cricketers' Annual*. The link with John Lilywhite led to Alcock establishing *Lilywhite's Football Annual* in 1868, which quickly became simply *The Football Annual*. His editorship gave him tremendous influence across football and the annual was through-out the 1870s and early 1880s the most important football publication in Britain.[12]

No sooner had Alcock been appointed than the FA arranged an England versus Scotland match to take place on 5 March 1870 at the Kenning-ton Oval cricket ground, the home of Alcock's Surrey CCC. Although the match was not at all representative – the Scotland side fielded only one Scottish-born player and the entire side played for London clubs, not least because the FA version of football was barely played north of the border – it raised the FA's profile significantly, as a journalist like Alcock probably anticipated. The match's social status can be gauged by the *Morning Post*'s comment that the game was 'numerously attended by gentlemen, most of whom had been educated at the various public institutions' and that the players were 'old Wykehamites, Etonians, Harrovians, Carthusians and other gentlemen'.[13] The 1–1 draw was sufficient for another match to be arranged in November, which England won 1–0 against a slightly more representa-tive Scots team which this time fielded three native-born players. Their presence was not enough to distract attention from the somewhat provoca-tive, or perhaps desperate, selection of Charles Nepean, who was deemed to be Scottish because his cousin had married a Scot.[14]

These two matches not only raised the FA's profile but also gave it, in an era of rising imperial nationalism, the prestige of being able to repre-sent England and Scotland. National and regional jealousies, real or imag-ined, could now be played out on an international stage, and the FA was the pioneer this new development in football. Its declaration of itself as the representative of nations came as a shock to the complacent disdain of rugby-playing clubs. Especially in Scotland, where rugby was unquestion-ably the dominant code, the FA's internationals seemed to be an affront to the football status quo. Rugby, according to Loretto School headmaster

H.H. Almond, was the 'parent code' and the FA had no right to claim to be representing the Scottish nation. Stung by the FA's impertinence, rugby clubs on both sides of the border began to organise.

Two weeks after the second FA international, the captains of Scotland's five leading rugby clubs challenged rugby players in England to an international match to take place in Glasgow or Edinburgh.[15] Soon after that, Benjamin Burns and Edwin Ash, the secretaries of the Blackheath and Richmond clubs, respectively, published an appeal in *Bell's Life* to 'the supporters of Rugby Football' to meet and 'join with us in framing a code of rules to be generally adopted'.[16] A month later, on 26 January 1871, thirty-two delegates representing twenty rugby-playing clubs met at the Pall Mall Restaurant in London's Charing Cross and in little more than two hours agreed a constitution and appointed a committee of three old Rugbeians to draft what they referred to with typical pomposity as 'the Laws of the Game'. The Rugby Football Union had been founded. Two months later, on 27 March, 8,000 people assembled at Edinburgh's Raeburn Place to watch Scotland defeat England in the first rugby international. The honour of the Scottish nation was upheld, and the position of rugby as its most important code of football was re-established. Or so it seemed.

PLATE 3   Soccer or Rugby? The 1872 England versus Scotland rugby international (*The Graphic*, 24 February 1872)

Alcock's ambition for the FA had not been sated however. In the same month that Burns and Ash had issued the call for a rugby union, the FA organised a North versus South match, once again seeking to capitalise on existing regional rivalries while emphasising that the FA was a truly national organisation. But Alcock's biggest initiative came on 20 July 1871 when the FA Committee met and backed his proposal that 'a Challenge Cup should be established in connection with the Association, for which all clubs should be invited to compete'. Cup tournaments in public schools at this time were commonplace – in the 1870 *Football Annual*, Alcock noted that Eton, Harrow Rugby, Cheltenham and Haileybury all staged knock-out competitions for teams in their respective schools – and the aim of the FA Cup was to stimulate interest in the game among young men in the professions and increase the attractiveness of the FA to unaffiliated football clubs.

The new competition was endorsed by the clubs on 16 October and a little over three weeks later, on 11 November 1871, the first round of the Football Association Challenge Cup kicked off with fifteen teams.[17] Two matches in the first round resulted in walkovers when their opponents failed to turn up. Queen's Park were awarded a bye in the first two rounds and so did not play a game in the tournament until the semi-finals, which they drew 0–0 with Alcock's Wanderers FC in Glasgow. They then withdrew from the competition when faced with a mid-week journey down to London for the replay. Wanderers therefore met the Royal Engineers in the final, dominating the game and running out 1–0 winners, thanks to a goal after fifteen minutes from Morton Betts, who like Alcock was an Old Harrovian. Scoring the winning goal was just about the only thing Alcock did not do, although he did have one effort disallowed. He not only captained the Wanderers side, but the final, like the England versus Scotland matches, was also staged at Surrey cricket club's Kennington Oval. The FA Cup was truly his creation.

The consequences of Alcock's initiative would eventually revolutionise football, yet this was neither the intention of, nor apparent to, him or the other leaders of the FA at the time. But what was completely clear to all was that the Association and Rugby organisations were going their own separate ways. Football was now irrevocably split. There would never be a universal game.

Notes

1 R.H. Graham, 'The Early History of the Football Association', *Badminton Magazine*, VIII (1899), p. 87.
2 Collins, *Rugby's Great Split*, pp. 11–12. For Stoke, see Martyn Dean Cooke and Gary James, 'Myths, Truths and Pioneers: The Early Development of Association Football in the Potteries', *Soccer and Society*, vol. 19, no. 1 (2018), pp. 9–10.

3 FA figures form Harvey, *Football: The First Hundred Years* (Abingdon: Routledge, 2006), p. 169. For his survey of 27 southern clubs (plus rugby-plying Manchester Athletic, who I have excluded from the number) see p. 176.

4 *Bell's Life*, 29 October 1864.

5 *Nottinghamshire Guardian*, 7 January 1870.

6 *Yorkshire Evening Post*, 9 February 1901.

7 Letter from FA secretary RG Graham, reprinted in R.H. Graham, 'The Early History of the Football Association', *Badminton Magazine*, vol. VIII (1899), pp. 80–1.

8 *Bell's Life*, 2 March 1867.

9 C.W. Alcock, *The Football Annual* (London: John Lilywhite, 1870), p. 37.

10 Adrian Harvey, *Football: The First Hundred Years*, p. 125.

11 R.H. Graham, 'The Early History of the Football Association', *Badminton Magazine*, VIII (1899), p. 80.

12 The only current biography of Alcock is Keith Booth's *The Father of Modern Sport: The Life and Times of Charles W. Alcock* (Manchester: Parrs Wood Press, 2002).

13 *Morning Post*, 7 March 1870 because of the unrepresentative nature of the sides, neither this nor the subsequent three internationals are regarded as 'official' internationals.

14 For the backgrounds of the players, see Andy Mitchell, *First Elevens: The Birth of International Football* (Edinburgh: CreateSpace, 2012).

15 *Bell's Life*, 8 December 1870.

16 *Bell's Life*, 24 December 1870.

17 C.W. Alcock, *Football: The Association Game* (London: George Bell, 1906), pp. 16–17.

6

FROM THE CLASSES TO
THE MASSES

The majority of Yorkshire teams are composed of working men, who
have only adopted football in recent years and have received no school
education in the art. The majority of members of London clubs have
played it all their lives, yet when the two meet there is only one it – the
Yorkshireman.

—'A Londoner', 1892[1]

In January 1871, *Bell's Life*, Britain's leading sports weekly, wrote confi-
dently that 'every year has increased the superiority in point of numbers and
popularity of the rugby clubs over those who are subject to the rule of the
[Football] Association'. It saw no reason why rugby's place as the premier
winter sport would not continue. After all, at its last annual general meeting,
the FA had just twenty-six adult clubs and thirteen schools and colleges in
membership. In contrast, at its founding meeting a few days after the *Bell's
Life* article, the Rugby Football Union (RFU) would bring together twenty
adult clubs, and by the time the 1874–75 season kicked off it would boast
113 clubs under its banner. The FA, despite the innovation of the FA Cup,
could count only seventy-eight members, and of those eighteen were clubs
of the Sheffield Association.[2]

Yet, a mere twenty-five years after *Bell's Life*'s assured statement, the football world could not have been more different. Thousands of clubs now
played the association game. Over 200 had entered that season's FA Cup,
which culminated in almost 49,000 people cramming into London's Crystal Palace stadium to see The Wednesday of Sheffield defeat Wolverhampton

Wanderers 2–1 in the final. Every week, tens of thousands played the game and hundreds of thousands more paid to watch it. Almost 700 young men were engaged as full-time professional players with Football League clubs, each of which was run as a commercial operation and were organised into leagues that ensured high-quality matches every Saturday afternoon for their paying customers.[3] National and local newspapers alike employed journalists solely to report on the daily doings of the sport, almost every town had a Saturday night newspaper devoted to the day's football activity, and railway companies ran excursions that criss-crossed the country taking players and supporters to and from matches. No longer the game of exclusive gentlemen's clubs, the association game was now the sport of the multi-millioned masses. It had, as Eric Hobsbawm would note, become 'a sort of lingua franca' of working-class men the length and breadth of Britain.[4]

In contrast, rugby had no national cup tournament. In 1877 Calcutta FC had disbanded and donated a trophy as 'a challenge cup to be annually competed for by all rugby union clubs' on the lines of the FA Cup. The RFU declined the suggestion because of 'difficulties of all clubs playing together', and instead awarded the 'Calcutta Cup' to the winners of the annual England versus Scotland match.[5] It was a decision that would play no small part in rugby's reversal of fortune. By 1895, rugby's clubs still numbered in the hundreds; with few exceptions its crowds could not compare with those of soccer, and the RFU had also forbidden league competitions. Worst of all, there were now two rugby unions – the RFU and the Northern Union (which would become known as rugby league) – the result of a bloody decade-long battle fought over the legalisation of payments to players that shattered the game into separate middle- and working-class constituencies. Any rugby player who played the northern game was banned for life by the RFU from ever playing the union code again. In the war of the football codes, rugby was the indisputable loser.

A generation after the FA's attempt to create a single universal game, Britain now had three versions of football. Not only had the face of football utterly changed, but it had happened with startling rapidity. The 1870s saw the game leave the world of exclusive gentleman's clubs to become a sport played and watched by all classes. The 1880s saw it further transmogrify into a commercial juggernaut that commanded the attention of millions. And just when people thought it could not become any more popular, its appeal expanded yet further. Like the railways in the 1830s or the internet in the 2000s, the normally slow alchemy of historical change was compressed into a few short years, transforming the rocks of public school football into the diamonds of mass spectator sport.

This new football was a product of Britain's second industrial revolution, the result of railways transforming travel and industry and technologies like the telegraph making news almost instantaneous. Mass-market daily newspapers now brought everyday stories to a population that had become almost universally literate due to educational reforms like the 1870 Forster Act, and rising wages and shorter working hours brought new leisure opportunities for the working classes. This new football had almost nothing in common with the old folk football games of custom, tradition and festivity. Whether association or rugby, this sport was highly structured on the pitch, commercially driven off it, and was a cultural phenomenon that had never been seen before. This was a modern sport for modern times, a scientific game for a scientific age, a mass entertainment for the era of the masses.

Football's radical metamorphosis into a mass spectator sport was not the intention of its leaders. The privately educated young professional men who played the game in the 1860s and 1870s had no desire to see it spread to the great mass of the population. Their clubs were for their own recreation, places where one could relax and entertain oneself in the company of one's peers. The FA and the RFU wanted to extend the game horizontally across men of similar circumstance, not vertically down to the lower classes. The early 1870s saw the game expand quickly among the middle classes of London and the provinces. From fifteen entrants in its first season the FA Cup grew to forty-three sides in 1877, augmenting its London and south-eastern base with Sheffield FC, Notts County, Shrewsbury's Shropshire Wanderers and Lancashire's Darwen FC.

Throughout the 1870s, football was a self-consciously middle-class sport. In December 1872 the *Sporting Gazette* published a list of twenty-four 'recognised gentleman's football clubs', including the FA's Barnes and Wanderers clubs, and the RFU's Harlequins and Wasps, with whom it advised that fixtures 'can generally be accepted with safety'. There were 'no doubt very many other clubs composed entirely of gentlemen', the *Gazette* reported, 'but it is almost impossible to obtain information on this point'. So that its readers might avoiding socially embarrassing fixtures in other sports, the magazine also provided similar lists of athletics, rowing and cricket clubs.[6]

Such concerns reflected football's growing fashionability among those who considered themselves gentlemen. In 1874 *The Goal*, a weekly founded in 1873 and probably the first publication devoted solely to football, remarked that almost every cricket club now 'assembles its members in the winter months behind the goal posts, to supplement and utilise the muscle gained in their summer exercises'. 'Do we not all recognise', it went on to say,

> with surprise and pleasure the faces of old school companions, who had long since renounced active and vigorous exercise, and resigned themselves to the dust and dyspepsia of business; but who . . . have

rushed responsive to the football field, and have returned to their work on the Monday with lighter hearts and clearer heads by reason of their Saturday's exercise.[7]

Many football clubs – including Derby County, Preston North End, Halifax and Widnes – were the product of cricketers' desire to continue playing sport after the summer had ended. Like the early development of football in Sheffield and Nottingham, the link with cricket also provided football clubs with the administrative models with which to organise the sport. In 1874, Yorkshire's five leading football clubs came together to form the Yorkshire County Football Club. Shortly after, in 1875, the Birmingham District FA was founded to bring together ten local sides. It was followed within eighteen months by the creation of county associations in Shropshire, North Staffordshire and Walsall and District. As in cricket, these associations also

PLATE 4 *The Goal*: launched in 1873 as probably the first dedicated football weekly

sought to organise inter-county matches, a tradition that became more important in rugby, which eventually started its own county championship tournament in 1889.

Most importantly, local administrators also took a lead from the FA and created local FA Cup-style knock-out competitions. The 1876–77 season saw the start of the Birmingham Senior Cup in soccer and the Yorkshire Cup in rugby. In 1876 rugby clubs in Cheshire formed their own county union, which then launched its own cup competition in 1878. The same year saw the Durham Rugby Union formed by seven clubs, its cup starting in the 1880/81 season. The Lancashire Football Association was also founded in 1878 and Darwen became the first winners of the Lancashire Cup the following year. In the same year, Darwen fought out a tumultuous battle with Old Etonians in the quarter-final stage of the FA Cup, drawing with them 5–5 and 2–2 before finally succumbing 6–2. It was a match that captured the national imagination, not simply because of its epic nature but also because it pitted representatives of the British ruling class against representatives of a northern working-class textile town. Such a meeting of the two classes was impossible in any other sphere of British life, and it gave soccer a social meaning that resonated far beyond a contest for a sporting trophy. 'There was not a large amount of interest taken in [association] football so far as the North was concerned' wrote 'A Free Critic' in 1892, 'and it was not until Darwen made their journey to play the Old Etonians in the English cup ties that we in Lancashire commenced to think of popularising the game'.[8]

In the industrial towns and cities of the English midlands and north, cup competitions had a revolutionary impact on football. Introduced to add some competitive seasoning to the diet of friendly matches that clubs then played, knock-out cups rapidly and unexpectedly became a focus for local pride and civic rivalries. From being private groups of select young men enjoying the company of their social peers, football clubs quickly became representatives of a community, carrying the honour of their neighbourhood into battle on the football pitch. By the end of the 1870s, dozens of clubs were playing in cup competitions across the industrial regions of Britain, and their success spurred the creation of other even more localised tournaments. The Yorkshire Cup led to the establishment of local cups in every major town in West and East Yorkshire, while the success of the Birmingham Senior Cup inspired the Walsall Cup, the Staffordshire Cup, the Mayor's Charity Cup, the Campbell Rovers Cup, the Wednesbury Charity Cup, the Birmingham Junior Cup and the SH Strollers Cup in the West Midlands alone.[9] By the early 1880s, a vast thicket of football cup tournaments had enveloped the expanding urban centres of industrial Britain, and these became the means by which football was transformed into a mass spectator sport.

The appeal of playing in the FA Cup and the regional competitions of both codes led to increasing numbers of clubs joining the FA or RFU. The importance of victory in cup tournaments meant that clubs had to specialise in one code or the other to maximise their chances of winning, and as a consequence the Sheffield FA found itself squeezed between the two national organisations. Sheffield joined the FA with hopes of converting it to their own rules but the FA proved impervious. For Sheffield, games against London and Glasgow were the highlight of the local season, but differences in the rules left these matches unsatisfactory as a true test of intercity pride. Sheffield's insistence on only one defender – who could be the goalkeeper – between the goal and the attacking players, as opposed to London and Glasgow's three defenders, essentially meant its game had no offside rule. Eventually, the Sheffield FA abandoned its own rulebook and adopted the FA's rules. Football had discarded the last of its local variations and was now consolidated around the twin poles of the FA and RFU.

It was no coincidence that four of the most important football centres of the 1880s – Sheffield, Leeds, Birmingham and Glasgow – were also the cities that experienced the highest percentage annual population growth in the second half of the nineteenth century.[10] Like Sheffield, Birmingham was a city of small industrial, predominantly engineering, factories, where working practices such as Saint Monday were difficult to suppress and left a strong sense of entitlement to leisure among skilled workers.[11] Leeds and Glasgow were cities of large-scale factory-based industry, whether it be the woollen trade and engineering in Leeds or shipbuilding and heavy engineering in Glasgow. As people flocked to these cities in search of employment, an entertainment industry emerged to provide amusement outside of work. Music halls, which had emerged in London in the 1850s, dominated the leisure landscape by the 1880s, by which time every major town and city had at least one 'palace of varieties'.[12] The brewing industry also expanded rapidly, building new pubs of unprecedented size and luxury.[13] Mass literacy boosted the popularity of local and regional newspapers, which responded by publishing Saturday night entertainment specials – one of the earliest being Birmingham's *Saturday Night*, which first appeared in 1882 – that soon became devoted to sport and especially to the afternoon's football results. And as well as the fortunes of the top sides, much of that newsprint space was devoted to local tournaments and junior clubs.

This explosion of interest in the game was made possible by the increased leisure time and rising standard of living of the industrial working class. Textile workers in northern England, such as in the future cradles of football in the cotton towns of Lancashire and the woollen producers of West York-shire, had secured a two o'clock end to work on Saturdays in 1850, and the August Bank Holiday was made law the following year. In 1874 parliament passed another Factory Act that made the one o'clock end to work on Saturdays the norm. The impact of this reduction in working time was described by Moses Heap, a Lancashire cotton spinner:

> for a while we did not know how to pass our time away. Before it had been all bed and work; now in place of seventy hours a week we had fifty-five and a half. It became a practice, mostly on Saturdays, to play football and cricket, which had never been done before.[14]

From the early 1870s, wages also began to rise and provided working people with disposable income to spend on leisure, adding a further stimulus to the development of the entertainment industry. But this increased spending power and leisure time did not automatically mean that football would become the sport of the working class.[15] Writing about the early 1870s in York, Jack Shaw, one of York FC's pioneering players, recalled that

> all the sport in which the working men of York seemed interested was rabbit coursing. Hundreds of them used to assemble on the Knavesmire [one of York's main public spaces] on a Saturday after-noon to indulge in this so-called sport and when they saw the football players they made jeering references to the 'silly fools who kicked the ball about in the wet'.[16]

Although residual enthusiasm for football did undoubtedly exist in certain regions, the great mass of working-class participants did not spontaneously take up the game in the second half of the nineteenth century but came to it through the institutions of the church, the workplace and the pub.

By the last third of the Victorian era, Muscular Christianity had come to be seen not merely as a means of inculcating masculine nationalist values in the future masters of the British Empire, but also into its servants. 'We must educate our masters', the Liberal politician Robert Lowe reputedly said as the 1867 Reform Act brought the vote to the better-off skilled minority of the working class. Moreover, the relative harmony between the classes that existed in Britain from the defeat of the Chartists in the 1840s to the emergence of 'new unionism' in the 1880s – what Engels called the 'forty years of hibernation' of class conflict – meant that sport across the classes was not impossible.[17] Thus Lancashire's Turton FC in the early 1870s could field teams with Old Harrovians and manual workers playing Harrow School rules, while the Pilkington works rugby team in St Helens on Merseyside contained both shop-floor workers and the heirs to the Pilkington fortune.[18] Such workplace-based teams were created by employers as an early form of what became known as 'welfare capitalism', using sport to foster a sense of corporate unity and esprit de corps.

In a similar way, the Anglican church viewed football as the apple to tempt working-class youths away from idleness, crime and immorality, and towards Christian duty. The list of football clubs that emerged from church organisations is a roll-call of subsequently famous clubs of all codes: Aston Villa, Bolton Wanderers, Everton, Northampton Saints, Leeds Rhinos, Wakefield Trinity, to name just a handful. The vast majority of these new working-class footballers remained steadfastly inured to the church's appeal to piety, and church clubs usually succumbed eventually to the exigencies of competitive football and abandoned their evangelical mission. Not even the spiritual power of the Anglican church could now stand in the way of football.

Within fifteen years of the first FA Cup final, soccer would be dominated by clubs that drew their players and supporters from the industrial proletariat. In rugby, the very same process would break the game into two hostile camps. In both soccer and northern rugby, the game's tactics, rules and culture were transformed by the invention and enthusiasm of working-class people. This was recognised by contemporary commentators, such as A.A. Sutherland, the football columnist of the weekly *Clarion*, who in 1893 celebrated the contribution of the working class to football over the previous two decades:

> The prosperity and popularity of the game dates from the time the working man commenced to interest himself in it, both physically and mentally. His success at the game may not be quite suitable to the tastes of the Corinthian, but it is nevertheless a fact that since he poked his nose into the recreation, football has come on in leaps and bounds.[19]

Notes

1 'A Londoner', 'Metropolitan Football', in Rev. Frank Marshall (ed.) *Football: The Rugby Union Game* (London: Cassell, 1892), p. 329.
2 *Bell's Life*, 7 January 1871. Membership figures from RFU minute books, 1871–75 and C.W. Alcock, *The Football Annual* (London: Lilywhite, 1874).
3 Professional player figures from Tony Mason, *Association Football and English Society 1863–1915* (Brighton: Harvester, 1981), p. 38, and Matthew Taylor, *The Leaguers: The Making of Professional Football in England, 1900–1939* (Liverpool: Liverpool University Press, 2005), p. 85.

4 Eric Hobsbawm, *Worlds of Labour* (London: Weidenfeld & Nicolson, 1984), p. 206.

5 RFU committee minutes, 22 January 1878.

6 *Sporting Gazette*, 28 December 1872.

7 *The Goal*, 7 February 1874.

8 The Free Critic, 'The Past and the Future', *Athletic News Football Annual*, 1892–3, London 1892, p. 107.

9 For Birmingham cups, see *Saturday Night* [Birmingham] 26 April 1884.

10 A.F. Weber, *The Growth of Cities in the Nineteenth Century: A Study in Statistics* (London: Macmillan, 1899), p. 450.

11 For a comparison of the working and leisure practices of Sheffield and Birmingham see Dennis Smith, *Conflict and Compromise: Class Formation in English Society, 1830–1914: A Comparative Study of Birmingham and Sheffield* (London: RKP, 1982).

12 See, for example, Dave Russell, *Popular Music in England, 1890–1914: A Social History* (Manchester: Manchester University Press, 1987), ch 5.

13 Tony Collins and Wray Vamplew, *Mud, Sweat and Beers: A Cultural History of Sport and Alcohol* (Oxford: Berg 2002), ch. 1.

14 Moses Heap, *My Life & Times*, typescript in Rawtenstall Library, RC942 ROS.

15 For the contrary view that football 'only needed a nudge to set it going viral', see Roy Hay, Adrian Harvey and Mel Smith, 'Football Before Codification: The Problems of Myopia', *Soccer & Society*, vol. 16, no. 2–3 (2015), p. 168.

16 *Yorkshire Evening Post*, 21 February 1903.

17 Engels, 'May 4 in London', in Karl Marx and Frederick Engels, *Collected Works*, vol. 27, p. 61.

18 For Turton see C.E. Sutcliffe and F. Hargreaves, *History of the Lancashire Football Association 1878–1928* (Blackburn: Toulmin & Sons: Blackburn, 1928), pp. 17 and 32–3. For Pilkington's, see *The Lantern* (St Helens), 13 December 1889.

19 *Clarion*, 7 October 1893. A similar point is made in Gavin Kitching, 'The Origins of Football: History, Ideology and the Making of "The People's Game"', *History Workshop Journal*, first published online February 1, 2015, doi:10.1093/hwj/dbu023, 22.

7

GLASGOW

Football capital of the nineteenth century

One has got to be in Glasgow on International day to realise adequately how tremendous is the hold the game has on the Scottish mind. The enthusiasm of the Scot for the Association game is without parallel in any other race for any particular sport or pastime.

—R.M. Connell, 1906[1]

Nowhere could the face of modern football be seen more clearly than in Glasgow. If Sheffield's football culture of the 1860s was the first cuckoo of the football spring, Glasgow's football culture from the 1870s blossomed into the most glorious summer to create the archetypal football city. Its population doubled to over 760,000 between 1851 and 1901, and it became home to almost 20 per cent of Scotland's entire population.[2] The rapid growth of the shipbuilding industry – by 1913 the city was producing more shipping tonnage than the entire national output of Germany or the United States – and other engineering trades saw working-class living standards rise between a third and a half.

Organised football was probably first played in the city in 1864 under rugby rules at Glasgow Academy, the city's elite private school. In 1866, the school's old boys formed the Glasgow Academicals club, following the creation of the West of Scotland club the previous year. Both sides yet again emerged from cricket clubs. Association rules were brought to the city in 1867 when Queen's Park FC was founded, again by privately educated young professional men. In 1871 Queen's Park joined the FA and in 1872 organised the first official Scotland versus England soccer match at

Glasgow's Hamilton Crescent cricket ground. This was to prove the catalyst for soccer's immense popularity in the city.

Over the next fifteen years, Scotland won nine and England just two of their encounters. It was not merely that Scotland won, but the exuberant manner in which they did it. Between 1876 and 1882, the scorelines read 3–0, 3–1, 7–2, 4–5, 5–4, 6–1, 5–1. It wasn't until 1888 that England managed their first win in Glasgow. Every Scotland versus England match was played in Glasgow, and consequently the city became co-terminus not merely with the association game but also with Scottish identity itself. From 1906 onwards, there would never be less than 100,000 people attending Scotland versus England matches, none of which would be lost by Scotland, and these matches would make up five of the six matches in Britain that drew more than 100,000 spectators.[3] In contrast, with the exception of a desultory rain-sodden 0–0 draw with England in 1873, the Scottish Rugby Union team kept itself to its Edinburgh heartland, with the result that rugby in Glasgow stood loftily aloof from the explosion of interest in football in the city; a mere eleven rugby clubs were formed in the city between 1874 and 1900.[4]

Yet by 1890 there were hundreds of soccer clubs playing in every corner of Glasgow, with major club matches regularly attracting crowds in excess of 10,000, and many more for important cup matches. The city had become, in the words of Keith Angus in 1880,

> a veritable home for football. Few but those who have been present at the Scottish matches can realise the extraordinary enthusiasm displayed by the spectators. Thousands and thousands witness even minor contests, and consequently the contrast is wonderful to one accustomed to the sprinkling of onlookers at a metropolitan contest.[5]

By the early 1900s, Glasgow's three major football stadia – Hampden, Ibrox and Parkhead – could together accommodate over 300,000 spectators, almost half of the city's population of 762,000.[6] Nor was it just as spectators that football captured the imagination of the population. Matthew McDowell has calculated that by 1900 a soccer club existed for every 160 males aged between 15 and 29 living in central Scotland.[7]

The passion that gripped urban Scots for soccer was facilitated by the works of the municipal age. The trams that had been introduced to the city in 1871 allowed players and spectators to travel across the city to play and support their teams. The public parks that had been created provided ample space for the playing of football, not to mention the name for Queen's

Park FC. And the local press provided the daily sustenance for the unending conversations about the game throughout the workshops and offices of the city. In 1884 the *Scottish Athletic Journal* claimed sales of 20,000 a week, undoubtedly a factor in the *Glasgow Herald* publishing its first local Saturday sports' edition that year, the first of many the city would see.[8]

Other industrial regions could boast similar levels of interest to that in Glasgow, but none could match the completeness with which football enveloped the city. In 1886, 20,000 people crammed themselves into the Yorkshire Cup semi-final between Halifax and Batley, larger than any FA or Scottish FA Cup final crowd thus far.[9] In Birmingham, its *Saturday Night* newspaper in 1883 could list 107 local clubs of sufficient standing to warrant a place in its unofficial merit tables, alongside seven local cup competitions.[10] But Glasgow was unique in its huge number of clubs, the immensity of its crowds and, lacking any rivalry from rugby or cricket, the complete identification of the city with soccer. Moreover, because the Scottish national team played almost all its home matches in the city, usually resulting in the defeat of the English, the identification of Glasgow, Scotland and soccer became one and indivisible. National, local and, given the dominance of the sport by working-class players and spectators by the 1880s, class pride became intertwined so much so that Glasgow *was* Scottish football. If Paris was the capital of the nineteenth century, as Walter Benjamin described it, Glasgow was the football capital of the age, setting the template not only for the world football cities such as Rio de Janeiro, Buenos Aires, Milan or Barcelona, but also providing the archetype for the relationship between football and the city.

Glasgow's experience underlined a deeper truth about football's appeal. As its economy expanded, people moved into the city in search of work. It was a city of immigrants, from Ireland, England, and the Scottish countryside. In 1881 almost half of its population had been born outside of the city. As people poured into Glasgow's tenement blocks, football provided Saturday afternoon entertainment they could share with their neighbours and workmates, strengthening the collective bonds of local solidarity. Up until the legalisation of professionalism in 1893 by the Scottish FA, it was quite likely that the players they cheered also lived and worked alongside them, further enhancing a sense of belonging. Local patriotism and civic pride could be expressed on an almost continual basis through football, whereas outside of the stadium it was usually confined to elections or war-time.[11]

But football also brought something that was new. For perhaps the first time in human history since the age of the Roman colosseum, one could pay a small amount of money to experience extremes of emotion. For two hours or so, the world of work and daily life could be set aside while the spectator rode a collective roller-coaster of intense highs and lows, joy and despair, exultation and frustration. People did not merely watch football from the terraces, they experienced it alongside thousands of other people. Unlike the theatre, the concert or the music hall, football allowed participation for both the player and the audience. The spectator chose a side and then, through shouting, singing, chanting, cheering and booing with their fellow fans, sought to affect the outcome of the match. The win or loss was felt as intensely by the fan as it was by the player.

The weekly cycle of matches meant that the game could be discussed throughout the week, anticipating the new experience of the following weekend. Even the sheer size of the crowds that attended matches became part of its unique and new appeal. 'Monster crowds' were not unknown for great civic or political occasions, but football offered the opportunity to be part of a huge collective throng, with its unconscious rhythms, spontaneous flows and sense of belonging, every other week. Such a level of personal involvement was something that no other form of entertainment could provide. Indeed, it allowed the spectator to experience intense emotions that, outside of matters of life and death, would be unavailable to them in everyday life. The constant military references in sports reports were not just an expression of the jingoism of the times but also an attempt to convey an emotional palette that most people would only experience in wartime. But football replicated the potency of those feelings without harm or repercussion.

Although the game offered the most visceral experience, this 'commodification' of the emotions was not unique to football and could also be seen in many of the newly commercialised forms of leisure of the late nineteenth century. The 'sensation novel', in which the reader was drawn into worlds of sex, murder and insanity, sought to stimulate the emotions, a phenomenon given additional impetus with the rise of the Gothic novel, perhaps most famously with the success of Bram Stoker's *Dracula* in 1897. The growth of the popular press and the attention it paid to murders, especially the Jack the Ripper killings of 1888, also sought to capitalise on this stimulation of emotion. For the well-heeled middle classes, opera offered the same emotional intensity at a somewhat higher price. But until the rise of the cinema and popular music in the twentieth century, nothing could compete with the ability of football to offer a capsule moment of intense emotion without consequence.[12]

The unique and multi-faceted appeal of football of whatever code led to an exponential growth in the numbers of people attending matches in the last two decades of the Victorian era. Barely 2,000 people watched Wanderers' victory over the Royal Engineers in the 1872 FA Cup Final. The crowd wouldn't reach five figures until Blackburn Rovers' second successive win in 1885. But from then on attendances ballooned, reaching 45,000 in 1893 and 101,000 in 1901. Scottish crowds reached five figures as early as 1877, when Vale of Leven prevailed over Rangers in an epic final that was drawn twice, and expanded to over 40,000 for the first time in 1892. Although rugby's Yorkshire Cup final outdrew the FA Cup final until the mid-1880s, the civil war that fractured rugby effectively scuppered its ability to attract crowds approaching six figures until the inter-war years.

Glasgow's impact on the game was as great on the field as it was off it. The intensity of its competitions forged highly skilled players and created a style of play based on team-work, combination and close passing that became known as the 'scientific' game. Reflecting everyday life in the factories, shipyards and working-class communities of the region, collectivity underpinned the Scottish way of football. As the regular victories over England demonstrated, Scottish players and tactics were far more advanced than the individual play of the English public schools or the long-ball game of the Sheffield clubs.[13]

This did not go unnoticed by the ambitious association clubs of Lancashire. In January 1878, Glasgow's Partick FC travelled down to play Darwen in the heart of Lancashire's cotton district, the third match that the two sides had played over the previous two years. A few months later, at the start of the following season, Partick's Fergus Suter and James Love joined the Lancastrians. It was widely suspected that both were being paid by the club. When Suter then transferred to Blackburn Rovers at the end of the 1879–80 season, no-one was in any doubt.[14]

Football was on the cusp of another revolution.

Notes

1 R.M. Connell, 'The Association Game in Scotland', *The Book of Football* (London: Amalgamated Press., 1906), p. 45.

2 Figures and much of the detail of this chapter can be found in Peter Bilsborough's outstanding *The Development of Sport in Glasgow, 1850–1914* (MLitt thesis, University of Glasgow, 1983).

3 The other being the drawn 1901 FA Cup final Between Tottenham and Sheffield United at Crystal Palace.

4 Bilsborough, *Development of Sport in Glasgow*, p. 111.

5 J. Keith Angus, *The Sportsman's Year Book* (London: Cassell, 1880), p. 19.

6 Bill Murray, *The Old Firm* (Edinburgh: John Donald Publishers, 1984), p. 35.

7 Matthew L. McDowell, *A Cultural History of Football in Scotland* (New York: Edwin Mellen Press, 2013), p. 14.

8 Bilsborough, *Development of Sport in Glasgow*, p. 236. Murray, *The Old Firm*, p. 47.

9 *Athletic News*, 1 June 1886.

10 *Saturday Night*, 2 February 1884.

11 For a discussion of these themes, see Richard Holt, 'Football and the Urban Way of Life in Nineteenth-century Britain', in J.A. Mangan (ed.) *Pleasure, Profit and Proselytism: British Culture and Sport at Home and Abroad 1700–1914* (London: Frank Cass, 1988), pp. 67–85.

12 On the importance of emotion in sports spectators, see Matthew Klugman, *A New Mania? Tracing the Emergence of Passionate Modern Spectator Sport Cultures in Manchester, Melbourne and Boston*, presented at the Centre for the History of Emotions, Queen Mary University of London, June 2014.

13 See Scottish FA secretary Archibald Rae's critique of the Sheffield game in *Bell's Life*, 8 September 1877.

14 The nature of payments to players in the 1870s make it impossible to know who was the first paid player. In the 1876–77 season Peter Andrews and James Joseph Lang moved from Scotland to play for Sheffield's Heeley and Wednesday clubs but there appears to be no evidence about their status. see Matthew Taylor, *The Association Game*, p. 48. For more on Suter and Love, see Andy Mitchell, *From Partick with Love – The Story of Jimmy Love and Fergie Suter, The First Professional Footballers* at www.scottishsporthistory.com/sports-history-news-and-blog/from-partick-with-love-the-story-of-jimmy-love-and-fergie-suter-the-first-professional-footballers, accessed 22 November 2017.

8

THE COMING OF PROFESSIONALISM

Football is played more scientifically than it ever was, and that is solely due to the fact that in a professional team the men are under the control of the management and are constantly playing together.

—William Suddell, Preston North End manager, 1887[1]

As Glasgow showed, the explosion of public interest in football across all sections of society from the late 1870s, especially among the great mass of the industrial working class, brought significant amounts of money into the sport for the first time. Moreover, the importance that cup competitions now assumed for both national and local pride also injected a competitive imperative into the sport. These were the twin engines that would propel football into a different and completely new era.

Fergus Suter and James Love's move to Lancashire laid down a path that would be followed by thousands of other Scottish footballers over the next decades. Known as 'Scotch Professors' because of their footballing expertise, no northern soccer club was complete without at least a Scottish leavening. The extent to which the professors came to dominate English football was shown in December 1884 when the Scottish FA wrote to fifty-eight players then playing with English clubs, informing them that they were to be considered professionals and would not therefore be eligible for selection for Scotland.[2] Eleven of them played for Preston North End, nine for Burnley and the rest, with the exception of Aston Villa's Archie Hunter, all played for clubs in Lancashire cotton towns. Despite the Scottish FA's best efforts, the migration of Scots players to rich English clubs continued unabated, perhaps the most egregious example being when Liverpool kicked off their first season in 1892 with every member of their inaugural side was a Scot.

The same emergence of professionalism was taking place in rugby. When Suter and Love were on their way to Darwen, Harrogate rugby player and professional cricketer Teddy Bartram was joining Wakefield Trinity in exchange for a job as the assistant secretary of the club at £52 per annum. The role of 'assistant secretary' was a common ruse of cricket clubs to enable amateurs to be paid without being classed as professionals. Other players followed, tempted to change clubs for payments and also for jobs, at first in the cotton and woollen factories that speckled both sides of the Pennines, and then increasingly by the prospects of becoming a pub landlord.

A migration of footballers to northern England was also seen in rugby, although instead moving south from Scotland it was from industrial south Wales that players 'went north' to play in Lancashire and Yorkshire. Although this began slightly later than in Scotland – the first recorded player to play for a northern club was future Welsh international Harry Bowen in 1884 – it also highlighted the rapid development of football beyond England. As with Glasgow and the English industrial cities, Cardiff, Swansea and industrial South Wales had experienced exponential population growth. Cardiff grew from 20,000 people in 1851 to 182,000 by 1911 while the Rhondda Valley, the beating heart of Welsh coal production, went from 2,000 people to 152,000 in the same period. In 1878 the South Wales Cup tournament began and, as was the case everywhere else that a cup competition took hold, the game spread like wildfire, with Cardiff alone having 220 teams playing by 1890.[3] By then, Welsh players in northern English rugby sides were a common sight, attracted by the jobs and money that could be provided by cash-rich northern sides.

It wasn't only imported players from Scotland and Wales that benefited from football's commercial success. As the case of Teddy Bertram demonstrated, skilled footballers could receive substantial rewards from clubs seeking cup success, regardless of their origins. In the 1882–83 season Bolton Wanderers' outgoings were almost £1,100. Where, wondered the *Athletic News*, had this money been spent? The clear implication was that most, if not all, of it had gone to the players. Eighteen months later, the football correspondent of *The Yorkshireman* weekly magazine could report with little fear of contradiction that 'I could mention some dozen players who (if report is to be believed) all receive money over and above their actual expenses'.[4] It wasn't only cash that players received. Gifts of legs of mutton, bottles of port, cloth for suits were all made to players and teams for outstanding individual performances or simple victories in cup ties.

Many of these practices came from the working-class leisure culture of the players and spectators who were increasingly dominating both types of football. Pubs were the well-spring of commercial sport within working-class communities, supplying pitches, changing rooms and publicity for teams in return for the opportunity to sell beer to crowds, but also providing prizes, stake money and gambling facilities.[5] In this community, money, sport and entertainment were inextricably linked. To football's new mass audience, the idea that successful athletes should receive rewards, whether monetary or otherwise, was a self-evident fact of life.

But this view was not shared by those who governed football. Educated in the public school tradition that sport was a character-building source of moral education, they instinctively rejected the idea that the playing of a game should have a monetary reward. Professionalism, they believed, would inevitably lead to corruption of sport's ideals by gambling and match-fixing. They feared that professionalism would undermine the structure of football, and allow professional players – by which it was understood to mean working-class athletes – to dominate the sport. This had in fact almost been the case in cricket, when the popularity of professional touring sides such as William Clarke's All-England Eleven had briefly threatened the MCC's authority over the game in the mid-nineteenth century.

Underlying these fears was an acute sense of social snobbery and a desire to use sport to maintain the status quo between the classes. Two years before the formation of the FA the *Rowing Almanack* had categorically excluded 'tradesmen, labourers, artisans or working mechanics' from events under its jurisdiction. Shortly after, the Amateur Athletic Club, the forerunner of the Amateur Athletic Association, also barred anyone who was 'a mechanic, artisan or labourer' from membership.[6] Both sports had long traditions of working-class involvement and it was the need to ensure that lower-class athletes did not threaten upper- and middle-class control that led to such explicit statements of class prejudice.

In football, the sudden popularity of cup competitions in the late 1870s brought all of these concerns to the fore. Defeating local rivals and winning cups now had a wider social importance, causing clubs to seek out players who could bring cup glory to their communities, regardless of whether the player came from that community. Knock-out tournaments also meant that clubs could no longer choose their opponents, undermining the social networking aspect that had been so important in the formation of the early gentlemen's football teams. A club could not only now find itself playing a team that it considered to be socially inferior, but it could quite possibly lose to them. For many this was unacceptable, as highlighted in 1884 when *The Athlete* contemptuously declared that the 'employment of the scum of the

Scottish villages has tended, in no small degree, to brutalise the game'.[7] Cup competitions therefore tended to undermine the informal social codes that had previously governed the sport. As a Birmingham FA committee member bemoaned in 1884, cups were 'the root of the evil' of professionalism.[8]

So it did not come as a surprise that when the first reports of men being paid or offered employment to play football appeared in the late 1870s, the leaders of both codes felt something had to be done. The concern was heightened by the fact that the popularity of the sport was based on its appeal to civic identity, and this appeared to be threatened by what was known as the 'importation' of players from outside the area. To counteract the threat of paid players, the initial impulse of both codes of football was, once again, to follow the lead of cricket.

Consequently, in late November 1879 the Yorkshire Rugby Union committee decided that

> no player who is not strictly an amateur shall be allowed to play in the Challenge Cup ties, or in any match under the direct control of the County Football Committee; the definition of the term 'amateur' shall be the same as that adopted by the MCC.

But the MCC's definition of an amateur was simply a player who took 'no more than his expenses for a match'. This was deliberately vague – in reality, an amateur cricketer was by definition a gentleman, a term easy to understand but impossible to define – and it did nothing to resolve the issue.[9] Likewise, the Lancashire FA also turned to cricket's rules to stem the flow of imported players from Scotland. In 1882 it adopted cricket's County Championship qualification rules and insisted that players born outside of Lancashire were not eligible to play in the Lancashire Cup until they had lived in the county for two years.[10]

Both the association and rugby codes of football took the same approach to payments to players at this time. The differences that emerged in the mid-1880s had not yet appeared. Some historians have suggested that it was Charles Alcock's experience as secretary of Surrey CCC that gave the FA a more flexible approach to professionalism than that of the RFU, while sociologists have argued that the FA had a more patrician leadership than the RFU, so they did not feel 'status anxiety' when confronted with working-class professionals.[11] But initially soccer's leaders were more determined to fight the danger than the RFU. Only in Yorkshire, where the cup tournament had become widely popular, did the rugby authorities take measures to combat the problem. The RFU itself did not seriously debate the issue until 1886, possibly because the lack of a national rugby cup competition meant that its leading clubs did not play against clubs suspected of paying their players. However, in soccer there were numerous discussions about the issue and in 1882 the FA passed a resolution declaring that

> Any member of a club receiving remuneration or consideration of any sort above his actual expenses and any wages actually lost by any such player taking part in any match, shall be debarred from taking part in either cup, inter-Association or International contests, and any club employing such a player shall be excluded from this Association.[12]

But it was already too late to stop it. Barely eighteen months later, the issue came to a head when Upton Park, a London gentlemen's club, drew 1–1 with Preston North End in the fourth round of the FA Cup. Upton Park appealed against the result, claiming that Preston had fielded paid players, contrary to the 1882 resolution. When confronted with the charges, Preston's secretary William Sudell cheerfully admitted that they had found jobs for their players and that this was standard practice in Lancashire. The class element behind the dispute was illustrated by the *Preston Guardian*, which pointed that 'no working man can be an amateur football player. A working man cannot afford to absent himself from work in order to take part in a game without remuneration'.[13] Preston were suspended from the FA but, seeing the writing on the wall, Alcock proposed that the FA legalise professionalism. He was in a minority so, at the urging of the FA's assistant secretary N.L. Jackson, a journalist like Alcock and also something of a sporting entrepreneur, a committee was set up to consider the matter. The urgency of the issue was underlined shortly after when the FA suspended Burnley for exactly the same offence.[14]

Jackson's committee reported back in June 1884 and recommended that payments be allowed to players who took time off work to play, known as 'broken-time payments', but outlawing all other forms of payment on pain of expulsion from the FA. Just as drastically, it also suggested that only English players should be allowed to play in the FA Cup. It was not only supporters of the public school ethos who opposed professionalism. The Birmingham FA also vigorously objected to paying players, not least because they feared that their players would be picked off by rich Lancashire clubs, a concern shared by the Sheffield FA.[15] Tellingly, Birmingham's concerns about professionalism did not extend to Aston Villa captain Archie Hunter, who happened to be one of the first Scotch professors to make his way south.

However, as the attitude of William Sudell demonstrated, the Lancashire clubs were not passively prepared to accept the strictures of the FA. News of Preston's suspension was met by Lancashire clubs voting that 'a northern association be formed which will promote the interest of football generally in the northern districts'.[16] The Lancastrians bided their time until the start of the 1884–85 season when the FA announced that it would bar clubs from the FA Cup if they fielded or played against a club fielding an ineligible imported player.[17] The northern network immediately sprang back into life and on 23 October the British Football Association (BFA) was founded by seventeen clubs. The following week BFA advertisements appeared in the sporting press inviting clubs to a meeting in Manchester to 'promote and consolidate a powerful organisation which will embrace clubs and players of every nationality'.[18] Battle had commenced.

The new FA regulations were an existential threat to the top Lancashire clubs. If they were barred from playing clubs with imported players, their fixture lists would quickly dry up and their income shrivel. Football for them was a commercial business and the loss of attractive fixtures against leading clubs with star players would bring financial ruin. This was also apparent to those commercially based clubs that on paper opposed professionalism, so despite its formal support for the FA, the Birmingham FA decided to send a representative to the BFA meeting in Manchester on 30 October.[19]

The meeting was an impressive display of club power, attracting seventy delegates representing thirty-seven clubs. Faced with the now real threat of the formation of a rival association, the FA backed down. Four days after the BFA meeting, the FA suspended its proposed ban on imported players and called a special general meeting to discuss professionalism.[20] Eight days later, Alcock and Jackson's proposal that it was 'now expedient to legalise professionalism under stringent conditions' was endorsed by the full FA committee. However, the vote for professionalism at the FA's special general meeting in January 1885 failed to reach the necessary two-thirds majority, as did another special meeting was held in March. But the tide had clearly turned, and by the time a third special meeting convened on 20 July 1885, the inevitability of professionalism had been accepted and the two-thirds majority was comfortably achieved.

Professionalism was now legal but, as in cricket, the role of the professional player was stringently controlled. All professional players had to be registered by the FA, they could not change clubs without permission and they were subject to a residential qualification before they could play in the FA Cup. Professionals could not sit on FA committees nor could they be a club representative to the FA. In short, players would be paid to play football, and play was all that they would be allowed to do.

But if professionalism removed any danger that working-class professionals might dominate the administration of the FA, it meant precisely

PLATE 5 Football turned upside-down. Blackburn Olympic defeat Old Etonians to win the FA Cup in 1883 (*Illustrated Sporting and Dramatic News*, 7 April 1883)

the opposite on the field. In April 1885 Queen's Park lost 2–0 to Blackburn Rovers in that season's FA Cup final. It would be the last time that a gentleman's club would ever play in the final. Indeed, with the exception of the Slough-based Swifts club the following year, they would be the last such club to appear even in the semi-finals. This was the culmination of a trend that had emerged in 1882 when Blackburn Rovers became the first northern side to appear in the final. They lost 1–0 to Old Etonians but the following season their local rivals, Blackburn Olympic, upheld the pride of the town with an extra-time 2–1 win over the Etonians, and the cup stayed in Blackburn for the next four years as Rovers completed a hat-trick of wins. The age of the professional had arrived, and there would be no turning back.

The coming of the league

If cup competitions were the launchpad for football's popularity, professionalism was the rocket fuel that propelled soccer into the stratosphere. Although it had been the quest for cup glory that had caused clubs to import and pay players, it was soon apparent that knock-out tournaments were not enough to support the financial burden that they had brought. Players' wages had to be met and the huge increase in spectators also meant constructing grandstands, laying down terraces and installing turnstiles. The administrative responsibilities of running what were now businesses meant that a club had to employ at least a paid secretary. A good cup run would bring cash flooding into a club, but it could just as easily find itself eliminated in its first match and having to rely on friendly matches for its income. This was rarely enough. One of the reasons for Blackburn Olympic's abrupt demise in 1889 was the simple fact that, after the legalisation of professionalism in 1885, they never won another FA Cup tie. As Stoke-born novelist Arnold Bennett noted about the football crowd in 1911, 'if it could see victories it would pay sixpence, but it would not pay sixpence to assist at defeats'.[21]

The only way to avoid the same fate as the Olympic was to have regular high-quality fixtures that would be consistently attractive to spectators. Once again, cricket provided part of the answer. Since the 1860s there had been an unofficial county championship, largely tabulated by the cricket press, although the official MCC county championship began in 1890. This was advocated by some professional soccer administrators as a useful model. It is also likely, as Stefan Szymanski has pointed out, that they were influenced by the success of baseball's National League, founded in 1876 by America's leading professional clubs.[22] These discussions came to fruition on 2 March 1888 when Aston Villa director William MacGregor proposed the formation of a league competition based on home and away fixtures. Matters moved quickly and on April 12 teams from Lancashire and the Midlands met to found the Football League.[23] Selection of teams for the new league was made using strict business criteria. There was to be only one team in each town (another contributory factor in the downfall of Blackburn Olympic who lost out to Rovers) and stadia had to be easily accessible to ensure good crowds (Nottingham Forest seemingly lost out to Notts County because the latter had a better tram service from the city centre).

The new league kicked off on 8 September 1888 and proved to be every bit as successful as its founders had hoped. Preston carried off the first championship and also won the FA Cup. Most importantly, the league fulfilled the financial hopes of its founders, attracting 602,000 spectators. As had been the case with cup competitions a decade previously, the Football League's successful proof of concept immediately led to emulation, and a plethora of leagues sprang up across the country. In 1892 the Football League merged with one of these, the Football Alliance, which became its second division. In 1894 the Southern League was formed. Although Woolwich Arsenal, the first professional side in the south of England, had joined the Football League's second division in 1893, football in the south of England remained dominated by amateur clubs, restricting the development of the game as a mass spectator sport. The Southern League initially combined both amateur and professional sides but quickly became an incubator for the spread of professional soccer below its traditional north and midlands' heartlands.

The impetus that professionalism and the league system had given soccer can be gauged by the huge growth in attendances. By 1895 aggregate attendances at Football League matches had more than doubled to 1.5 million and a decade later had ballooned to 5 million. Just as strikingly, crowds at FA Cup finals rocketed from 22,000 in Preston North End's double-winning season of 1888–89 to 73,000 ten years later, reaching a previously unimaginable 110,820 that saw Spurs draw 2–2 with Sheffield United in 1901. The impact of the speed with which the association game was launched into modernity was reflected by the fact that of the thirty-two clubs playing the Football League in 1896, only eight had been founded before 1871, and three of those would not survive by 1901.

Outside of gentlemen's clubs for whom amateurism was a rationale for social exclusivity, soccer clubs which hesitated about embracing professionalism were thrown into turmoil. For a sport whose popularity was based on civic pride, the competitive imperative made professionalism inescapable. Supporters, whether working class or middle class, often demanded that their sides turn professional to remain competitive and uphold local honour. 'If we cannot depend upon native talent, then by all means let us have some of these stray Scotchmen who can be picked up so easily by our neighbours', wrote one Middlesborough supporter in 1889. 'Has the noble game, now that it has got such a hold on the public, to die out, and have we to dwindle into a fourth rate club after all our grand achievements?' Such was the clamour for professionalism that a new professional club, Middlesborough Ironopolis, was created in opposition to the hesitancy of the Middlesborough FC.[24]

Some clubs found the financial pressures of professionalism too much to bear. In the 1892–93 season Everton paid £3,529 and Blackburn Rovers £2,156 in wages alone, figures way beyond the reach of those sides outside of the successful elite.[25] Blackburn Olympic found it impossible to survive as a second professional side in a relatively small town – Blackburn's population in 1891 was just 120,000 people – as eventually did Middlesborough Ironopolis. In Manchester, both of its Football League sides, Ardwick and Newton Heath, collapsed under extensive debts in 1894 and 1902, respectively, leading to them being reformed as Manchester City and Manchester United. Newton Heath was bought by local brewing magnate J.H. Davies for £500 and effectively became a subsidiary of his Manchester Breweries, perhaps the most prominent example of the close relationship that developed between professional football and the brewing industry, one for the primary providers of capital for ground developments, stadium advertising and players' jobs for numerous clubs across Britain.

For many, professionalism brought untold sums of money into the club's coffers. Everton made a profit in every season bar one between 1891 and 1914. Liverpool, the side created when Everton split into two in 1892 over a financial dispute, also recorded a profit every season from 1900. In London, its belated football boom led to the creation of Chelsea by sporting entrepreneur Gus Mears, a purely business proposition that returned profitable seasons from 1908 to 1915, including a gargantuan £22,826 in 1908. By the 1890s it had become common for clubs to become limited liability companies. This made it easier to raise funds for capital investment and to adopt an organisational model that was appropriate for the substantial enterprises they had now become.[26] No-one could now be in any doubt that football was now a business.

But the adoption of professionalism had also led to a subtle but fundamental change to soccer. Amateur sport was based on status, hierarchy and deference. The authority of governing bodies like cricket's MCC, rugby's RFU and soccer's FA rested ultimately on their social status – they had appointed themselves the governing bodies of their respective sports.

Relationships between amateur clubs were based on social gradations. Gentlemen preferred to play against gentlemen and restricted their fixture lists to clubs they felt to be their peers. Cup competitions undermined these distinctions because clubs could not choose their cup-tie opponents, one of the underlying reasons for the RFU's refusal to organise a national knock-out tournament. And players were also judged on status as well as merit, most tellingly in the tradition that captains of the England cricket team had to be amateurs, regardless of ability. Under amateurism, sport operated according to social codes that were unwritten and understandable only to those who shared the same social background.

Professionalism dissolved these unspoken 'structures of understanding'. The contract system placed soccer on a legal basis that was ultimately beyond the authority of the governing body. The payment of wages meant that players were assessed on merit rather than status. The introduction of leagues meant that fixtures were arranged by strictly objective criteria rather than social connection. And as commercial enterprises, clubs had legal obligations beyond the requirements of the governing body. Professionalism and the league system gave soccer the appearance of being meritocratic, in contrast to the aristocratic basis of amateurism. As the creation of the Football League and countless other leagues demonstrated, soccer no longer belonged to the FA.

In little more than a decade, association football had undergone a social and economic revolution. It had thrown off the straitjacket of gentlemanly amateurism to become a commercial juggernaut that engaged the passions of millions of men and women. This allowed it to conquer nineteenth-century Britain, and laid the basis for its subsequent conquest of the planet.

Notes

1 William Suddell, Preston North End manager in 1887, quoted in Neil Carter, *The Football Manager* (Abingdon: Routledge, 2006), p. 18.
2 *Saturday Night* (Birmingham), 13 December 1884.
3 Gwyn Prescott, *The Birth of Rugby in Cardiff and Wales: 'This Rugby Spellbound People'* (Cardiff: Ashley Drake Publishing Ltd, 2011), pp. 42–69.
4 Tony Mason, *Association Football and English Society 1863–1915* (Brighton: Harvester, 1981), p. 72. *The Yorkshireman*, 10 January 1885.
5 Tony Collins and Wray Vamplew, *Mud, Sweat and Beers: A Cultural History of Sport and Alcohol* (Oxford: Berg, 2002).
6 For examples of amateur regulations, see appendix two of Wray Vamplew, *Pay Up and Play the Game* (Cambridge: Cambridge University Press, 1988), pp. 302–7.
7 *The Athlete*, 29 September 1884, quoted in Steven Tischler, *Footballers and Businessmen: The Origins of Professional Soccer in England* (New York: Holmes & Meier, 1981), p. 45.

8 *Saturday Night* [Birmingham], 29 March 1884.

9 *Yorkshire Post*, 25 November 1879.

10 Tony Mason, pp. 71–2. For cricket's 1873 residential rules, see Christopher Martin-Jenkins, *The Wisden Book of County Cricket* (London: Queen Anne Press, 1981), p. 17.

11 For example, Richard Holt, *Sport and the British* (Oxford: Clarendon Press, 1989), p. 107, and Eric Dunning and Kenneth Sheard, *Barbarians, Gentlemen and Players* (Abingdon: Routledge, 2005, Second Edition), pp. 136–8.

12 Dave Russell, 'From Evil to Expedient: The Legalization of Professionalism in English Football, 1884–85', in Stephen Wagg (ed.) *Myths and Milestones in the History of Sport* (Basingstoke: Palgrave, 2011), p. 35.

13 Preston Guardian, 6 February 1884, quoted in Tischler, *Footballers and Businessmen*, p. 45.

14 *Saturday Night* [Birmingham], 29 March 1884.

15 *Saturday Night* [Birmingham], 25 October 1884.

16 *Saturday Night* [Birmingham], 2 February 1884.

17 *Football Field*, 11 October 1884.

18 *Saturday Night* [Birmingham], 25 October 1884.

19 *Saturday Night* [Birmingham], 25 October 1884.

20 *Athletic News*, 5 November 1884.

21 Arnold Bennett, *The Card* (London: Methuen, 1911), p. 85.

22 Stefan Szymanski and Andrew Zimbalist, *National Pastime: How Americans Play Baseball and the Rest of the World Plays Soccer* (Washington: Brookings Institution, 2005).

23 Matthew Taylor, *The Association Game: A History of British Football* (London: Pearson, 2008), pp. 65–7. Graham Williams, *The Code War* (Harefield: Yore, 1994), p. 106. The history of the Football League is in Matthew Taylor, *The Leaguers: The Making of Professional Football in England, 1900–1939* (Liverpool: Liverpool University Press, 2005).

24 *North-Eastern Daily Gazette*, 2 February 1889, quoted in Catherine Budd, *Sport in Urban England: Middlesbrough, 1870–1914* (Lanham, MD: Lexington, 2017), p. 104.

25 'Professionalism in Football', *The Yorkshireman*, 6 October 1893.

26 For a detailed discussion of the economic evolution of football clubs, see Wray Vamplew, *Pay Up and Play the Game*.

9

KICKING AGAINST THE PRICKS

Women and football

> We are organised to show that the game of Association football can be
> played by women as scientifically as by men.
> —Helen Graham, captain and secretary of the Original
> Lady Footballers' team, 1895[1]

Unsurprisingly, it was the Scottish cauldron of football that produced the
first recorded examples of women playing organised soccer. In May 1881 two
teams of women from Glasgow began a series of Scotland versus England
matches.[2] The first attracted 1,000 people to the Easter Road ground in
Edinburgh while the following week 5,000 saw the teams at Shawfields in
Glasgow. This was a purely commercial venture designed to profit from the
novelty of women playing what was perceived as a 'man's game' and the male
organisers made no attempt to disguise its nature. According to press reports,
there were almost no women spectators at the Glasgow match, in contrast to
the large numbers of women watching men's matches, and it was abandoned
after fifty-five minutes due to a pitch invasion when the women players
were attacked.[3] The organisers' aim was not to encourage women to play
football but to make money from the mockery and misogyny of the crowd.
Five further matches were played in the football heartlands of Blackburn,
Manchester, where the match was ended after another pitch invasion, and
Liverpool, where the sides appear to have switched to rugby rules.[4] Having failed to make money the venture folded less than two months after it
started, leaving the male chauvinism of football as strong as it had ever been.

Although women were firmly excluded from all versions of the game on the pitch, they were still a significant presence off the pitch. Few reports of major matches failed to note the significant presence of 'ladies'. As early as the first Yorkshire versus Lancashire match in 1870 the press had noted the 'large number of the fair sex' in attendance, and as the sport's popularity exploded, women were an integral part of football crowds. In both codes, women could be found in the grandstands, where higher admission charges created a middle-class enclave, and on the terraces, where they were often admitted for free, allowing working-class women more opportunity to attend.[5]

> Don't imagine that all the spectators were men, for they were not. Indeed, the female element was very largely represented and the comments from this portion of the gathering were as numerous and as critical as those of their brothers, husbands and fathers,

commented *The Yorkshireman* about the 1883 Yorkshire versus Cheshire rugby match.[6] The following year it was estimated that a quarter of the 5,000 crowd at the Manningham versus Hull rugby match were women. As with men, football was an opportunity for women to step out of their traditional roles for a couple of hours each week. In 1888 the chairman of Swinton criticised the side's female supporters for their 'bad manners and rowdiness', and in 1884, the victorious Batley team found themselves being pelted with red-hot coals by a woman as they left the vanquished Horbury team's ground.[7]

In 1887, as part of the football boom that followed in the wake of the legalisation of professionalism, another attempt was made to profit from women playing soccer. Madame Well's Grimsby Town Team and Madame Kenny's Famous Edinboro' Team played each other for a silver cup during Easter 1887 in Grimsby, Hull and possibly Wakefield. Once again, this was a commercial venture closely linked to local music hall entrepreneurs. The Hull match was organised by the manager of Alhambra Palace Music Hall and, as had happened in 1881, this match was abandoned after a pitch invasion and assaults on the players. It was most definitely not an attempt to promote football for women or to encourage them to take up the sport. Once again, the idea was to make money from titillation and mockery.[8] Rather than challenge gender stereotypes, these commercial matches of the 1880s reinforced them. It is also quite possible that such events discouraged women from playing football. As Patrick Brennan has discovered, when the Southwick Lilies' young women's side in Sunderland advertised for opponents, they received two replies from other women's teams but could not organise a match due to parental opposition. Eventually, in February 1889, two women's sides from a local glass factory – Greener's Violets and Greener's Cutters – played a six-a-side game that was won 8–2 by the Violets.[9] Almost thirty years were to pass before working-class women once again played organised football.

It would be middle-class women who made the most sustained attempt to play soccer in the Victorian era. In late 1894 the British Ladies' Football Club was created by Nettie Honeyball, and its president was Lady Florence Dixie, an aristocrat who was a prominent advocate of the rational dress movement, which sought to make women's clothing less restrictive and more practical. She was also the sister of the Ninth Marquess of Queensberry, the sports enthusiast who infamously brought about jailing of Oscar Wilde.[10] Thirty women responded to an advertisement for players, all of whom were, as Honeyball informed the press, 'educated ladies and belong to what I term the upper middle-class'. Indeed, Honeyball openly refused applications from working-class women: 'if I accepted all the girls from the masses that made application to join us, why our list would have been filled long ago', inadvertently demonstrating the pent-up demand for the game among working-class women.[11] On 23 March 1895 the club divided its players into North and South teams to play its first match in front of 10,000 spectators at London's Crouch End. Although the club had been formed to capitalise on the ever-increasing national obsession with football, its business model was the touring All England cricket elevens of the 1860s.

The British Ladies played forty-three matches across Britain in the next three months as North versus South, or more usually Reds versus Blues. By the time the following season had kicked off, the club had split in two, with both factions claiming to be the Original Lady Footballers. Nevertheless, the two sides played 101 matches in the 1895–96 season, dwindling to nineteen the next season as interest, both from players and public, waned. Although Honeyball's teams were nothing like the music hall–inspired sides of the 1880s – they trained seriously and when confronted with chauvinist opposition in the press responded with a resolute defence of soccer's value to the health of women – the British Ladies was primarily a money-making exercise that sought to capitalise on the novelty of watching women playing football. Although its leaders were vocal in their belief that football was a game for women as much as it was for men, they did little to encourage other women to take it up and left behind no legacy. Even though it was a product of the age of the New Woman, in which young women challenged conventional views about dress, sex and work – perhaps most notably through the extraordinary popularity of cycling – the BLFC did not challenge the fundamental gender order of football.

The phenomenon of the 'New Woman' was a transnational movement and moves to organise women's football were not confined to Britain. In San Francisco, businessmen sought to profit from the popularity of football and the growing awareness of women's rights by organising two women's soccer matches in December 1893. Part of an attempt to bring crowds to the newly opened Central Park stadium, the two matches did not attract enough spectators and the experiment failed. In 1897 two matches of women playing modified American football were also commercial failures and women's football was abandoned.[12] In New Zealand, where women won the right to vote in 1893, an attempt was made to establish two women's rugby teams in 1891. As would be the case with the British Lady Footballers, Mrs Nita Webbe sought to combine the campaign for women's rights among middle-class women with the commercial popularity of football by setting up two women's sides to tour New Zealand. 'In this age are not my sex coming to the front in every line? As doctors, lawyers, scholars, are they not successful?' she asked. 'Yet it is only after years of bitter opposition that their right to the professions has been acknowledged. In athletics a similar prejudice used to prevail in even a stronger degree, but is not that rapidly dying out?'[13] Sadly, prejudice was not dead and Nita Webbe's plans never left the drawing board.

Football's hostility to women playing the game was not simply based on the personal misogyny of the male leaders of soccer and rugby. It was structurally embedded in the DNA of all forms of the sport. The modern game had emerged in the public schools not merely as a means of instilling masculinity into young men, but also as a way to inure them against femininity, and especially effeminacy and homosexuality. The Reverend Frank Marshall, president of the Yorkshire Rugby Union in the 1880s, was speaking for more than himself when he roared at a committee meeting that 'we have no dealings with women here!'[14] Arthur Kinnaird, who played in nine FA Cup Finals between 1873 and 1883, and served a thirty-three-year stint as FA president, was also a high commissioner of the Church of Scotland, an enthusiastic supporter of organisations such as the National Vigilance Society – which was behind the jailing of an English publisher for publishing 'obscene' works by Zola and Flaubert in 1889 – and a cheerleader for the persecution of Oscar Wilde in 1895. He was not alone in his bigotry. Football had been established to be a resolutely male sphere with the explicit intention of excluding women. The very fact that on the rare occasions that women did play the game it was in segregated games – an arbitrary division derived from the sport's origins in all-male schools that was unquestioningly accepted as the norm – underlined the role that football played in upholding and reinforcing the gender-segregated order of capitalist society.[15]

Although there were occasional reports of women playing organised soccer in the 1900s, it would not be until World War One that the game again became a participation sport for women. The war quickly became an insatiable charnel house demanding more and more men for the carnage at the front, and as they left for the trenches, they were replaced in the factories by women. The rising demand for armaments also created new work in engineering factories, and, especially after conscription for men was introduced in 1916, women poured into jobs once seen as exclusively male. By the summer of 1918, over one million women were employed in munitions industry alone. The work was arduous, dangerous and long, with a working week that could be as much as sixty-five hours.[16] Consequently many of these factories sought to improve employee morale and health by providing welfare facilities, such as sports halls, playing fields and even time off work for their workers to take part in all kinds of sporting and recreational activity, of which soccer was one of the most popular.

Having been brought into heavy industry to do what was traditionally seen as 'male work', the barrier to women taking part in what was also viewed as 'male sport' was considerably lowered. From 1916 a number of factories started women's football teams, often at the initiative of women workers, such as Grace Sibbert at Dick, Kerr's huge engineering factory in Preston, and within the space of eighteen months dozens of women's soccer teams had been formed at factories across Britain. Finally, the door had been opened and thousands of young working-class women flooded enthusiastically into the new teams. Cup tournaments, international matches, particularly against teams from France where the women's sports movement had become influential, and eventually local leagues sprang up in almost every industrial region of Britain.[17] Women were at last playing a game they loved in large numbers.

But their participation was strictly controlled. As far as is known, every club was coached and managed by men. Even the Dick, Kerr's team that had been initiated by Grace Sibbert was controlled by company manager Alfred Frankland.[18] Moreover, almost every match was organised to support the war effort by raising funds for military or other patriotic charities. Women's soccer was framed as being another way in which women could support their menfolk, thus reinforcing traditional gender roles and pacifying all but the most reactionary critics of women's sport. It is also the case that many factory soccer sides were set up in industrial towns in the north of England such as Barrow, Wigan, Leigh, St Helens, Huddersfield and Whitehaven where rugby league was the dominant code of football and the round-ball game was widely regarded as un-masculine, underlining the way in which the gender order was not fundamentally threatened.[19]

The growth of women's football must also be seen in the industrial context of World War One. Many of the factories that formed sides were also noted for the militancy of their workforce. In Glasgow, William Beardsmore's engineering factory dominated the east end of Glasgow and took the initiative in organising women's football from 1917, including non-representative Scotland versus England matches.[20] It was also one of the most militant factories in an already militant city. Following a strike in March 1916, the chief shop steward, future MP David Kirkwood, was arrested and deported to England. Across the city in Govan, the previous year had seen over 20,000 households take part in a rent strike. The bringing together of women to play and watch football was seen by the employers as a way of defusing class tensions. The same point can be made about the Vickers' engineering factories in Barrow and Sheffield, both of which had a reputation for militancy and established well-known women's teams in the aftermath of strikes in 1916. In Australia, where women began to play Australian Rules football for war-time charities at the same time as in Britain, the game was encouraged by notoriously anti-trade union and pro-conscription companies such as the Boan Brothers' department stores and the Commonwealth Clothing Factory.[21] From the perspective of the employers, it was hoped that women's football would be a patriotic antidote to rising levels of class conflict, especially after the October Revolution of 1917.

When the war ended, women's soccer seemed to be primed to become even more popular. For major charity matches, five-figure crowds could be attracted, including a famous 53,000 crowd at Everton's Goodison Park on 26 December 1920 that watched Dick, Kerr's defeat local side St Helens Ladies 4–0 in support of ex-servicemen's charities. This was not far short of the 59,964 who watched Everton men's side take on West Bromwich Albion later that week on New Year's Day.[22] In a much more limited way, women also played rugby union in Cardiff and Wellington in New Zealand, rugby league in New South Wales and Auckland, and Australian Rules in Perth and Victoria. In France, a modified form of rugby called Barette became popular among women and continued throughout the 1920s, and soccer also continued to be played in small pockets throughout the 1930s. In September 1921 over 20,000 people turned out to watch the Metropolitan Blues and Sydney Reds women's rugby league sides play each other in Sydney.[23]

It was not to last. Women's football of whatever code was viewed by the footballing authorities as nothing more than a charitable fund-raising exercise. Even the huge crowd for the Dick, Kerr's match at Goodison Park got barely a single column inch in the *Lancashire Daily Post*, Preston's local newspaper. Despite the number of women's sides across the country, there was no attempt to set up a national league or cup competition. The government's post-war drive to remove women from the factories and re-assert their roles as wives and mothers was reflected in football. Now that the 'special circumstances' of the war were over, soccer was once more a male domain, unsuitable for women. All the spurious arguments of the pre-war years re-emerged: 'the periodicity of a woman's life and their delicate organism emphasises the danger of accident, strain and the ordinary risks of violent exertion', one doctor informed the press.[24]

Using the excuse of unauthorised broken-time payments being made to women players, in October 1921 the FA Council warned clubs that they must have FA permission before staged women's matches and provide a full statement 'showing how the whole of the receipts are applied' after each match. Later that month Spurs apologised to the FA for allowing the Edis-wan versus Lyons women's game to be played at White Hart Lane without seeking FA approval. Shortly after, Winchester City were censured for host-ing Plymouth Ladies against Seaton and ordered to pay the whole of the gate receipts to charity.[25] The campaign against women's football reached its climax on 5 December 1921 when the council of the Football Association passed a resolution that read:

> Complaints having been made as to football being played by women, the council feel impelled to express their strong opinion that the game of football is quite unsuitable for females and ought not to be encouraged.
>
> Complaints have also been made as to the conditions under which some of these matches have been arranged and played, and the appro-priation of the receipts to other than charitable objects.
>
> The council are further of the opinion that an excessive proportion of the receipts are absorbed in expenses and an inadequate percentage devoted to charitable objects.
>
> For these reasons the Council request the clubs belonging to the Association to refuse the use of their grounds for such matches.[26]

Initially it was felt that the ban on using FA-affiliated grounds would make little difference. 'The decision of the FA does not affect us very seriously unless our firm decide to ban the game', said Miss Long, the captain of the Strand Corner House side. Alice Kell, the Dick, Kerr's captain, attacked the FA's insinuation of financial wrongdoing and defended the broken-time payments she and her teammates received: 'it was absolutely impossible for working girls to afford to leave work to play matches . . . [and she] saw not the slightest reason why they should not be recompensed for loss of time'.[27]

PLATE 6 Women footballers defy the FA ban: match programme for Stoke versus Dick, Kerr's in 1923

Less than a fortnight after the FA decision, fifty-seven clubs met in Blackburn to form the English Ladies' Football Association.[28] In March 1922 the English Ladies' FA Cup kicked off with twenty-three sides. But the men who led the ELFA – the president was Stoke's Len Bridgett and only one of the five vice-presidents was a woman – were businessmen who hoped to emulate the financial success of the women's game during the war. Yet without the legitimacy of patriotic charitable fund-raising, the women's game struggled to pay its way. Unable to succeed commercially and weighed down by male chauvinist scorn, the ELFA lasted little more than a year, and mass participation in women's football withered.

Dick, Kerr's and a handful of other teams continued as itinerant sides and women played other football codes sporadically over the next decades, but it would not be until the 1960s that, facilitated by workplace recreational provision and inspired by the rise of the women's liberation movement, large numbers of women began to play the football code of their choice once again. And once again, just as during World War One, the impetus came largely from working-class women.

Notes

1 *Hull Daily Mail,* 28 October 1895.
2 *Blackburn Standard,* 28 May 1881.
3 *Nottinghamshire Guardian,* 20 May 1881.
4 *Manchester Guardian,* 22 June 1881. *Liverpool Mercury,* 27 June 1881.
5 For more on East Lancashire soccer crowds see Robert Lewis, '"Our Lady Specialists at Pikes Lane": Female Spectators in Early English Professional Football, 1880–1914', *International Journal of the History of Sport,* vol. 26, no. 15 (2009), pp. 2161–81.
6 *The Yorkshireman,* 3 March 1883.
7 *Salford Reporter,* 2 June 1888. *Yorkshire Evening Post,* 29 November 1902.
8 *Cardiff Times,* 2 April 1887. *Hull Daily Mail,* 11 April 1887. I am grateful to Dr Victoria Dawson for drawing my attention to this.
9 The details of the Sunderland events are at www.donmouth.co.uk/womens_football/1889.html (accessed 27 June 2017), which also mentions the 1887 Wakefield match, although I have not been able to locate a newspaper report for it.
10 For more on sport and rational dress, see Jihang Park, 'Sport, Dress Reform and the Emancipation of Women in Victorian England: A Reappraisal', *International Journal of the History of Sport,* vol. 6, no. 1 (1989), pp. 10–30.
11 *Maidenhead Advertiser,* 17 April 1895, quoted in James F. Lee, *The Lady Footballers: Struggling to Play in Victorian Britain* (Abingdon: Routledge, 2008), p. 109.
12 *San Francisco Call,* 21 & 26 December 1897. I am grateful to Dr Brian Bunk for bringing this to my attention.
13 Quoted in Jennifer Curtin, 'Before the "Black Ferns": Tracing the Beginnings of Women's Rugby in New Zealand', *International Journal of the History of Sport,* vol. 33, no. 17 (2016), p. 2075.
14 *The Yorkshireman,* 18 December 1889.
15 The FA banned matches between women's and men's teams in August 1902. Football Association, minutes of the FA Council, 25 August 1902, National Football Museum, Manchester. I am grateful to Dr Alex Jackson for pointing this out.

16 Alethea Melling, *'Ladies' Football': Gender and the Socialization of Women Football Players in Lancashire 1916–1960* (PhD thesis, University of Central Lancashire, 2000), p. 34.

17 Wendy Michallat, 'Terrain de lutte: Women's Football and Feminism in "Les anneés folles"', *French Cultural Studies*, vol. 18, no. 3 (2007), pp. 259–76.

18 Melling, *'Ladies's Football'*, p. 54.

19 Victoria S. Dawson, *Women and Rugby League: Gender, Class and Community in the North of England, 1880–1970* (PhD thesis, De Montfort University, 2017).

20 Jessica Macbeth, *Women's Football in Scotland: An Interpretive Analysis* (University of Stirling PhD, 2004), pp. 104–8.

21 Rob Hess, 'Missing in Action? New Perspectives on the Origins and Diffusion of Women's Football in Australia during the Great War', *International Journal of the History of Sport*, vol. 31, no. 18 (2014), pp. 2330–3.

22 *Lancashire Daily Post*, 28 December 1920. Over 31,000 saw Dick, Kerr's defeat Bath Lady Footballers 12–0 at Old Trafford on 8 January 1921, *Bath Chronicle*, 15 January 1921.

23 Katherine Haines, 'The 1921 Peak and Turning Point in Women's Football History: An Australasian, Cross-Code Perspective', *International Journal of the History of Sport*, vol. 33, no. 8 (2016), pp. 828–46; Peter Burke, 'Patriot Games: Women's Football During the First World War in Australia', *Football Studies*, vol. 8, no. 2 (2005), 5–19; Charles Little, '"What a Freak-Show They Made!": Women's Rugby League in 1920s Sydney', *Football Studies*, vol. 4, no. 2 (2000), pp. 25–40; Jennifer Curtin, 'More than Male-Gazing: Reflections of Female Fans of Rugby Union in New Zealand, 1870–1920', *International Journal of the History of Sport*, vol. 32, no. 18 (2015), pp. 2123–34; Barbara Cox, 'The Rise and Fall of "The Girl Footballer" in New Zealand in 1921', *International Journal of the History of Sport*, vol. 29, no. 3 (2012), pp. 444–71; Rob Hess, 'Playing with "Patriotic Fire": Women and Football in the Antipodes During the Great War', *International Journal of the History of Sport*, vol. 28, no. 10 (2011), pp. 1388–408.

24 *Lancashire Daily Post*, 6 December 1921.

25 Football Association, Minutes of the Emergency Committee, 4 October to 28 November 1921 and 29 November to 12 December 1921. National Football Museum, Manchester.

26 Football Association, Minutes of meeting of the Consultative Committee, 5 December 1921, held at the National Football Museum, Manchester.

27 *Lancashire Daily Post*, 6 December 1921.

28 For more on ELFA, see Patrick Brennan's excellent site at www.donmouth. co.uk/womens_football/elfa.html.

10

RUGBY FOOTBALL

A house divided

> The English Rugby Union . . . will never stand professionalism in the game, whatever name it is cloaked under. . . . It would have to sacrifice many fine exponents of the game doubtless, but it would not hesitate. It would lose a good many international games, but it would still not hesitate.
> —*Yorkshire Owl*, 1893[1]

The eclipse of gentlemen's clubs by working-class professionals was exactly what the supporters of amateurism had feared. Writing in the 1886 *Football Annual*, Arthur Budd, an RFU committee member who would become its president in 1888, summed up the lessons of the past four years:

> Only six months after the legitimisation of the bastard [of professionalism] we see two professional teams left to fight out the final [FA] cup tie. To what does this all end? Why this – gentlemen who play football once a week as a pastime will find themselves no match for men who give up their whole time and abilities to it. How should they? One by one, as they find themselves outclassed, they will desert the game and leave the field to professionals.

He ended by promising the RFU would 'throttle the hydra' with 'no mercy but iron rigour'.[2] Until this point the only action the RFU committee had ever taken against professionalism was the unspoken refusal to pick Wakefield Trinity's Teddy Bertram for representative teams, but soccer's short experience with professionalism caused the leaders of the RFU to abandon their previous policy of turning a blind eye and undertake a scorched earth policy to resolve the problem.[3]

At its 1886 annual general meeting the RFU outlawed any form of payment to players for playing or training, with the exception of second-class rail fares for travel to matches. Players were banned from working for a club or for any member of that club. Rugby union was now a strictly amateur sport, and any person or club violating its grandly titled 'Laws As To Professionalism' faced a ban from the sport. As if to underline its class bias, when a Yorkshire delegate to the meeting pleaded that 'the very existence of his club, composed almost entirely of working men, would be threatened if they were held to the letter of the new laws', Bradford's Harry Garnett, Budd's successor as RFU president, bluntly replied, 'if working men desired to play football, they should pay for it themselves, as they would have to do with any other pastime'.[4]

The stridency of the language used by rugby's supporters of amateurism reflected a rising sense of panic among public school footballers about the consequences of the FA's decision. FA committee member N.L. Jackson, who had seconded Charles Alcock's motion that the FA legalise professionalism, changed his mind and advocated the most lily-white amateurism. He became one of the principal organisers of the opposition to the northern rugby clubs' demands for broken-time payments and, more famously, the organiser of Corinthians FC, the touring amateur soccer club which demanded the strictest amateurism while at the same time requiring considerable expenses payments for the right to play against them.[5] Jackson's entrepreneurial spirit meant that the Corinthians became one of the few gentleman's clubs that played socially mixed sides. The social divide between middle-class sides and working-class clubs, whether professional or amateur, became an unbridgeable gulf. Middle-class clubs retreated into their own networks in an attempt to recreate the football world of the early 1870s.

In 1893 the FA Amateur Cup was started to provide a competition for amateur sides, but when that was quickly overwhelmed by amateur working-class sides, the gentlemen retreated further and in 1903 started the Arthur Dunn Cup exclusively for teams of old boys of private schools. Four years later, frustrated at what they saw as the FA's refusal to act against professionalism, 500 club representatives from London and the South East met in July 1907 to form the Amateur Football Association (AFA), dedicated to upholding socially exclusive soccer for those

> who by their bringing up and training can play it as it should be played . . . and do not want a vast and ignorant crowd of partisans to egg them on to all kinds of malpractices to win, tie or wrangle, for pocket-filling purposes.[6]

Viewing itself as soccer's analogue to the zealous amateurs of the RFU, the AFA quickly discovered that without control of its sport, amateur rigour was nothing more than self-enforced marginalisation. It crept back into the FA in January 1914.[7] By then, the war against professionalism in soccer had long been lost.

In rugby however, the game remained firmly in the hands of the opponents of professionalism. In the north of England, rugby had experienced some of the explosive growth seen in soccer. Indeed, in late Victorian Britain, soccer and rugby were two parts of a single social phenomenon. Exactly the same social, cultural and economic processes took place in each code. With the exception of a handful of clauses in their rulebooks, soccer and rugby were viewed by the press and the public as two variants of the same sport. Newspapers and magazines covered them both under the generic heading of 'Football', journalists, officials and supporters referred to each version as 'football', and all players, regardless of whether they could legally handle the ball, were referred to as 'footballers'. Only the aficionado cared about which set of rules were employed to engage the teams and to attract the public to the thrill of the spectacle.

Even by the early 1890s, rugby could still be compared favourably to its round-ball rival in terms of crowds and public interest. When in 1893 the Inland Revenue investigated the finances of football, it chose to examine the accounts of Aston Villa and Bradford rugby club, arguably the two richest clubs in football. The leading rugby clubs made covert payments to players that could be compared to the legal wages of contracted soccer professionals – England rugby international three-quarter Dicky Lockwood appears to have been paid £1 per match by Heckmondwike in 1887, which was significantly more than the eleven shillings per away match that Sheffield Wednesday paid their players when they turned professional in the same year. And regardless of the status of their players, rugby clubs had to make the same investments in grounds and facilities as their soccer cousins.

In Yorkshire where, outside of Sheffield and Middlesborough, rugby ruled supreme, the leading clubs felt exactly the same pressures as the top soccer sides. In May 1889, inspired by the success of the Football League's first season, Wakefield Trinity called for the formation of a 'Yorkshire Football League' to ensure regular high-quality competitive rugby. But whereas soccer's Football League and the other minor leagues were created quickly without any intervention from the Football Association, it took three years of intense wrangling between the clubs and the rugby authorities before the Yorkshire Senior Competition, as the league was named, kicked off. The league question had become one of the battlefields in rugby's decade-long war over professionalism.[8]

The RFU's 1886 decision to become a purely amateur organisation marked the start of an all-out assault against the threat to the gentlemanly control of rugby. Unlike soccer, where the discussion about professionalism was compressed into just three years, the long debate in rugby was not resolved until 1895, allowing the arguments and their practical implications to be fully drawn out. Much of the short debate in soccer focused on the threat posed to sport by 'imported' players and commercialism, which it was thought would undermine the spirit of genuine competition. This view was shared both by clubs threatened by richer rivals, which animated much of the Birmingham FA's initial opposition to the proposals of the richer Lancashire clubs, and by defenders of the public school ethos who understood that commercialism would inevitably loosen the grip of the gentlemanly clubs. This was also how the debate began in rugby, but as it unfolded it peeled back the underlying fears of working-class domination of sport.

Indeed, once the amateur tocsin had been sounded, class prejudice flowed freely. 'The Rugby game, as its name implies, sprang from our public schools', wrote the international cricketer and Cambridge University rugby 'blue' Frank Mitchell. 'It has been developed by our leading London clubs and universities; and why should we hand it over without a struggle to the hordes of working men players who would quickly engulf all others?'[9] The fact that rugby was fracturing along class rather than North-South lines was highlighted by the fact that Mitchell had been born and educated in Yorkshire.

And it was in the White Rose county that the campaign against professionalism was waged most mercilessly. Two dozen trials of players and clubs for violations of the RFU's amateur regulations took place between 1887 and 1894, resulting in the suspensions of leading players such as England international John Sutcliffe, who promptly switched to soccer, and of senior clubs such as Leeds and Wakefield Trinity. The slightest indiscretion was pursued: JW Moore of Leeds and George Broadbent of Holbeck were investigated for receiving wedding presents from their club. Even Leeds Parish Church's rugby club was suspended in January 1890 for its numerous professional sins.

Unsurprisingly, this unceasing auto-da-fé did little to extend rugby's appeal in the face of soccer's burgeoning popularity. But for many in the RFU leadership, the popularity of rugby was indeed the problem. Noting that 'the Rugby game is losing ground among the working class and Association spreading in its place, owing to the pecuniary advantages to be reaped from the latter game', the *Football Annual*'s review of the 1888–89 season said that 'the loss of followers to the grand old game is regrettable, yet looking at the present state of all professional sports we cannot but think that this possible loss is far preferable to legalising professionalism'.[10]

Most people in northern rugby thought the opposite. Wakefield Trinity's call for the formation of a rugby league in 1889 was based on the desire to reverse the sport's declining fortunes, as were the repeated calls by Lancashire clubs for a cup tournament for the county, where rugby was being forced out of its traditional hotbeds of Liverpool and Manchester due to the appeal of soccer's cup and league competitions. Calls emerged for rugby's rules to be made more attractive, such as reducing the number of players from fifteen to thirteen. Most significantly, in February 1889, Halifax called for the RFU to allow players to be compensated for taking time off from work to play the game, so-called broken-time payments. This was a deliberate attempt to avoid the financial chaos that full professionalism had brought to many soccer clubs and to revive the informal practices of the northern clubs before the imposition of amateurism in 1886. But the RFU refused to compromise and at its 1893 annual general meeting, thanks to a well-organised campaign orchestrated in part by N.L. Jackson, it decisively rejected broken-time payments.

The RFU's hostility to payments for players was not merely based on its dislike of the development of soccer since 1885. Britain since the early 1880s had changed dramatically. A huge upsurge in industrial militancy and working-class self-confidence had taken place, highlighted by the great dockers' strike of 1889 that led to the rapid growth of militant 'new unionism' and the foundation of the Independent Labour Party in Bradford in 1893. This was the crucial factor in the contrasting attitudes of the FA and the RFU to professionalism. Soccer's 1884–85 debate took place in a period of relative social harmony, but rugby's dispute over broken-time payments became a proxy for wider concerns about the rise of the working class. If rugby players in the north wanted to be paid, a correspondent to the *Yorkshire Evening Post* argued, they should

> start a union of their own, where they can quarrel amongst themselves, find employment for the many out of work, and indulge in strikes, trades unions, and a general disinclination for honest work so dear to the average north country working man.[11]

In contrast, supporters of broken-time payments argued that working-class players

> were constantly called upon to lose their wages in order to play for their county or their club and at the same time they were debarred from recompense for the loss of time involved. Why should not the working man be able to play the game on level terms with the gentleman?[12]

Having won a decisive victory in 1893, the leaders of the RFU went on the offensive, suspending leading clubs such as Huddersfield, Wigan and Salford. The two sides prepared themselves for the inevitable split, the catalyst for which was the RFU's declaration that it would amend its rules so that clubs could be suspended for accusations of professionalism and would have to prove their innocence before being reinstated. This was too much for the northern clubs, who realised that they would be picked off one by one by the RFU, and so, on 29 August 1895, twenty-one clubs met at the George Hotel in Huddersfield and resigned from the RFU to create the Northern Rugby Football Union. By the turn of the century, almost all rugby clubs in its Lancashire and Yorkshire heartlands had joined the rugby league, as the new organisation would become known. There were now three codes of football in England, and rugby's dominance of the football world was nothing more than an increasingly distant memory.

THE YORKSHIRE OWL.

KEPT IN.

PLATE 7   Rugby on the verge of split: cartoon satirising the RFU's suspension of Huddersfield (*Yorkshire Owl*, 15 November 1893)

Notes

1 *Yorkshire Owl*, 4 October 1893.
2 Arthur Budd, 'The Rugby Union Game', in *The Football Annual* (London: Lily-white, 1886), p. 52.
3 Collins, *Rugby's Great Split*, pp. 53–4.
4 *Yorkshire Post*, 5 October 1886.
5 For the debate on the Corinthians, see *Yorkshire Post*, 4 October and 13 December 1893.
6 L.A.M. Fevez letter in *The Sportsman*, 6 March 1906.
7 The full story of the AFA can be found in Dilwyn Porter, 'Revenge of the Crouch End Vampires: The AFA, the FA and English Football's "Great Split", 1907–1914', *Sport in History*, vol. 26, no. 3 (2006), pp. 406–28.
8 Tony Collins, *Rugby's Great Split* (London: Frank Cass, 1998), pp. 62–3.
9 Frank Mitchell, 'A Crisis in Rugby Football', *St James's Gazette*, 24 September 1897.
10 An Old Player, 'The Rugby Union Game in 1888–89', in *The Football Annual* (London: George Bell & Sons, 1890).
11 *Yorkshire Evening Post*, 30 September 1893.
12 *Leeds Mercury*, 21 September 1893.

11

MELBOURNE

A city and its football

> A good football match in Melbourne is one of the sights of the world;
> old men and young get equally excited; the quality of the play too
> is much superior to anything the best English clubs can produce. . . .
> [T]here is much more 'style' about the play of half a dozen clubs in Vic-
> toria than about the Old Etonians or Blackheath, which are the two best
> clubs I have seen play in England.
>
> —'Follower', 1885[1]

By the time that modern football codes began to emerge in the 1860s,
Britain stood unchallenged as the most powerful nation on earth. It had
conquered more than 8 million square miles of territory, exerted political
and economic influence over a significant section of what remained, and by
1870 commanded an empire that produced almost a quarter of the world's
gross domestic product. From its birth, football became a symbol of the self-
confidence and self-satisfaction of British imperial nationalism.[2]

'What! Talk of *danger* to British boys! To the descendants of those men
who were at Waterloo and Trafalgar?' exclaimed a youthful footballer in
Rugby School's *New Rugbeian* magazine.[3] At the FA's founding meeting,
Blackheath's F.M. Campbell told the delegates if they banned hacking from
football, it would 'do away with all the courage and pluck of the game, and
I will be bound to bring over a lot of Frenchmen, who would beat you
with a week's practice'. It was during the Napoleonic Wars at the start of the
nineteenth century, when ideas of 'British fair play' first emerged to counter
the French Revolution's 'Liberty, Equality, Fraternity', that sport became

fused with British nationalism. Cricket and boxing were elevated from mere games into metaphors for the British character and way of life. And within a generation, football had also become, in the words of the *Yorkshire Post*, one of 'those important elements which have done so much to make the Anglo-Saxon race the best soldiers, sailors and colonists in the world'.[4]

Across the British Empire, this nationalist ideology was articulated by Muscular Christianity and carried across the English-speaking world by *Tom Brown's Schooldays*. In the Empire's white settler colonies – Australia, Canada, New Zealand and South Africa – *Tom Brown* quickly acquired the status of a cultural bible. Despite living thousands of miles from what they referred to as the 'Mother Country', these colonists were proudly British in all but geography and rushed to embrace the message of the book, making it a best-seller across the empire. As soon as copies arrived from London, the *Sydney Morning Herald* was lauding its tone 'so hearty, its good sense so strong and so thoroughly national, its morality so high, and yet so simple and practical, that . . . we venture to prophesy for it an extended and permanent popularity'.[5] In the southern state of Victoria – Australia was until 1901 a collection of individual colonies rather than a single nation – Melbourne's *Argus* newspaper chided readers who did not understand the value of football: 'let those who fancy there is little in the game, read the account of one of the Rugby matches which is detailed in that most readable work, *Tom Brown's Schooldays*, and they will speedily alter their opinion'.[6]

Although more than 13,000 miles from London, the economic and cultural integration of the Australian colonies with the Mother Country meant they functioned as a 'suburb of Britain', in the words of the economist Lionel Frost.[7] Football emerged in Melbourne at the same time as it did in Britain as a seamless part of the same social process. Many of the city's young middle-class men had been educated in British public schools, returning home with great enthusiasm for the now fashionable football. One typical example was Tom Wills, the son of one of Victoria's biggest landowners, who had been sent to Rugby School as a 14-year-old in 1850. Not much of a scholar, he distinguished himself on the cricket field and his name can still be seen today in the school cricket pavilion as a captain of the first XI.

Back home in Australia, in 1858 Wills wrote to *Bell's Life in Victoria* – itself an antipodean clone of *Bell's Life in London* – bemoaning the lack of exercise for cricketers in the winter months. 'Rather than allow this state of torpor to creep over them, and stifle their now supple limbs, why can they not, I say, form a foot-ball club, and form a committee of three or more to draw up a code of laws?', he suggested, in just the same way as many of his cricketing contemporaries were advocating in Britain.[8] Almost a year later in May 1859, Melbourne Football Club was formed and Wills, schoolteacher Thomas Smith, and two journalists, William Hammersley and J.B.

Thompson (all of whom had been educated in Dublin or Cambridge) met to draw up a set of football rules.[9]

Melbourne was one of the youngest but also one of the most dynamic cities of the empire. It had been founded barely twenty years earlier and by the time it was declared a city in 1847, settlers had driven almost all Aboriginal people from the land that was named Victoria. Four years later, gold was discovered less than 100 miles north-west of the city, transforming Melbourne into a boom town. From just 23,000 inhabitants in 1851, the gold rush ignited a demographic explosion that resulted in a population of 445,000 by 1889. Made rich by gold and the wool trade, it became known as 'Marvellous Melbourne', a comment on its success and perhaps also about the self-satisfaction of its elites.[10] As in Britain, the city developed a network of middle-class associations that fostered both business and recreation. Foremost among the latter was the Melbourne Cricket Club, founded just three years after settlement, of which Wills, Hammersley and Thompson were members. By 1842 the club had been joined by a side from nearby Brighton and over the next decade more cricket clubs were formed as the city and its suburbs grew. By 1870 there were so many teams that a challenge cup competition began.

So when Melbourne FC was formed in 1859, it brought football into a pre-existing sporting culture in much the same way as football in Sheffield and Nottingham. Just as would be the case in the industrial regions of Britain, but in an even more concentrated form, tens of thousands of people flocked to Melbourne looking for work. And once people had found employment, they next looked for entertainment, excitement and a sense of belonging. Although Melbourne football had begun as recreation for the young men of the local elite, the growth of the city meant that the game soon captured the imagination of all classes. By the early 1870s, crowds of 10,000 were being seen at major matches, especially those featuring the city's two major sides, Melbourne and Carlton. In 1879 10,000 people even turned out to watch two local military sides, Collingwood Rifles and East Melbourne Artillery, play under floodlights. In 1886, the interest in football had reached such heights that a claimed 34,000 crushed into South Melbourne's ground to see their championship-deciding clash with Geelong, making it probably the largest crowd that had ever assembled to watch a game of football anywhere in the world.

Asa Briggs observed in his classic *Victorian Cities* that the popularity of football in Melbourne 'pre-dated the rise of the football leagues in England', highlighting the depth of 'the general interest in sport among all sections of the population. Australia led Britain in this direction and Melbourne led Australia'.[11] But it was more than simply a matter of timing. Football in Melbourne was unique. In Britain, the sport had come to cities that, however much they were changing, had been founded centuries earlier and already had their own distinctive cultures. But in Melbourne, football was appeared at the same time that the city itself was in the process of being born. Rather than merging with a city's pre-existing culture as in Britain, the game was an organic part of Melbourne culture, as integral to the pulse of the city as its climate and geography. Football encompassed all of Melbourne's classes, from Scotch College's elite upper-class schoolboys to Collingwood's unskilled labourers who had to queue to find work every morning. Nowhere, not even in Glasgow, was football so completely intertwined with the life of a city.

Such was the gravitational pull of Melbourne that nearby cities were drawn into its football orbit. In the neighbouring state of South Australia, Adelaide's first football club had been formed in 1867 and played its own version of football. But as the city grew and developed business and trade links with Victoria, South Adelaide FC argued that 'it was possible that someday an inter-colonial [between Australian states] football match might be played, and it was desirable in that case that South Australian players should play the game as it was played in other colonies'. In 1877, the clubs of the South Australian Football Association voted to adopt the same rules as Melbourne clubs – and it was this prospect of intercolonial football that helped spur the formation of the Victorian Football Association later that year.[12] Two years later, footballers in Hobart, the capital of Tasmania, initially rejected a request for a match from Melbourne's Hotham (now North Melbourne) club in the hope that a proposed British football tour would take place. Although hopes for the British tour evaporated, the enthusiasm for matches against visiting teams did not diminish, and to enable them to play their neighbours, Hobart football clubs voted to abandon their own rules and adopt those played in Victoria.[13]

Melbourne's position as the main entrepôt to the south island of New Zealand also saw its football code being played in the future stronghold of rugby, establishing a presence in the 1870s that was not finally extinguished until World War One.[14] Sydney, and the northern state of Queensland, remained largely immune, partly because it looked down on the upstart city to its south, but also because rugby had already laid down stronger roots, and the Southern Rugby Union, the forerunner of the Australian Rugby Union, was created in 1874. Soccer, although widely played, lacked the Melbourne game's deep roots or rugby's imperial links and was unable to achieve the cultural significance or national importance of its two rival codes.

There was one other factor that made Melbourne football unique. It was the only city in the world that maintained its own code of rules. Unlike Sheffield, which had abandoned its rules to become part of the FA, Melbourne's rulebook became the basis for a national sport. The fact that Wills and his colleagues began drawing up their rules four years before the creation of the FA – and more than a decade before the RFU – meant the Melburnians did not have to defer to a football governing body in the Mother Country, unlike in cricket where the authority of London's MCC was unchallenged. If Wills and his compatriots had met ten years later, after the consolidation of the English football codes had begun, it is quite possible that the city would have been a stronghold of rugby or soccer. But without the direction of an authoritative governing body, the exigencies of competing in cup competitions or the need to compete in internationals, Melbourne football rules developed in something of a football Galapagos Island where isolation caused the evolution of the sport to take its own unique path.

This also meant that Australian Rules had a relatively untroubled path to professionalism. Two years after the Victorian Football Association had introduced a formal league system in 1894, its best supported clubs broke away in opposition to its proposals for greater revenue sharing and stricter amateur restrictions, and formed the Victorian Football League (VFL). Despite intense rivalry, the two leagues ran in parallel without the deep ideological hostility that affected the rugby codes, and eventually the greater economic strength of the VFL came to eclipse its parent association.

A game of our own?

The formation of Melbourne FC raised the obvious question of how its members would play football. As one of the club's founders, William Hammersley, later recalled, 'Tom Wills suggested the Rugby rules but nobody understood them except himself' and so the committee used Rugby School rules as a template for their own ideas about the best way to play game.[15] From this starting point the club initiated the development of what would become the distinctive Australian Rules code of football. Over the next thirty years, the Victorian football clubs abandoned the offside rule, forbade running with the ball in the hands, and gradually elevated the mark – catching the ball directly from a kick before it hit the ground – into one of the game's most distinctive features. It was this supposed deviation from football rules in Britain that for future generations appeared to make Melbourne football distinctively Australian, a game that uniquely reflected the Australian way of life. In contrast to soccer and the rugby codes, it seemed to be, as Tom Wills was claimed to have said, 'a game of our own'.[16]

In fact, there was nothing uniquely Australian about the way Tom Wills and his associates chose to play the game. Like the football clubs created in the British Isles in the 1850s and 1860s, Melbourne and the other Victorian sides were merely looking for the most enjoyable method of playing the sport between themselves. Indeed, all of the supposedly distinctive rules that were eventually embraced by Melbourne could be seen in embryo in one or more forms of football played in Britain during this formative period.

One Rugby School rule immediately discarded by the Melburnians was offside. For many followers of Australian Rules this is one of the most distinctively Australian features of the game.[17] But in the primordial soup of football's early evolution during the 1850s and 1860s, offside rules everywhere were fluid and changing. Although the major public school codes of football had rules regulating offside play, Sheffield FC had no offside rule at all until 1863.[18] Gaelic football also never had offside rules. Ice hockey, which originally also took its inspiration from rugby rules, abandoned its offside rules in the 1930s, highlighting that dissatisfaction with offside restrictions was not unique to Australia.[19]

The second feature of Australian Rules most commonly assumed to be uniquely different from soccer and rugby is the mark, the 'one aspect of the Australian game that distinguishes it from all other codes'.[20] But the mark was commonplace across almost all codes in the early years of football. Usually known at the time as a 'fair catch', it allowed a player who caught the ball cleanly before it touched the ground to claim a 'free kick', the right to kick the ball unimpeded by his opponents. The second edition of C.W. Alcock's *Football Annual* in 1868 outlined its widespread use, detailing that catching the ball was allowed in the public schools of Harrow, Rugby, Winchester, Marlborough, Cheltenham, Uppingham, Charterhouse, Westminster, Haileybury and Shrewsbury, as well as the FA and the Sheffield FA.[21]

Indeed, the original 1863 rules of the Football Association specified that 'if a player makes a fair catch he shall be entitled to a free kick, provided he claims it by making a mark with his heel at once'. Even the early Cambridge University version of football − seen by some as a precursor of modern soccer − originally allowed the ball to be handled, as an 1863 description of one of the first matches played under Cambridge rules highlights: 'any player may stop the ball by leaping up, or bending down, with his hands or any part of the body'.[22]

Although the mark disappeared from the rulebooks of the London and Sheffield associations by the late 1860s, the fair catch was already embedded as a major feature of the rugby game. Indeed, the definition of a fair catch was the very first rule in Rugby School's *Football Rules* of 1845.[23] The mark also appeared in the 1862 rules of Blackheath FC and in the rules adopted by the RFU at its foundation in 1871, although its complexity meant its governance stretched across five other rules. It was not until 1892 that the RFU outlawed an airborne player catching the ball, thus ending what in Australian Rules would be called a high mark.[24]

The early Melbourne footballers also disliked running with ball in hand, which led to a third distinctive feature of Australian Rules, the fact that a player could only run with the ball if it was bounced or touched on the ground regularly, originally 'five or six yards'.[25] But even this was not unknown in other types of football in the 1860s. The 1864 rules of football as played at Bramham College in West Yorkshire also had this rule. Carrying the ball by hand was not permitted but the college's football Rule 14 stated that 'the ball may "bounced" with the hand, and so driven through the opposite side'.[26] This rule was in use at least two years *before* it was introduced into the Australian game in 1866.

Moreover, emphasising how early football developed in similar ways across the English-speaking world, a similar rule existed in Princeton University's first football rules. As alumnus W.J. Henderson recalled in 1899, Princeton's own code did not allow players to run with ball in their hands:

> You were positively forbidden to carry the ball in your hands a greater distance than one yard. You must kick it, or else throw it upon the ground, causing it to bound; and by catching it again and bouncing it again, you might advance it.

And in a further similarity to the Melbourne game, the ball could not be passed from the hands but had to be batted between players using a closed fist.[27]

The Melbourne game was part of an international continuum of variations that stretched across the early football-playing world. The chosen rules of Wills, Thompson, Hammersley and their Melbourne compatriots no more represented a uniquely Australian view of football than the Sheffield FA's code reflected the distinctive characteristics of Yorkshire. The desire for 'a game of our own' was not an expression of Australian uniqueness but one more example of the widespread frustration with the rules of football as played at the various public schools, and an expression of the desire for a set of rules that was both understandable and enjoyable to its players. Australian Rules football was not a declaration of independence. It was a symbol of Australia's place in the British Empire.

Notes

1 Follower, 'Australasian Football', *The Age* [Melbourne], 27 June 1885.

2 This and the following chapter is largely based on my article, 'National Myths, Imperial Pasts and the Origins of Australian Rules Football', in Stephen Wagg (ed.) *Myths and Milestones in Sports History* (London: Palgrave, 2012), pp. 8–31.

3 *The New Rugbeian*, vol. 3, no. 8, November 1861, p. 296.

4 *Yorkshire Post*, 29 November 1886. For an excellent transnational analysis see Patrick F. McDevitt, *'May the Best Man Win' Sport, Masculinity and Nationalism in Great Britain and the Empire, 1880–1935* (Basingstoke: Palgrave Macmillan, 2004).

5 *Sydney Morning Herald*, 16 October 1857.

6 *The Argus*, 16 August 1858.

7 Lionel Frost, *Australian Cities in Comparative View* (Victoria: Penguin, 1990), p. 4.

8 *Bell's Life in Victoria*, 10 July 1858.

9 Gillian Hibbins, 'The Cambridge Connection: The English Origins of Australian Rules Football', in J.A. Mangan (ed.) *The Cultural Bond* (London: Frank Cass, 1993), pp. 108–27.

10 Graham Davidson, *The Rise and Fall of Marvellous Melbourne* (Melbourne: Melbourne University Press, 1978).

11 Asa Briggs, *Victorian Cities* (London: Odhams, 1964), p. 302.

12 See Shane Pill and Lionel Frost, 'R.E.N. Twopeny and the Establishment of Australian Football in Adelaide', *International Journal of the History of Sport*, vol. 33, no. 8 (2016), pp. 802–5.

13 For more, see Ian Syson 'The "Chimera" of Origins: Association Football in Australia before 1880', *International Journal of the History of Sport*, vol. 30, no. 5 (2013), pp. 456–7. The tour was probably that discussed but never organised by the RFU MINUTES REFERENCE.

14 See Chris McConville and Rob Hess, 'Forging Imperial and Australasian Identities: Australian Rules Football in New Zealand During the Nineteenth Century', *International Journal of the History of Sport*, vol. 29, no. 17 (2012), pp. 2360–71.

15 *Sydney Mail*, 25 August 1883.

16 It appears to have been J.B. Thompson who first used the phrase in the *Victorian Cricketers' Guide for 1859–60*. See Hibbins and Mancini, p. 18. It seems to have been first attributed to Wills in the 1923 autobiography of fellow rule-framer H.C.A. Harrison, *The Story of An Athlete* (Melbourne, 1923), reprinted in Hibbins and Mancini, p. 119.

17 Rob Pascoe, *The Winter Game* 2nd Edition (Melbourne, 1996), p. xiv.

18 For the Sheffield FA, see *Rules, Regulations & Laws of the Sheffield Foot-Ball Club* (Sheffield, 1859), Brendan Murphy, *From Sheffield With Love* (Sheffield: Sports Books, 2007), pp. 37–41, and Adrian Harvey, *Football: The First Hundred Years* (Abingdon: Routledge, 2005), pp. 11 and 162–3.

19 See Joseph Lennon, *The Playing Rules of Football and Hurling 1884–1995* (Gormanstown: Northern Recreation Consultants, 1997), p. 10.

20 Robin Grow, 'From Gum Trees to Goal Posts, 1858–76', in Rob Hess and Bob Stewart (eds) *More Than A Game* (Carlton: Melbourne University Press, 1998), p. 21.

21 C.W. Alcock (ed.), *Football Annual* (London: Lilywhite, 1868), p. 74.

22 Rule 8, reprinted in *The Rules of Association Football 1863* (Oxford: Bodleian Library, 2006), p. 49. John D. Cartwright, 'The Game Played by the New University Rules', reprinted in reprinted in Jennifer Macrory, *Running with the Ball: The Birth of Rugby Football* (London: Collins, 1991), p. 164.

23 *Football Rules* (Rugby School, 1845), p. 7.

24 RFU rules of 1871, reprinted in O.L. Owen, *The History of the Rugby Football Union* (London: Welbecson Press, 1955), pp. 65–72, Royds, pp. 6–8.

25 Rule 8 of the 1866 rules, in Geoffrey Blainey, *A Game of Our Own*, 2nd Edition (Melbourne: Black Ink, 2003), p. 225.

26 'Bramham College Football Rules, October 1864', in *The Bramham College Magazine* (November 1864), p. 182.

27 W.J. Henderson, 'College Football Twenty-Five Years Ago', *Outing*, vol. 37, no. 1 (October 1899), p. 16.

12

AUSTRALIAN RULES AND THE INVENTION OF FOOTBALL TRADITIONS

> Many there are who cry 'we have too much sport in Australia', but if the [Australian Rules] League can use sport as the ladder-way to a higher patriotism breathing loyalty to Australian institutions, high manly ideals, and practical education, it is surely doing a service to our country.
> —The Young Australia League, c. 1906[1]

The history of any sport is a palimpsest. Meanings, interpretations and purposes are written and rewritten over that history as people seek to give a broader significance to the act of play. Details and fragments are reassembled and rearranged to create a story that meets the desires and demands of different generations, social groups and ideologies. The deep attachment that people have to football and the emotional resonance it generates means that it can become an effective carrier for creation myths and invented traditions that seek to share not just our view of the past but also our understanding of the present.

The isolated nature of Australian Rules football offers a laboratory to explore how these invented traditions evolve according to the society in which they operate. From its inception, the game acted as a barometer of changing ideas about Australian national identity. Until the second half of the twentieth century, the game was viewed as Australia's contribution to British culture. 'It is the very element of danger in our own out-of-doors sports that calls into action that noble British pluck which led to victory at Agincourt, stormed Quebec and blotted out the first Napoleon at

Waterloo', wrote one Australian commentator about the value of the Melbourne game.[2] In 1908, addressing the sport's 1908 Silver Jubilee carnival, Australian prime minister Alfred Deakin quoted from Henry Newbolt's militaristic poem *Vitai Lampada* to proclaim that football prepared Australians to fight in Britain's wars.

> When the tocsin sounds the call to arms, not the last, but the first to acknowledge it will be those who have played, and played well, the Australasian game of football before they play the Australian game of nation-making and nation-preserving *to stand by the old land*. [my emphasis][3]

Following World War Two, Australia's traditional relationship with the 'Mother Country' began to break down. In 1958 the journalist C.C. Mullen published a history of the Australian Rules that speculated, on the flimsiest of evidence, that the game had been popular in Scotland before World War One, a reflection of the prevailing sense of 'different but equal' Britishness then prevalent in Australia. Like Scotland, it saw itself as loyally British but with its own role to play in the world.[4] In the 1960s and 1970s, after Harold MacMillan's government effectively broke the imperial link by ending Australians' rights to unrestricted entry to Britain and by applying to join the European Common Market without consulting Australian trade partners, a more radical nationalist outlook sought to draw parallels between Australia and Ireland. The idea that Australian Rules was derived from Gaelic football became fashionable, despite the fact that Melbourne rules were codified twenty-five years before those of the Gaelic game. In 1967 and 1968 an Australian Rules side undertook short tours of Ireland, where 'Waltzing Matilda' was played before matches instead of 'God Save The Queen', the then-official Australian national anthem.[5]

Since the 1990s the dominant liberal view of Australian national identity is based on reconciliation between European and Aboriginal Australians. In 1993 the Paul Keating-led Labour government passed the Native Title Act that paid lip-service to Aboriginal land claims. In 2008 the then-Labour prime minister Kevin Rudd apologised to the Aboriginal population for what he described euphemistically as past 'mistreatment'. Thus it became popular to imagine that Australian Rules has its roots not in Australia's imperial past but in Aboriginal culture. The Aboriginal pre-history of Australian Rules has become an article of faith for many liberal-minded Australian Rules' fans and has been crucial in validating the claim of the Australian Football League (AFL, as the sport's governing body has been known since 1990) to be Australia's true national, and multicultural, football code.[6]

This belief is based on the claim that Tom Wills was heavily influenced by the Aboriginal ball game known as Marn Grook when he and his fellow Melbourne FC members drew up their first rules of football. According to nineteenth-century descriptions of Marn Grook written by white European colonists, the game featured high kicking and leaping for a ball. 'The ball is kicked high in the air, not thrown up by hand as white boys do, nor kicked along the ground, there is general excitement who shall catch it, the tall fellow stands the best chance', wrote James Dawson in 1881. 'When the ball is caught it is kicked up in the air again by the one who caught it, it is sent with great force and ascends as straight up and as high as when thrown by hand'. [7] Such descriptions of punting the ball were combined with accounts of Wills' boyhood activities with Aboriginal children to claim that the true origins of Australian football were in Aboriginal ball games. [8]

However, there is no evidence to suggest Wills was influenced by Aboriginal ball games. Gregory de Moore's exhaustive biographical research found no mention of them in any of his private or public writings. Quite the opposite, as Wills favoured rules that followed those of Rugby School, such as a cross bar between the goal posts and a designated kicker to take kicks at goal. [9] Moreover, the 'high mark' only started to become a significant feature of Australian Rules in the mid-1870s, almost twenty years after

PLATE 8 Scrummaging in early Australian Rules football (*The Australasian Sketcher*, 12 June 1875)

the first rules were drawn up. Even then it was not popular. In 1876 *The Footballer* advised players to avoid 'jumping for marks' because it was danger-ous.[10] Loose scrummaging was a much more important part of the game in its early years, and as late as the 1890s complaints were common that the game was dominated by scrums.[11]

It is easy to see why the Wills/Marn Grook story of cultural exchange between European colonists and Aboriginal peoples became popu-lar. It offers a sanitised version of the genocidal reality of race relations in nineteenth-century Australia. Wills' own father, Horatio S. Wills, was respon-sible for the murder of several Aboriginal people as he enforced his claim to own the land they had lived on for generations.[12] Like all sports, Austral-ian football was no less racist than the society which nurtured it. One of its most famous clubs, Essendon, was for most of its early history known as 'the blood stained n–s'. Aboriginal football clubs were often excluded from local competitions and even the greatest of aboriginal footballers faced racist taunts and humiliations.[13] Doug Nicholls, a future governor of South Australia, transferred from the Carlton club in the late 1920s because his teammates claimed he smelled. The Marn Grook story views Aborigi-nal involvement in Australian Rules football through the spectacles of the twenty-first century, sanitising the racial politics of both the past and the present, and inventing a tradition from which the modern game can claim a moral authority.

More generally, Australian Rules' shifting sense of its own past is perhaps the most complex example of how a sport invents its own traditions. As Eric Hobsbawm and Terence Ranger suggest in *The Invention of Tradition*, invented traditions

> normally attempt to establish continuity with a suitable historic past . . . the peculiarity of 'invented' traditions is that the continuity with ['a historic past'] is largely factitious . . . they are responses to novel situations which take the form of reference to old situations, or which establish their own past by quasi-obligatory repetition.[14]

Sport's invented traditions acquire their power because they articulate the desires of each particular game for its own distinctive social significance. William Webb Ellis' picking up that ball and running with it for the first time at Rugby School in 1823 or Abner Doubleday's 'invention' of baseball at Cooperstown in 1839 have no foundation in historical fact.[15] But for rugby union, the Webb Ellis story demonstrated that this was a game cre-ated by and for the middle classes, while for baseball, Doubleday confirmed that it was truly a uniquely American game. The emergence of the belief that Sheffield football rules are the true precursor of modern soccer rules reflects the belief that English soccer has been taken away from its authentic working-class roots by businessmen and self-interested administrators.

The Tom Wills/Marn Grook story also illustrates the key characteristics of invented sporting traditions. The first is that the founder of the sport must have had minor rather than extensive involvement in it. Webb Ellis had no involvement in rugby after he left school. Doubleday's career in the U.S. military was apparently untroubled by any entanglement with baseball. Similarly Wills' major contribution to the development of football took place while he was secretary of the Melbourne Cricket Club. The lack of substantive long-term engagement with the sport is an important factor in such invented traditions because it opens narrative space for speculation and supposition.

Second, the evidence to support the invented tradition is based on hearsay or personal affirmation. Webb Ellis' role was founded on nothing more than the testimony of Matthew Bloxam, a Rugby School old boy who did not know Webb Ellis and relied entirely on undocumented 'enquiries'. The Doubleday story was based on a letter by Abner Graves, who was a 5-year-old child in Cooperstown in 1839. Wills' famous claim that Australia now had 'a game of our own' is a recollection of his cousin H.C.A. Harrison some sixty years later. Claims that Wills' boyhood interactions with Aboriginal youths inspired his football rules also lack any evidence.[16] And in the case of Sheffield football, there is no evidence that the FA took any notice of its rules. Again, the plasticity of the argument allows the story to be fashioned according to the needs of the advocate.

The third common feature is these traditions emerge at pivotal moments in the history of the sport. The Webb Ellis myth came to prominence when rugby union felt the threat of working-class influence in the sport. This led to rugby's split of 1895, precisely the year the Old Rugbeian Society declared Webb Ellis to be rugby's inventor. The Doubleday myth emerged in response to the 1908 Mills Commission report on the origins of baseball. This was the period in which baseball was emerging from labour relations turmoil and intra-league disputes, leading to the National League's alliance with the American League and the first World Series in 1903. In Australian Rules, the Wills/Marn Grook tradition gained traction in the early 2000s as the AFL sought to position itself as the national football code of Australia.

Fourth, supporters of the invented tradition ultimately base their position on an unverifiable belief rather than historical fact. 'What these materialists are unable to understand is that not only are we unable to prove it, but also that this fact does not bother us at all' wrote the RFU's official history in response to those seeking proof of the Webb Ellis story.[17] Similarly, the

Doubleday exhibit in baseball's Hall of Fame at Cooperstown claimed that 'in the hearts of those who love baseball, he is remembered as the lad in the pasture where the game was invented. Only cynics would need to know more'.[18] Defending the idea that Australian Rules is derived from an Aboriginal game, Jim Poulter wrote that 'we should reverse the onus and accept the indigenous origins to our game, unless somebody can clearly prove otherwise', putting those who disagree in the position of having to prove a negative.[19] All three statements serve to insulate their arguments from critical enquiry, elevating the invented tradition to an article of faith.

Finally, the invented tradition projects back into the past a picture of how its supporters see the modern world. For rugby union followers, Webb Ellis confirmed their belief that theirs was a game for the privately educated middle classes. For baseball, Doubleday supported their ideas of American exceptionalism and difference from the 'old world' of Europe. And for Australian Rules, the Wills/Marn Grook story of games being played between Aboriginal and European children offers an alternative narrative to the bloody reality of white settlement.

The apparent historical legitimacy of invented traditions also plays an increasingly important commercial role in the business of sport. Rugby union's world cup is fought for the Webb Ellis trophy. Well-heeled spectators at Twickenham can enjoy luxury corporate hospitality in the stadium's exclusive 'Webb Ellis Suite'. Visitors to Cooperstown can stay in Doubleday-inspired hotel suites, visit the Doubleday exhibit in the Hall of Fame and watch a game at Abner Doubleday Field.[20] 'Dreamtime at the 'G', an annual Australian football match between Essendon and Richmond, is one of the highlights of the contemporary AFL season. Commercial exigency today plays a major role in the shaping of sporting history and heritage. The re-fashioning and even the falsification of history for commercial, publicity or political reasons is just as likely in sport as it is in any other activity.

Perhaps this is only to be expected. The importance of football to national identity increases the power of the invented traditions of sport. Stories which are re-woven from the historical fabric of sport are not merely narratives about sport, but are projections of how nations want to perceive themselves and their history. As Hobsbawm commented about the invented traditions of the United States, they became important because 'Americans had to be made'.[21] So too did Australians in the final third of the twentieth century as the umbilical link with 'Mother' Britain was cut. Just as the culture of football in the mid-nineteenth century offered supporters of the British Empire, whether at 'Home' or in the colonies, the reassurance of their superiority over other races, today each football code provides comfort to and confirmation of its ideology to its supporters. In the constant reinvention of national identity, sport occupies a central position.

Notes

1 *Australia Junior* [*Journal of the Young Australia League*], no. 2, undated, c. 1906, p. 10.
2 Quoted in Leonie Sandercock and Ian Turner, *Up Where Cazaly?* (Melbourne, 1981), p. 33. See also W.F. Mandle 'Games People Played: cricket and football in England and Victoria in the Late-nineteenth Century', *Historical Studies*, vol. 15, no. 60 (April 1973), pp. 511–35.
3 Deakin's speech of 28 August 1908 is reprinted in full in Richard Cashman, John O'Hara and Andrew Honey (eds), *Sport, Federation, Nation* (Sydney, 2001), pp. 111–13. For similar sentiments expressed by British Rugby Union writers in the years before 1914, see Tony Collins, 'English Rugby Union and the First World War', *The Historical Journal*, vol. 45, no. 4 (2002), pp. 797–817.
4 C.C. Mullen, *History of Australian Rules Football from 1858 to 1958* (Carlton, 1958). The Scottish link is examined in John Williamson's *Football's Forgotten Tour* (Applecross, 2003). There was an 'Edinburgh Australasian Football Club' formed in 1886, but this played rugby football; see *Otago Daily Times*, 4 December 1888.
5 For the tours to Ireland, see Peter Burke, 'Harry and the Galahs', *ASSH Bulletin*, no. 29, December 1998, 9–17. Barry O'Dwyer, 'The Shaping of Victorian Rules Football', *Victorian Historical Journal*, vol. 60, no. 1, pp. 27–41, argues the case for the Irish origins of the game, but see Blainey, *A Game of Our Own*, 2nd Edition (Melbourne: Black Ink, 2003), pp. 187–96. for a debunking of this myth.
6 Much of the debate can be seen in the controversy surrounding Gillian Hibbins' chapter in Geoff Slattery (ed.) *The Australian Game of Football* (Melbourne, 2008). Martin Flanagan defence, 'Football Ebbs and Flow with Tide of Society', *The Age* (Melbourne), 9 August 2008.
7 James Dawson, *Australian Aborigines: The Language and Customs of Several Tribes of Aborigines in the Western District of Victoria, Australia* (Melbourne, 1881), p. 85.
8 Perhaps the most representative example can be found in Martin Flanagan, 'A Battle of Wills', *The Age*, 10 May 2008.
9 Greg de Moore, *Tom Wills: His Spectacular Rise and Tragic Fall* (Sydney, 2008), p. 161 (for his support for a rugby-style cross bar and designated kicker), and pp. 283–6 for lack of mention of Aboriginal ball games. As Rob Hess has pointed out, Wills involvement in the 1868 Aboriginal cricket tour of the United Kingdom make it unlikely he would seek to disguise any aboriginal influence.
10 Blainey, pp. 118–22.
11 Blainey, pp. 64–5 and 227. For a discussion on scrummaging, See Robin Grow 'From Gum . . .' in Hess, pp. 15, 30 and 78.
12 Gregory de Moore's research has documented that H.S. Wills was 'listed as having murdered several aborigines' in the western district of Victoria. Gregory de Moore, *In From the Cold: Tom Wills – A Nineteenth Century Sporting Hero* (PhD thesis, Victoria University, Melbourne, 2008), pp. 119–21.
13 For example, see the accounts of Aboriginal footballers in the 1920s and 1950s in Richard Broome, *Aboriginal Victorians: A History Since 1800* (Sydney, 2005), pp. 224–5. For a post-war example, see Peter Read, *Charles Perkins, A Biography* (Melbourne: Penguin revised edition, 2001), pp. 51–2.
14 Eric Hobsbawm and Terence Ranger (eds), *The Invention of Tradition* (Cambridge, 1983), pp. 1–2.
15 For Doubleday, see Harold Seymour, *Baseball: The Early Years* (Oxford, 1960), pp. 8–12 and James A. Vlasich, *A Legend for the Legendary: The Origin of the*

Baseball Hall of Fame (Wisconsin, 1990), pp. 162–8. For Webb Ellis, see Tony Collins, *Rugby's Great Split* (London: Frank Cass, 1998), pp. 5–8 and William Baker, 'William Webb Ellis and the Origins of Rugby Football', *Albion*, vol. 13, no. 2 (Summer, 1981), pp. 117–30. Douglas Booth his *The Field* (Abingdon, 2006), ch. 6, pp. 111–26, discusses sporting myths but in typical post-modern fashion draws no distinction between actuality and invention.

16 In reality it was J.B. Thompson, one of the four Melbourne rule-framers who used the phrase in the *Victorian Cricketers' Guide for 1859–60*. See Hibbins and Mancini, p. 18.

17 U.A. Titley and R. McWhirter, *Centenary History of the Rugby Football Union* (London: Rugby Football Union, 1970), p. 9.

18 Quoted in Stephen Jay Gould, 'The Creation Myths of Cooperstown' in his *Triumph and Tragedy in Mudville* (New York: Jonatahn Cape, 2003), p. 199.

19 Jim Poulter, *From Where Football Came. . .* (September 2007) at www.sporting pulse.com/assoc_page.cgi?client=1-5545-0-0-0&sID=75914&news_task=D ETAIL&articleID=5854332&sectionID=75914 accessed 13.05, 25 May 2009.

20 The importance of the Doubleday myth to baseball's Hall of Fame is described in Vlasich, *A Legend for the Legendary: The Origin of the Baseball Hall of Fame*.

21 Eric Hobsbawm, 'Mass Producing Traditions', in Eric Hobsbawm and Terence Ranger (eds) *The Invention of Tradition* (Cambridge: Cambridge University Press, 1983), p. 271.

13

IRELAND

Creating Gaelic football

> No movement having for its object the social and political advancement
> of a nation from the tyranny of imported and enforced customs and man-
> ners can be regarded as perfect if it has not made adequate provision for
> the preservation and cultivation of the national pastimes of the people.
> —Michael Cusack, 1884[1]

Michael Cusack didn't hang up his rugby boots until he was 35. A self-
described 'sterling lover of the game', in 1879 the burly forward had introduced rugby football into the Dublin academy school he had established to
train the sons of the capital's well-to-do. The school team joined the Irish
Rugby Football Union in 1880 but Cusack became frustrated by his side's
lack of success and wound up the team the following year. But the experience didn't dampen his enthusiasm for the game and he joined a local adult
rugby club, Phoenix FC. In his final season as a player he packed down for
Phoenix against Dublin University in the first-ever Leinster Senior Cup
competition match before retiring in 1882. From that point, he would
spend the rest of his life trying to destroy his first sporting love.

Rugby was the first modern football code to be played extensively in
Ireland. A club playing a game seemingly based on Rugby School rules was
formed at Trinity College Dublin as early as 1854 and by the early 1870s
Irish rugby clubs were sufficiently well established to host visiting clubs
from England and Scotland. In 1875 Ireland played its first international
match. It ended in an embarrassing defeat to England but the very fact that

internationals could be played against the English and Scots gave rugby a national prominence. In Leinster, Munster and Ulster, knock-out cup tournaments were established for the leading Catholic and Protestant private schools.[2]

But Ireland was a very different place to the rest of that nineteenth-century Anglophone world. In contrast to Australia, Canada, New Zealand and English-speaking South Africa, the majority of the population did not think of themselves as British or even as sharing a common set of Anglo-Saxon cultural values. Indeed, the majority Catholic population wanted some form of political and cultural independence from the British crown, and during the mid-nineteenth century Ireland underwent a 'Gaelic Revival'. In 1877 the Society for the Preservation of the Irish Language was formed to campaign for Irish to be taught in schools. Two years later, widespread discontent about rent and land ownership among Ireland's impoverished tenant farmers led to the creation of the Land League, based on the slogan of 'the land of Ireland for the people of Ireland'. In 1882 the Irish nationalist MP Charles Stewart Parnell gave new life to the 'Land War', as the struggle of the tenant farmers against their landlords had become known, by establishing the Irish National League. At the same time, he transformed the Home Rule League, a loose grouping of Irish MPs in the House of Commons, into the well-organised and influential Irish Parliamentary Party. The *Gaelic Journal*, the first significant bilingual journal in Ireland, also began publication in English and Irish in 1882. At the 1885 general election the Irish Parliamentary Party increased its representation to eighty-five MPs and unequivocally had the support of a large majority of the Irish population. The demand for separation from Britain in politics and culture was growing increasingly loud. Rugby was therefore born into an Ireland that was rejecting much of the British culture from which the game had emerged.

One of those Irishman who had come to reject the British nationalism of sport was Michael Cusack himself. His love of games led him to journalism and, among many other publications, he wrote regularly for the *Irish Sportsman*, *The Irishman* and *United Ireland*. In 1887, partly because of his unerring ability to fall out with everyone, he began his own weekly, *The Celtic Times*. As part of his increasingly nationalist outlook he joined the Society for the Preservation of the Irish Language in 1882, by which time he had abandoned his former love of rugby and cricket in favour of what he viewed as traditional Irish sport. In this, he saw himself as the sporting equivalent of cultural nationalists seeking to preserve the Irish language, literature and culture.

It was this that animated his historic 'A Word about Irish Athletics' article that he published in *The Irishman* and *United Ireland* on 11 October 1884.

This rallying cry denounced 'the tyranny of imported and enforced customs and manners' and called on the Irish people to

> take the management of their games into their own hands, to encourage and promote in every way every form of athletics which is peculiarly Irish, and to remove with one sweep everything foreign and iniquitous in the present system.[3]

The following week the *Irishman* published a supportive letter from Maurice Davin, arguably Ireland's leading athlete. Whereas Cusack's letter had focused on athletics, Davin called for the revival of all Irish sports, especially football and hurling:

> Irish football is a great game, and worth going a very long way to see, when played on a fairly laid-out ground and under proper rules. Many old people say that hurling exceeded it as a trial of men. I would not care to see either game now, as the rules stand at present. I may say there are no rules, and, therefore, those games are often dangerous. I am anxious to see both games revived under regular rules.[4]

Cusack and Davin issued a call for a meeting to discuss 'the formation of a Gaelic Association for the preservation and cultivation of our National Pastimes and for providing rational amusement for the Irish people during their leisure hours', to be held at Hayes Hotel in Thurles on 1 November.[5] Accounts vary, but it is generally accepted that Cusack and Davin were joined at the meeting by five others.[6] Together, they agreed to create the Gaelic Athletic Association (GAA).

The men who formed the GAA were typical of those who became leaders of the nationalist movements across Europe in the second half of the nineteenth century. Confirming Eric Hobsbawm's observation that 'the battle-lines of linguistic nationalism were manned by provincial journalists, schoolteachers and aspiring subaltern officials' three of the seven founding GAA members, including Cusack, were journalists, one was a policeman and another a solicitor'.[7]

The formation of the GAA was not simply a political act to create a specifically Irish nationalist sports organisation.[8] Both Cusack and Davin were genuinely concerned for the future of Irish athletics. The Amateur Athletics Association (AAA) nominally regulated athletics in Ireland but it was seen to be interested only in privately educated British sportsmen. Sport in Ireland, believed Cusack and Davin, was badly organised and needed root-and-branch reform in order for traditional Irish games to be revived.

This was more difficult to accomplish than it first appeared. Of the sports mentioned by Cusack and Davin, only hurling was uniquely Irish. It appeared in Celtic myths such as those of Cú Chalainn and Diarmuid Ua Duibhne, giving it a historical authenticity that few sports could match, and match advertisements and reports appeared in the Irish press from the early eighteenth century. No-one could doubt that hurling was a distinctively Irish sport.[9]

But the same could not be said for football. The game in various forms had been played in Ireland since at least the fourteenth century. In the early eighteenth century the British authorities suspected that football matches were being used as cover for political gatherings.[10] In parts of Ireland football was known as Caid, but unlike hurling, there was nothing distinctively Irish about how it or any other football game was played.[11] Reports and descriptions of matches in previous centuries were indistinguishable from those played in Britain. This presented a problem for Cusack and Davin. The GAA would have to invent its own game if it wanted a specifically Irish version of football.

Other codes of football developed invented traditions or creation narratives long after they had been codified to justify their origins and to position the game within a particular national culture. But in Ireland, the process was reversed. Gaelic football itself had to be invented to fit a tradition and a narrative that already existed. The task of creating a specifically Gaelic form of football seems to have fallen to Davin. He drew on the existing rules of rugby and soccer, while Cusack appears to have favoured playing football using the rules of hurling.[12] The first Gaelic football rulebook was unveiled at its second convention in December 1884 but its ten rules said next to nothing about how the game should be played. It differed from the two British codes only in technicalities such as the size of teams ('not less than fourteen or more than twenty-one players'), the size of the pitch (120 yards by 80), and the length of a match (one hour). There were no regulations about whether the ball could be handled. Other than requiring the ball to go under rather than over the cross bar for a goal to be scored, there was little to differentiate the new game from rugby.[13]

Indeed, in its early years, the GAA's version of football was largely defined in relation to rugby. This was largely a result of the GAA's nationalist response to the prominence that rugby had gained as Ireland's first significant football code. It viewed the Irish national team's inability to defeat the English as an affront to the nation. 'Rugby football has been played on many an international field, but Ireland has never yet scored against England', wrote Cusack in 1885. 'Therefore, of course, we are inferior to the English. The vast majority of those who play Rugby football believe in the superiority of the foreigner'. Another Irish defeat the following year led him to lament that 'imported games have been a source of humiliation to us'.[14]

Shortly after the formation of the GAA, this antagonism to rugby came into sharp focus in Cork. The Munster region was unique in Ireland for having a rugby culture that, like South Wales and the North of England, embraced all classes from labourers to lawyers. Predominantly played on a Sunday with cup competitions at the heart of its season, rugby quickly became a vehicle for popular civic pride in a way that sharply contrasted to the more patrician-inflected rugby of Dublin and Belfast. But this popularity also meant it was also affected by the great revival of nationalist feeling in the 1880s and a number of rugby clubs quickly became identified with the GAA. J.F. Murphy, a leading official of the Lee FC rugby club, even became a vice-president of the GAA. At the start of the 1885–86 season Murphy formed the 'Munster National Football Association' to play football under his own Irish 'national rules'.[15]

In reality, Murphy's rules were a very slightly modified version of rugby that sought to fill the vacuum in the GAA's football rules. Cusack was not fooled by Murphy's claims to be playing the national game. Railing against a 'foreign faction' in the GAA, he accused Murphy of wanting to 'stick to the games our masters permitted us to play when they had more control over the national life of Ireland than they have at present'.[16] When the Cork delegates presented their 'national rules' to the GAA at its first annual general meeting in October 1885, Cusack attacked the proposal as 'undisguised rugby'. Maurice Davin, the GAA chair, struck a more conciliatory note. He argued that clubs should be allowed to play any type of football and still be eligible to take part in GAA athletic meetings, but that football clubs playing their own rules could not themselves become branches of the GAA. To the Munster delegates, this implied that clubs like Murphy's Lee FC, which also had an athletics section, could remain in the GAA and still play their own football code.[17]

Cork was not the only GAA area that initially played a type of rugby. In 1886 Wexford GAA's county football championship was won by Rosslare, who beat Crossabeg by three tries to two, a scoreline that was impossible according to GAA football rules, which mentioned no such thing as a try. Davin's attempt at a compromise simply prolonged the increasingly fractious debate until the GAA's next general meeting in April 1886 resolved the issue by expelling the Lee club from the GAA. It and the other Munster Association clubs returned to rugby, while the Wexford results disappeared from the record books.[18]

The Munster football controversy was a pivotal moment in the development of the GAA's code of football. By forcing the GAA to define exactly how its code of football was played and how it differed from rugby, the debate was the catalyst for the codification of modern Gaelic football. Over the course of the next eighteen months, three decisive rule changes redefined Gaelic football in Ireland and laid the basis for the modern game.[19]

The first was to restrict handling of the ball. The 1884 rules said nothing about the use of hands by players, and this was a major reason why the Munster rebels thought their modified rugby was compatible with the principles of the GAA. By 1888 the use of hands had been tightly constrained and the new rules stated that it could be caught or hit with the hand but it could not be carried or thrown. There could now be no running with the ball in hand or passing it to teammates, as was allowed in rugby.[20]

Nor could there be bodily tackling. In 1886 'wrestling and handigrips [an older term for hand-to-hand struggles]' were outlawed. Although this has been presented as removing traditional Irish wrestling features from football, in reality it took the sport a further step from rugby by banning the tackling of a player around the body. It also opened the game by removing the potential for loose scrummages and mauls.

The third distinctive change was the 1886 introduction of 'point posts', single posts placed twenty-one feet apart at either side of the goal. Like soccer, and originally rugby, the only method of scoring at this time was the goal. The difficulty in actually getting the ball through the posts meant many matches ended up as 0–0 draws and concern was expressed that low-scoring games were not attractive to spectators. The RFU overcame this in the 1880s by making tries a method of scoring and eventually introducing a points system. This course of action was precluded by the GAA's antipathy to rugby and so point posts were introduced. A ball that was kicked over the goal line between the goal posts and the point posts scored a point. The result of a match continued to be decided by the most number of goals, but if both teams scored an equal number of goals, the match was decided by the number of points scored.

In developing its own rules, the GAA did not try to recreate Irish football as it existed the past. This was widely recognised at the time. One commentator claimed that 'Irish football as played prior to 1884 was quite a different game from that known now as Gaelic football' and GAA rules would 'divest the game of all the interest it might possess for an Irish country audience'.[21] Yet there was nothing in previous versions of football played in Ireland that could be identified as unique. The GAA was a product of the late nineteenth century and needed a football code that could be played in contemporary society, not the sprawling, haphazard folk football of earlier centuries that disrupted work and inconvenienced trade. It therefore had to base its rule-making on the experience of other codes and the trial-and-error process of actually playing football.

Once the distinctiveness of the game had been established, the GAA's rules evolved in response to the difficulties encountered by players or the frustrations of spectators. The lack of goal-scoring opportunities became a perennially acute issue. For example, in 1891 the fifty-five matches that took place in Westmeath managed to record just thirty-five goals.[22] To open up the game, the size of teams was reduced to seventeen-a-side in 1892 and to today's fifteen-a-side in 1913. Adjustments were made to the size of the goal and the distance of the point posts. Goals were assigned a points value, initially five as proposed by Kerry in 1889 but reduced to three in 1896, and matches would henceforth be won by the team scoring the most points.[23]

Although deeply hostile to rugby, the GAA was not averse to borrowing from soccer. It essentially revived the FA's original Rules 8, 9, 11 and 12, which allowed the ball to be caught or knocked down but not carried or passed by hand.[24] It also took soccer's throw-in rule, in contrast to the throw-in from rugby's line-out, and borrowed the shape of soccer's goals, albeit making them slightly narrower. But it also came to resemble Australian Rules football. Neither had an offside rule. Neither allowed carrying the ball but did allow it to be caught. And both introduced an additional set of posts, the Australians preceding the Irish by twenty years.[25]

Trans-hemispheric football influences

The similarities between Australian Rules and Gaelic football today are well known. Since 1984 an ill-fitting 'International Rules' tournament has been played between representative Australian and Irish national sides under a compromise set of rules. And, as we saw earlier, when Australia began breaking from the apron strings of its British 'Mother Country' in the 1960s, the idea that Australian Rules was derived from Gaelic football became popular. However, it is far more likely that Australian Rules had some influence on the rules of Gaelic football.

Ireland in the late nineteenth century had a multitude of links to Australia. Irish immigrants accounted for something like 25 per cent of the total Australian population in the nineteenth century, and familial and business links between Australia and Ireland were plentiful.[26] Michael Cusack's sister emigrated there in 1864, joining numerous cousins. [27] Michael Davitt, the founder of the Land League and one of the GAA's three original patrons, spent several months down under in 1895 and discussed what Ireland could learn from Australia in his 1898 book *Life and Progress in Australia*. Many Irish families settled in Melbourne, where jobs were plentiful, and became part of its football culture. Collingwood FC, based in industrial north Melbourne, was supported by many Irish Catholics, while the popularity of neighbouring Fitzroy FC among its Irish population earned the club the nickname 'The Fenians'.

Links with football in Ireland were common. Up until the 1870s, matches of indeterminate rules against visiting Irish regiments often took place in Melbourne, such as Hotham's 5–0 drubbing of the 18th Royal Irish Regiment in 1870.[28] News from 'home' often included sporting chat. In 1887 the Sydney edition of the *Freeman's Journal* published the GAA's latest set of football rules, while the following year *The Tasmanian* newspaper in Launceston discussed recent developments in Gaelic football.[29] Thus family ties, military visits and the easy availability of news meant that sport played a significant role in the cultural links between Irish citizens in Ireland and Australia.

This can clearly be seen in hurling. As Pat Bracken's painstaking research has uncovered, hurling was played extensively by Irish communities in Australia.[30] At least twenty hurling clubs were active in Victoria between 1877 and the formation of the GAA in 1884. In April 1878 clubs around Melbourne formed their own Victorian Hurling Club Association (VHCA) and drew up a code of rules for the game. Among its members were clubs in the Melbourne football hotbeds of Collingwood, Richmond, Prahan and Brighton. The VHCA's sixteen rules incorporated some of the features of Australian Rules football, including the distinctive goal posts with no cross bar and two accompanying side posts. When Maurice Davin came to draw up the GAA's rules, he used the same sized playing pitch, agreed that twenty-one would be the maximum size of a team, and in 1886 included the distinctively Australian second set of posts.[31]

Of course, this does not mean that the GAA simply copied the Australians. Rules for hurling were also drawn up in Ireland in the same period, for example by clubs in Killimor (1869), Trinity College (1870) and Dublin (1883).[32] Rather, the similarities in rules highlights the transnational nature of discussions about how to play the sport. The development of Gaelic football's distinctive rules was not simply an attempt to apply Irish nationalist principles to sport but was also influenced by what was happening in football games across the English-speaking world.

Indeed, the transnational exchange of football knowledge between Ireland and Australia may well have gone both ways. It was not until 1897 that the Australian game awarded a point for a ball that went between the goal and the behind posts (as they became known in Australia). The Australians also moved their behind posts closer to the goal, emulating the twenty-one-foot distance that the GAA had specified.[33] Ironically, shortly after the Australians

PLATE 9   Kerry GAA great Dick Fitzgerald's 1913 handbook for Gaelic footballers

had replicated the Irish post rules, the GAA abandoned them, opting instead in 1910 to extend the goal posts upwards in rugby style to award points for kicks over the cross bar and to bring in soccer-style goal nets.[34]

By the time the GAA abolished point posts, its football rulebook had grown from its original ten short points to twenty-one, with an additional twenty-five explanatory notes. The claim of the great Kerry football captain Dick Fitzgerald in his 1914 book *How to Play Gaelic Football* that 'Gaelic football is what might be called a natural football game . . . truly there is no artificiality about our game', was no more than wishful thinking.[35] Far from being a traditional sport played according to ancient custom, Gaelic football was as codified, as regulated, and as much a product of the modern world as any of its British rivals.

Notes

1 Michael Cusack, 'A Word about Irish Athletics', *The Irishman*, 11 October 1884.
2 For the history of Irish rugby, see Liam O'Callaghan, *Rugby in Munster* (Cork: Cork University Press, 2011) and Jean-Pierre Bodis, *Le rugby d'Irlande: Identité, territorialité* (Bordeaux: Maison des sciences de l'Homme d'Aquitaine, 1993).
3 *The Irishman*, 11 October 1884.
4 *The Irishman*, 18 October 1884.
5 *United Ireland*, 8 November 1884.
6 Paul Rouse, *Sport and Ireland: A History* (Oxford: Oxford University Press, 2015), p. 162.
7 E.J. Hobsbawm, *Nations and Nationalism Since 1870* (Cambridge: Cambridge University Press, 1990), p. 117.
8 Rouse, *Sport and Ireland*, pp. 162–5. More broadly, he takes issue with W.F. Mandle's thesis in his *The Gaelic Athletic Association and Irish Nationalist Politics: 1884–1924* (London: Gill and Macmillan, 1987). See also Richard McElligott, *Forging a Kingdom: The GAA in Kerry 1884–1934* (Cork: Collins Press, 2013).
9 See, for example, *Daily Journal*, 17 August 1722. A.B. Gleason, 'Hurling in Medieval Ireland', in Mike Cronin, William Murphy and Paul Rouse (eds) *The Gaelic Athletic Association 1884–2009* (Dublin: Irish Academic Press, 2009), pp. 1–14.
10 For the British suspicion of Irish football matches, see *London Gazette*, 4 April 1719.
11 Eoin Kinsella, 'Riotous Proceedings and the Cricket of Savages: Football and Hurling in Early Modern Hurling Ireland', in Mike Cronin, William Murphy and Paul Rouse (eds) *The Gaelic Athletic Association 1884–2009* (Dublin: Irish Academic Press, 2009), pp. 16–19. McElligott, *Forging a Kingdom*, pp. 62–4. More generally, see James Kelly's outstanding *Sport in Ireland, 1600–1840* (Dublin: Four Courts Press, 2014).
12 See Rouse, *Sport and Ireland*, p. 171 and Joseph Lennon, *The Playing Rules of Football and Hurling 1884–1995* (Gormanstown, 1997), p. viii.
13 The rules can be found in *United Ireland*, 7 February 1885.
14 *Freeman's Journal*, 31 January 1885. *United Ireland*, 13 February 1886.
15 *United Ireland*, 31 October 1885. See also Liam O'Callaghan, *Rugby in Munster: A Social and Cultural History* (Cork: Cork University Press, 2011), pp. 81–3.
16 *United Ireland*, 6 February 1886.
17 *Freeman's Journal*, 2 November 1885.
18 *Freeman's Journal*, 7 April 1886. For Wexford, see and Eoghan Corry, *The History of Gaelic Football* (Dublin: Gill & Macmillan, 2010), ch. 1.
19 For more on the centrality of the Munster conflict to the development of Gaelic football, see W.F. Mandle, *The Gaelic Athletic Association and Irish Nationalist Politics 1884–1924* (London: Christopher Helm, 1987), pp. 32–4.
20 For all of these rule changes, see Joe Lennon, *The Playing Rules of Football and Hurling 1884–1995* (Gormanstown: Northern Recreation Consultants, 1997), pp. 24–6.

21 *The Colonist* [Tasmania], 27 July 1889.

22 Tom Hunt, *Sport and Society in Victorian Ireland: The Case of Westmeath* (Cork: Cork University Press, 2007), p. 153.

23 For a discussion on the development of the rules, see McElligott, *Forging a Kingdom*, pp. 160–2.

24 For a comprehensive listing of the FA's rules, see Tony Brown's excellent, *The Football Association 1863–83: A Source Book* (Nottingham: Soccerdata, 2011), especially pp. 20 and 80.

25 First introduced in 1866, the history of supplementary posts in the Australian game is documented in Geoffrey Blainey, *A Game of Our Own: The Origins of Australian Football* (Melbourne: Black Ink, 2003), pp. 54–6.

26 Seamus Grimes and Gearoid O Tuathaigh, *The Irish Australian Connection* (Galway: UC Galway, 1988), p. 18.

27 Marcus de Burca, *Michael Cusack and the Gaelic Athletic Association* (Anvil Books, 1989), p. 15.

28 *The Australasian*, 4 June 1870. See also 'The Football Jubilee' in *The Argus* (Melbourne), 1 August 1908 which recounts other encounters with Irish military sides.

29 *Freeman's Journal* (Sydney), 12 February 1887. *The Tasmanian*, 19 May 1888.

30 Patrick Bracken, "The Emergence of Hurling in Australia 1877–1917", *Sport in Society*, vol. 19, no. 1 (2016), pp. 62–73.

31 Bracken, "Hurling in Australia", pp. 65–6.

32 For the history of the rules of hurling, see Lennon, *The Playing Rules of Football and Hurling 1884–1995*.

33 See Blainey, *A Game of Our Own*, p. 54 and pp. 235–6.

34 Mandle, *The Gaelic Athletic Association and Irish Nationalist Politics 1884–1924*, pp. 144–5.

35 Dick Fitzgerald, *How to Play Gaelic Football* (Cork: Guy & Co., 1914), p. 15.

14

FOOTBALL AND NATIONALISM IN IRELAND AND BEYOND

We trust that the chivalrous sense of fair play which the warrior heroes Cucullain and Ferdiad displayed towards each other will animate our Gaelic footballers and hurlers.

—Dick Fitzgerald, 1914[1]

In one important sense, it did not matter what the rules of Gaelic football were. Although the GAA rulebook now differentiated its own football from rugby and soccer, the actual rules of the game appear to have made little or no difference to its popularity. Almost from its founding in 1884, GAA events, which usually staged a number of football contests between local sides, were often capable of attracting crowds in excess of 10,000 spectators, emulating the crowds seen at major soccer and rugby matches in England at that time.

Whereas it had taken the British football codes two decades to reach this level, the GAA had emerged from the Hayes Hotel in 1884 almost fully formed as a mass spectator sport. The lateness of its birth meant it came into a world in which a deep-going culture of spectator sport had taken root over the previous two decades. The spread of literacy, newspapers and magazines meant that by 1884 awareness of sport was part of daily life for great sections of the Irish population. Even the fact that Ireland was a predominantly rural nation was no barrier to the popularity of football. Although it lacked the urban population and industrial economy that existed across the Irish Sea, Ireland was sufficiently integrated into the cultural and economic life of the Victorian era that sports mania captured the imagination of the rural labourer in Laois just as easily as it had the textile factory hand in Leeds or the miner in Leith.

Indeed, rural society may have given the GAA an advantage. The tradition of village sports and gatherings in Ireland had not been extinguished, as had happened during the industrial revolution in Britain. After the devastating impact of the Irish Famine of 1845–49, which killed around 800,000 people through starvation and disease, the popularity of Gaelic sports could be seen as part of the collective recovery of rural communities, which allowed the GAA to be embraced without controversy by Ireland's Catholic population.

The structure that the GAA adopted for its clubs and competitions was far more important to its popularity than any particular set of rules under which its rules might be played. From the start, the GAA organised its teams on the principle of locality, usually based on the Catholic church parish, and at a county level for representative matches. This meant it could immediately build on one of the cornerstones of modern football: the idea that a team was a representative of local identity. Its appeal was amplified further when in 1887 the GAA launched the All-Ireland Championships, heightening local rivalries, creating regional ones, and offering the opportunity, for the first time in any Irish team sport, of national glory. This was a heady cocktail that in Ireland only the GAA could provide.

The appeal of the GAA was also enhanced because, unlike the other football codes, it staged its matches on Sundays.[2] Whereas the leaders of rugby union and soccer refused to play on Sundays, the GAA had no qualms. It even received an imprimatur from Archbishop Thomas Croke, who enthusiastically endorsed Sunday sport as long as players and spectators were 'never unmindful' of their duty to attend mass. The GAA was therefore able to fashion a new type of Sunday entertainment, in which whole families and communities could gather for the day to eat, drink and cheer their local representatives.

A GAA Sunday resembled a local carnival, with brass bands, community singing and all manner of activity taking place alongside the football, hurling and athletic contests. Railway companies ran special trains for visiting supporters to travel to see their side in towns and villages they would normally have no reason to visit. On arrival supporters and players would often march behind a brass band as they made their way to their host's ground. For those who liked a drink, the GAA also offered a way to circumvent Ireland's ban on the sale of alcohol on Sundays. Anyone who travelled more than three miles from home to a match acquired the legal status of a traveller with the right to be served in a public house. For many, this in itself was probably more than enough reason to go to a match.[3] One can gain a flavour of the atmosphere at an early football match from the *Celtic Times'* description of the build-up to a match in the small village of Kilmacthomas in County Waterford in March 1887:

> Down the pretty, partly-wooded slopes which surrounded the town the sturdy peasants poured and thronged the single street; the roads were crowded with vehicles of all descriptions. The stirring notes of the excellent brass band from Dungarven was the signal for marching to the football field, situated about a quarter of a mile from the town. It was a stirring sight to witness the long procession of old men and young men, old dames and budding womanhood, boys and girls, as fine specimens of the Irish peasantry as could anywhere be found.[4]

Eventually, the report notes, 7,000 people from the surrounding area turned out that Sunday afternoon, approximately three times the village's population.

This was the key to the success of the GAA: its ability to stage events at which people could watch sport collectively in a highly convivial environment while at the same time expressing their local and national pride. The experience of Gaelic football is the most powerful counter-argument to the 'football historian's fallacy', the belief that it is the rules of a football code that determine its popularity. After the temporary decline of the GAA's fortunes in the early 1890s, when its reputation was damaged by its close association with the paramilitary Irish Republican Brotherhood (IRB) and its support for Parnell during his highly public divorce case, the popularity of Gaelic football followed an upward curve until the outbreak of World War One, regardless of what was written in its rulebook.

The nationalist imperative

Through the emotional resonance that it generated among its supporters, the GAA was seen as articulating a deep-rooted popular nationalism that did not exist in other sports. Its links to other nationalist organisations such as the Land League, Gaelic language associations, and other Irish cultural organisations, not to mention the support of the Catholic Church, gave it a unique national authority upon which its popularity was built. Its nationalism gave expression to national pride in a way that the poorly performing Irish soccer and rugby sides could not. The GAA offered national redemption on the sporting field, thanks to games in which the Irish could take pride in their own achievements without suffering the humiliation of defeat by the occupying power.

Rugby was viewed, at least outside of Munster, as a sport of the middle classes, while soccer's relatively late arrival in Ireland – the first recorded match under FA rules appears to have taken place as late as 1875 – meant it could not challenge the GAA's hold on the national imagination. In 1890 the GAA numbered 875 clubs while the Irish Football Association could muster just 124. Rugby had even fewer.[5] Nor did the national soccer side's dismal five wins and five draws in fifty-two matches before 1900 do much to rouse the blood of patriotic sports fans.[6]

The emergence of Gaelic football appears to be the most overt example of the rise of football in the service of nationalism in the second half of the nineteenth century. Just as nationalist politicians in Europe constructed their 'invented traditions' of language, ritual and customs, so too football offered a narrative that complemented the framework of nationalism. The spectacle, drama and binary nature of football provided a stage upon which the shifting stories of nationalism could be acted out.

Yet the nationalism of Gaelic football only appears to be unusual because the nationalism of those codes of football based on the British model of Muscular Christianity was taken for granted and did not have to be explicitly stated. British nationalism was at the heart of all types of football. Even American football drew on British cultural tropes to tell its story. But the GAA expressed the nationalism of those who opposed Britain, or at least its policy towards Ireland, and therefore its nationalism appeared to be aberrant in comparison to that of other football codes.

This difference in perception can be seen by examining the links between the GAA and militant Irish republicans. Paul Rouse has convincingly demonstrated that the Irish Republican Brotherhood played a marginal role at best in the formation of the GAA.[7] By 1889, however, it appears that supporters of the IRB had gained a majority on the GAA national executive. Yet even if 'physical force' Irish Republicans were a major influence in the organisation, this should not be surprising. As those familiar with Sir Henry Newbolt's *Vitae Lampada* will realise, the link between sport and the British armed forces was perhaps even stronger. Attendees at the founding of the FA in 1863 included five career soldiers, a future assistant under-secretary of state for war, and representatives of the War Office and the Royal Naval School clubs.[8] Sporting organisations across the British Empire shared similarly close ties to the military. The governing bodies of other football codes were no less political than the GAA, but their support for the status quo meant their politics were perceived as being within the spectrum of 'common sense'. In contrast, the GAA's nationalist opposition to the existing order in Ireland meant that its politics stood out sharply.

Recent scholarship on the GAA has tended to downplay its nationalism, emphasising instead the porous boundary between soccer, rugby and Gaelic sports.[9] Many people played one or another in contravention of the GAA's Rule 27, the GAA's 1901 ban on members playing 'foreign sports' such as soccer, rugby and cricket. But the ban was also the GAA's recognition of that permeable border and the need to regulate contact with other sports.[10] Without a clear demarcation between it and these other sports, the GAA felt that its nationalist mission would be diminished. Conversely, the back and forth between sports also indicated that the GAA's nationalism was acceptable to a broad spectrum of Ireland's Catholic population and did not create a barrier for athletes who did not share its nationalist politics. As history shows, the thrill of pursuing a ball around a field with one's peers was rarely inhibited by political considerations.

Yet, aside from the GAA's explicit desire to see an independent Ireland, its practical sporting politics barely differed from those of British sports organisations.[11] Thus Michael Cusack – who was ousted as secretary of the GAA in 1885 but remained the source of the GAA's worldview – praised the organisation for having 'followed the counsels of the philosopher, which is embodied in the well-known Latin phrase – *Mens sana in corpore sano* [a healthy mind in a healthy body]'.[12] Just like Walter Camp in America, Pierre de Coubertin in France or Max Nordau in his attempt to create a 'Muscular Judaism', Cusack admired the British attitude to games and believed it was a model for his nation. 'In England the physical education of the pupils is carefully provided for', he wrote in 1887. 'and the result is when the boy becomes the man and leaves school he has plenty of stamina and vitality in him to battle his way through life', arguing that games should be as central to Irish schools as they were to the British.[13] Indeed, one of the distinguishing features of the nationalism of Camp, Coubertin, Nordau and Cusack was their wholehearted support for the fundamental tenets of British sport. They did not seek to develop an alternative sporting ideology but simply to harness British sporting values to their own particular nationalism.

The GAA was also a vigorous supporter of the British amateur ethos. Cusack's 'A word about Irish Athletics' argued that the British were undermining amateurism and condemned professional athletes in England. The GAA leadership shared his distaste and echoed prejudices from across the Irish Sea. 'Professional players are the very vagabonds and outlaws of the sporting fraternity', declared the *Gaelic Athlete* in 1913, while its editor, Séamus Upton, contemptuously bemoaned the fame that 'Tommy Bulletskull from Rochdale' could acquire as a professional sportsman.[14] Such social snobbery was no different from that which dripped from the pens of such upper-class Englishman as Arthur Budd and N.L. Jackson, and, it might be added, was also regularly directed against the Irish themselves.

Although its leadership adopted many of the prejudices of English amateurism, the GAA's form of amateurism was less draconian than that of the RFU or other similarly zealous sports organisations. Small amounts of prize money were acceptable and those who had competed with or against professionals in other sports were allowed to compete in GAA events. Unlike many British sports, there was no machinery of compliance to hunt down suspected transgressors of the amateur catechism.

Did this less rigid regime mean that the GAA's amateurism was democratic and not based on class division, as the GAA itself and some historians have claimed?[15] In contrast to the rest of the English-speaking world, the GAA's amateurism was never tested by an internal revolt or external professional threat. Loyalty to parish and county, so crucial to the GAA's popularity, was therefore not threatened by the lure of greater rewards elsewhere. The rising tide of nationalism in Ireland also gave the leadership of the GAA an extraordinary level of moral authority. Disloyalty to its principles could be, and often was, portrayed as a lack of patriotism. Free of internal threats to its authority or external threats to its popularity, the GAA's amateurism could remain largely benign.

Michael Cusack, Maurice Davin and the GAA leaders who succeeded them were well aware that they had created a new form of football. Like those who made up the backbone of innumerable nationalist movements across nineteenth-century Europe, their lives and their politics had become one, the only difference being that the GAA had enabled them to do this through the medium of sport. As nation-builders, they understood the importance of sport for the nation in the modern world. Once they had differentiated their code of football from those of the British in the 1880s, they had little subsequent need to justify the rules of their game by reference to Irish traditions because they understood that Gaelic football, like every other type of football, was about far more than simply what was written in its rulebook or that which took place on the pitch.

Notes

1 Dick Fitzgerald, *How to Play Gaelic Football* (Cork: Guy & Co., 1914), p. 78.
2 Neal Garnham makes this point strongly in *The Origins and Development of Football in Ireland* (Belfast: Ulster Historical Association, 1999), pp. 3–5.
3 This appeal is best captured and explained in Paul Rouse's wonderfully evocative *Sport and Ireland*, pp. 179–81.
4 *The Celtic Times*, 12 March 1887.

5 Tom Hunt, *Sport and Society in Victorian Ireland: The Case of Westmeath* (Cork: Cork University Press, 2007), p. 1.

6 See Martin Moore, 'The Origins of Association Football in Ireland, 1875–1880: A Reappraisal', *Sport in History*, vol. 37, no. 4 (2017), pp. 505–28. The definitive history of the early years of Irish soccer is Neal Garnham, *Association Football and Society in Pre-Partition Ireland* (Belfast: Ulster Historical Association, 2004).

7 Rouse, *Sport and Ireland*, pp. 164–5.

8 I am grateful to the superb research of Andy Mitchell for the biographies of those who attended the FA's founding meetings at www.scottishsporthistory. com, accessed 4 December 2017.

9 For example, see Connor Curran's excellent *The Development of Sport in Donegal 1880–1935* (Cork: Cork University Press, 2015).

10 David Hassan, 'The Gaelic Athletic Association, Rule 21, and Police Reform in Northern Ireland', *Journal of Sport & Social Issues* vol. 29, no. 1 (2005), pp. 60–78.

11 See also Mike Cronin, 'Fighting for Ireland, Playing for England? The Nationalist History of the Gaelic Athletic Association and the English Influence on Irish Sport', *The International Journal of the History of Sport*, vol. 15, no. 3 (1998), pp. 36–56.

12 'The Physical Training of the Young', *The Celtic Times*, 9 April 1887.

13 *The Celtic Times*, 14 May 1887.

14 Quoted in Donal McAnallen '"The Greatest Amateur Association in the World"? The GAA and Amateurism', in Mike Cronin, William Murphy and Paul Rouse (eds) *The Gaelic Athletic Association 1884–2009* (Dublin: Irish Academic Press, 2009), pp. 161–2. For a broader discussion on GAA amateurism see John Connolly and Paddy Dolan, 'The Amplification and De-Amplification of Amateurism and Professionalism in the Gaelic Athletic Association', *The International Journal of the History of Sport*, vol. 30, no. 8 (2013), pp. 853–70.

15 See, for example, McAnallen, '"The Greatest Amateur Association in the World" pp. 158 and 273.

15

AMERICAN FOOTBALL

The old game in the new world

> Football has earned for itself a unique place in the life of this coun-
> try . . . it is the national autumn sport, without a rival, and as such will
> retain its position as long as Anglo-Saxon blood flows in the veins of the
> young American.
>
> —Fielding Yost, 1905[1]

In June 1857 the *New York Times* noted the average New Yorker was wealth-
ier than the average Londoner. However the position was reversed when it
came to health.

> There can be no reasonable doubt that one very prominent and effi-
> cient cause of this difference between ourselves and out transatlantic
> kinsmen in respect of physical development is to be found in the
> greater prevalence through England of a taste for all manner of manly
> and athletic exercises

It went on to argue that 'the young Englishman . . . begins his education
in self-reliance and fair-play, through the trying ordeal of foot-ball at Eton
or Rugby'.[2] Three years later the same newspaper commented with some
approval that 'with the steady preaching of the school of muscular Christianity during the past few years . . . the human body has attained to a dig-
nity and importance in the eyes of instructors of youth'.[3] The importance
of physical education to young men was highlighted by the extraordinary

success in America of *Tom Brown's Schooldays*, which sold 225,000 copies in its first year of publication.[4] In 1872 the *New York World* even printed in full the book's description of Tom's first football matches as part of its coverage of the inaugural Yale-Columbia game.[5] As in the rest of the English-speaking world, this was to be the model for modern football in the United States.

Informal games of football had been played at the elite universities of the U.S. east coast since at least the 1820s. By the 1850s it had become part of undergraduate life at Columbia, Dartmouth, Harvard, Pennsylvania, Princeton and Yale, key members of what would become known as the Ivy League. Often a component of initiation or 'hazing' ceremonies, such was the violence of early football that the Harvard authorities banned the game in 1860.[6] Two years later the Oneida Football Club was formed by pupils of Boston's elite schools playing rules of its own concoction, making it probably the first club to be formed in the United States specifically to play football.[7] Although it folded in 1864, football's popularity among America's middle classes continued to grow due to the increasing importance of sport in American schools and colleges.

The emergence of football in mid-nineteenth-century America was not only due to concerns about the health of young middle-class men. The end of the era of Reconstruction in the 1870s renewed interest in the overseas expansion of U.S. interests. Americans who sought to revive the spirit of manifest destiny gazed enviously at the imperial successes of their British cousins: 'The splendid empires which England has founded in every quarter of the globe have had their origin largely in the football contests at Eton, the boat-races on the Thames, and the cricket-matches on her downs and heaths', Chicago professor William Mathews argued in 1873.[8] The underlying racial link between this bond and sport was further elaborated by the prominent Republican statesman Henry Cabot Lodge: 'injuries incurred on the playing field are part of the price which the English-speaking race has paid for being world conquerors'.[9] Teddy Roosevelt himself, the very embodiment of restless American national interests, believed that *Tom Brown's Schooldays* was one of two books that every American should read.[10]

Underpinning these attitudes was a belief in Muscular Christianity. Although it originated as a form of British nationalism, it also provided a framework into which other forms of nationalism could be inserted, and found especially fertile ground across the Atlantic, best exemplified by the Young Men's Christian Association (YMCA). Although it had been founded in England in 1844, the YMCA would become a considerable force in the United States. Amos Alonzo Stagg, after Walter Camp probably the most influential figure in the formative period of American football, embodied the unity of Christian ideals and sport, being a graduate of divinity school and a seminal coach with the University of Chicago. As was the case in the white settler colonies of the British Empire, Muscular Christianity became the dominant ideology not only of American football, but also of American education. It integrated these two spheres so that sport was portrayed as a force for moral improvement, rather than mere entertainment, and thus rejected commercialism and professionalism.

Despite a century having passed since the American Revolution, cultural ties to Britain remained strong and a shared sense of identity persisted. Between 1871 and 1890, the two decades of football's dramatic emergence, more than 1.7 million people migrated from Britain to the United States, with a further 409,000 going to Canada.[11] In 1866 Britain and America were linked by a commercial transatlantic telegraph cable. Rapid advances in such communications technology, alongside ocean-going steamships, railways and printing meant that, along with many other aspects of culture, football could be reported, discussed and eventually played across the Atlantic. In sport, Britain remained the lodestone for the English-speaking nations.[12]

The Anglocentric nature of early American football can be seen most graphically in Parke H. Davis' 1911 exhaustive chronicle of the early years of the sport, *Football: The Intercollegiate Game*, itself directly inspired by the Reverend Frank Marshall's 1892 *Football: The Rugby Union Game*. The book stressed the enduring cultural and sporting ties between the U.S. White Anglo-Saxon Protestant (WASP) middle classes and their British equivalents. 'There are many places in England so endeared to Americans by the ties of sentiment that we feel an ownership therein by the title of fancy if not by the title of actual fact', explained Davis, who continued:

> Where is the [American] lover of letters that does not claim an interest in the town of Avon? Where is the lawyer that does not believe that he possesses an inalienable right in the Inns of Court? Where is the football man from the field, side line, or stand who does not feel that he is an inheritor in the glories of Old Bigside at Rugby?[13]

Consequently, the United States adopted and adapted the British model in which schools and colleges were central to the organisation of amateur sport. American school and college sport followed the template of sport in elite British institutions. In nineteenth-century Britain, Eton versus Harrow cricket and rowing contests, and Oxford versus Cambridge cricket, rugby and rowing contests occupied a central position in national, middle-class sporting culture. Football contests between

Harvard and Yale, which became known simply as 'The Game', mirrored the annual Oxford versus Cambridge university rugby match. However, unlike Britain, college-level education in America grew exponentially in the late nineteenth and early twentieth centuries, due in large part to the impact of the Morrill Land Grant Acts of 1860 and 1892, which provided universities with land on which to build. This was precisely the period in which football became identified as an educational asset, a marker of social distinction, and, not least, a significant revenue generator for U.S. universities.[14]

This intertwining of football and the universities provided the platform for the subsequent exponential growth of the college sports' system. In contrast, there were barely a dozen universities in the United Kingdom in 1900, and the expansion of higher education was slow and piecemeal until the 1960s. British university sport therefore never had the geographic spread or national significance that college sport acquired in early twentieth-century America. So, although college and high school sport in America would soon develop a very different culture to sport in Britain, football initially emerged in America of the 1860s and 1870s profoundly shaped by British culture and tradition. Without *Tom Brown's Schooldays*, there would have no been no *Friday Night Lights*.

Football emerges in America

In 1869 the popularity of football within America's elite colleges had grown to such an extent that the game became an important arena for intercollegiate rivalry. On 6 November 1869 Rutgers hosted Princeton. Both institutions had their own football rules and so agreed to play each other according to the home side's code. Rutgers won the first encounter 6–4 but Princeton prevailed in the return match the following week 8–0. Although some historians have viewed the match as a form of soccer because running with the ball was forbidden, Rutgers allowed the ball to be hit with hands while Princeton rules shared some features with Australian Rules football, including bouncing the ball while running and a closed-fist passing technique.[15]

The two sides played each other again the following year and were joined by a side from Columbia University. In December 1872 a football club was formed at Harvard and the game also reappeared at Yale. In October 1873 Yale invited Columbia, Harvard, Princeton and Rutgers to meet to agree to a common set of rules. Harvard declined but the other four agreed to a twenty-a-side game that allowed catching the ball but not running with it. As with most early codes of football, these rules were vague enough to allow a wide array of interpretations.[16] Only three matches were played under these rules. Yale themselves quickly became dissatisfied with them and, after playing and defeating a team of former pupils of England's Eton College in December 1873, decided that football should be played using the Etonian eleven-a-side formation.[17] The following year, in May 1874, Harvard, whose 'Boston Rules' allowed carrying the ball, hosted two matches with its Canadian equivalent, Montreal's rugby-playing McGill University. It would be these two Harvard-McGill games that set the tone for football's subsequent development in America.

The first game was played according to Harvard's own rules, which the home side won easily. The second was played under McGill's rugby rules, which Harvard surprisingly drew 0–0. More importantly, the experience convinced the Harvard footballers that, in the words of the *Harvard Advocate*, 'the Rugby game is in much better favour than the somewhat sleepy game played by our men' and they switched to the rugby code.[18] Feeling compelled to compete against its traditional foe, Yale dropped its own rules and played Harvard under amended rugby rules, known as the 'concessionary rules', in November 1875. Princeton adopted the new rules and invited Harvard, Yale and Columbia to create an Intercollegiate Football Association (IFA). As had been the case in Britain, pride in one's own football rules had been trumped by the desire to compete against one's fiercest rivals.

The formation of the IFA in November 1876 and the standardisation of football rules – 'essentially those of the Rugby Union' reported the *New York Times* – created an arena in which America's elite universities could play out their intense rivalries.[19] Football matches, especially those on Thanksgiving Day, became major social occasions. In 1878, 5,000 spectators watched Princeton's 1–0 victory over Yale at Hoboken. Three years later football had become so fashionable that the Princeton-Yale match was moved to the more expansive Polo Grounds in Manhattan where it was watched by over 10,000 people. The Thanksgiving Day game, which became the traditional meeting ground for the season's two top teams, was attracting 25,000 people by 1890 and 40,000 by 1893.[20] Elite universities now provided entertainment for the masses.

Like soccer and rugby in Britain, college football's rapid success was facilitated by the growth of the popular press and transport systems. Matches between Ivy League universities commanded the back and the front pages of the major newspapers. The huge profile of the game meant that American universities saw football as a route to publicity, status and reputation. This was especially true for those which benefited from the Morrill Land Grant Acts. Many of the names that would dominate college football in the twentieth century were established this way: California, Clemson, Michigan State, Penn State, Purdue, Ohio State, Texas A&M, Virginia Tech and many others began as land grant universities. Through the universities, the game

PLATE 10   Quarterback passing from the scrimmage during the 1889 Yale versus Princeton match (*Frank Leslie's Illustrated Newspaper*, 7 December 1889)

expanded east to west, where the University of California abandoned rugby rules for the revised rules in 1886, and north to south, where Vanderbilt and Nashville universities began their rivalry in 1890, four years after Vanderbilt had taken up the game. By 1900, fourteen regional football associations, the forerunner of today's conferences, had been formed across the United States.

College football was now the undisputed king of American winter sports. Hundreds of thousands of people flocked to matches every week, the leading players became media personalities, and the daily drama of the game became a staple of newspapers and magazines. In this, football mirrored soccer in Britain. But in contrast to British soccer, top-flight American football was exclusively amateur. The leaders of the college game were keen amateurs and committed to middle-class exclusivity. Caspar Whitney, the editor of *Outing*, one of America's leading sports magazines, attacked as 'quite incomprehensible' the desire to 'bring together in sport the two divergent [class] elements of society that never by any chance meet elsewhere on even terms'.[21] Dr John C. Loveland believed that football was invaluable to

> the man of the future [who] must be able to elbow his way among rough men in the foul air of primary elections; he may need courage enough to take his part in vigilant and safety committees and the like; he may need to 'tackle' an anarchist now and then and perhaps oftener.[22]

Openly professional football only emerged in 1892 outside of the universities when Pittsburgh's Allegheny Athletic Association club paid former Yale star William 'Pudge' Heffelfinger $500 to play for them against their rivals in the Pittsburgh Athletic Club. Far from being a crack in the dam of amateur football, this proved to be merely one in series of short-lived experiments. Based largely in smaller, working-class industrial towns in Pennsylvania and the Mid-West, professional football struggled to make headway against the popularity and status of the university game.[23] Of course, like all amateur sports, college football was underpinned by a regime of hypocrisy that turned a blind eye to the monetary and other benefits provided to players from 'boosters' or even universities themselves. But professional football could not compete against the institutional renown of shamateur college sides. It was regionally based, lacked the kudos of the elite university sides and, thanks to the prevailing ethos of amateurism, its players viewed as sporting mercenaries. It would not be until after World War One that a relatively stable and financially viable professional league was established by the American Professional Football Conference, which in 1922 would change its name to the National Football League (NFL).

The problems that stalled attempts to start professional football before World War One also afflicted American soccer. Widely played in the industrial regions of America, soccer appears to have been unable to escape the perception that it was a sport for European, especially Scottish, immigrants. In 1894 the owners of six National League baseball clubs created the American League of Professional Football, but it collapsed after just seventeen days. Soccer was continually beset by organisational wrangling and, ironically, disputes over immigrant players, and found itself unable to gain any deeper resonance with the American public.[24]

Andrei Markovits and Steven Hellerman have argued that soccer's failure was because it was 'crowded out' of the American sport space, and its plebeian image deterred American universities from taking it up.[25] But it was not until after the legalisation of professionalism in soccer in 1885 – after rugby-style football had taken hold of American universities – that soccer in Britain came to be viewed as plebeian sport. As late as 1884 *The Field* magazine was arguing that

> the lower classes prefer watching a Rugby Union game, but that the Association rules find more favour in the eyes of the middle and upper classes is made amply evident by the crowds of respectable people that assemble [for major soccer matches] even in apathetic London.[26]

More importantly, until the 1900s soccer had neither the significant international profile nor the ideological framework desired by the middle classes of the Anglophone world who promoted football as a moral force. By the time that the Fédération Internationale de Football Association (FIFA) was formed in 1904, American football already dominated U.S. winter sport. As was the case everywhere else, football's popularity was based on its ability to express forms of identity, provide compelling stories to the print media and generate an emotional resonance among its supporters. American soccer could do none of these in any substantive manner, while college football continued to provide a narrative that transcended its elite origins. Far from America being exceptional in its embrace of rugby-style football over soccer, it was conforming to the pattern of adoption of sport in the English-speaking world in the late nineteenth century.

Unexceptional exceptionalism

The rapid series of rule changes that college football underwent in the 1870s and 1880s led many of its followers to believe that it had travelled a singular path that reflected what became known as American exceptionalism. First discussed in Alexis de Tocqueville's 1840 *Democracy in America*, American exceptionalism viewed American society as unique because of its lack of a feudal past, the vastness of its geography and a supposed greater degree of social mobility, encapsulated as the 'American Dream'.[27] The most prominent advocate of the idea that American football was an expression of American exceptionalism also happened to be the game's leading coach and journalist, Yale's Walter Camp.[28]

Born in 1859 in Connecticut, Camp was an enthusiastic reader of *Tom Brown's Schooldays* as a youth. He attended Yale from 1876 to 1882, where he was half-back and captain of its football team, eventually becoming coach in 1888.[29] He was the outstanding coach of his era, the most prominent member of the Intercollegiate Football Association (the first governing body for college football) and a prolific football journalist, being a contributing editor at both *Outing* and *Collier's* magazines. More than anyone else, Camp was responsible for the narrative of the birth of American football, and his 1886 article 'The Game and Laws of American Football' acquired the status of a Rosetta Stone for understanding the game's emergence from rugby.[30] After initially adopting the English rugby rules, Camp argued, Americans noticed 'ambiguities' in the rules of the game which led them to reform it to suit American attitudes. The rules had to be amended, he argued in a later article, because of 'the absolute lack of any existing foot-ball lore or tradition on American soil. The English game was one of traditions'.[31] Very much the author of his own legend, Camp himself invented the creation myth of the American game to fit the narrative of American Exceptionalism.

Camp's account is almost universally accepted, yet it is less a Rosetta Stone and more a Piltdown Man. The IFA rules committee met in November 1876 and accepted almost completely the fifty-nine rules of the English RFU as they applied in the 1874–75 English rugby season. They amended just two minor rules – relating to scoring and match officials – and added another two, regulating the size of the pitch and specifying that each team must comprise fifteen players. The latter two anticipated two changes that the RFU would make to their own rules in 1879 and 1892.[32]

In fact rugby's rules at this time were not, as might be inferred from Camp, rooted in the stasis of tradition but in a constant state of flux. Indeed, 'ambiguities' in the RFU's rules were as much an issue in England as in America. The observation of an unnamed 'Yale Player' in 1889 that, under rugby rules 'it was frequently impossible to decide with certainty a disputed point, in which case play was suspended, often for fifteen to twenty minutes, while the referee held a watch in his hands and the judges and the captains wrangled', was just as true in Britain.[33] Here too, matches were regularly delayed while rules were disputed and, as one English rugby player from the 1870s admitted, 'the more plausible and argumentative a player was, the more likely was he to be considered as a captain'.[34] Indeed, the International Rugby Football Board was created in 1886 due to an on-field dispute during the 1884 England versus Scotland match about the ambiguity of the 'knock-on' rule.

Camp's key argument was that the scrum was the central difference between British and American footballing sensibilities, because 'English players form solid masses of men in a scrummage and engage in a desperate kicking and pushing match until the ball pops out unexpectedly somewhere, leaving the struggling mass ignorant of its whereabouts'.[35] To remedy this, in 1880 the IFA adopted Camp's proposal to abolish the scrum and introduce an orderly 'snapback' after the ball-carrier was tackled. The two sets of forwards therefore lined up opposite each other and the ball was put back into play by being heeled back by the centre to the quarterback. This, he argued, did away with the uncertainty and ambiguity of the scrum.

But Camp's innovation was neither unique nor revolutionary.[36] The problems of the scrum were also under scrutiny across the football-playing world. As we have seen, in Australia, football clubs in Melbourne were gradually reforming the scrum out of existence. Many British rugby players were arguing that the sport should move away from the scrum-dominated game. And just a few hundred miles from Camp's home, another group of footballers was also discussing the best way to play rugby football, and in 1875 decided to abolish the scrum. Yet these were not American footballers, but Canadian.

Notes

1 Fielding Yost, *Football for Player and Spectator* (Ann Arbor: University Publishing: 1905), p. 14.

2 *New York Times*, 5 June 1857. This chapter is based on my article 'Unexceptional Exceptionalism: the Transnational Origins of American Football', *Journal of Global History*, vol. 8, no. 2, July 2013, pp. 209–30.

3 *New York Times*, 30 August 1860.

4 Julie Des Jardins, *Walter Camp: Football and the Modern Man* (New York: Oxford University Press, 2015), p. 11.

5 *New York World*, 17 November 1872.

6 Scott Meacham, *Old Division Football, the Indigenous Mob Soccer of Dartmouth College*, Dartmo (2006), at www.dartmo.com/football.pdf (viewed 12 August 2017). Ron Smith, *Sports and Freedom: The Rise of Big-Time College Athletics* (New York: Oxford University Press, 1991), p. 13. For Harvard, see the *New York Times*, 15 October 1852.

7 Winthrop S. Scudder, *An Historical Sketch of the Oneida Football Club of Boston, 1862–1865* (1926) at https://babel.hathitrust.org/cgi/pt?id=wu.89098742257 ;view=1up;seq=3 (viewed 9 April 2012). The Oneida club has recently been the subject of much attention for claims that it was the first U.S. soccer club, but there is no evidence that it played any form of modern code.

8 William Matthews, *Getting On in the World* (Toronto: S.C. Griggs, 1876), p. 61.

9 Quoted in Elliott Gorn, *The Manly Art* (Cornell: Cornell University Press, 1986), p. 188.

10 The other was Thomas Bailey Aldrich's 1869 *Story of a Bad Boy*. See Gordon Hutner (ed.), *Selected Speeches and Writings of Theodore Roosevelt* (New York: Vintage 2014), p. 7.

11 Gary B. Magee and Andrew S. Thompson, *Empire and Globalisation* (Cambridge: Cambridge University Press, 2010), p. 69.

12 See also Roberta J. Park, 'Sport, Gender and Society in a Transatlantic Victorian Perspective', *The International Journal of the History of Sport*, vol. 24, no. 12 (2007), pp. 1570–603.

13 Parke H. Davis, *Football. The American Intercollegiate Game* (New York: Charles Scribner, 1911), p. 24.

14 For a discussion of the relationship between football and the growth of American higher education, see Brian Ingrassia, *The Rise of the Gridiron University: Higher Education's Uneasy Alliance with Big-time Football* (Lawrence, KS: University Press of Kansas, 2012) and Ron Smith, *Sports and Freedom: The Rise of Big-Time College Athletics* (New York: Oxford University Press, 1991).

15 Davis, pp. 51–2. For the soccer view see Ronald Smith, 'American Football Becomes the Dominant Intercollegiate National Pastime', *International Journal of the History of Sport*, vol. 31, nos. 1–2 (2014), pp. 109–19. For the similarity with Australian rules, see W.J. Henderson, 'College Football Twenty-Five Years Ago', *Outing*, vol. 37, no. 1 (October 1899), p. 16. It is also worth noting Yale alumni Rudolf Wurts, who worked in Melbourne in the 1890s, thought Australian football was 'as near as can be the game played at Yale' in 1879, quoted in Walter Camp, *Football Facts and Figures* (New York: Harper & Bros, 1894), p. 163.

16 See Davis, pp. 60–1.

17 *Bell's Life*, 3 January 1874. See also Andy Mitchell's *A Transatlantic Football Game in 1873* at www.scottishsporthistory.com/sports-history-news-and-blog, accessed 12 November 2017.

18 *Harvard Advocate*, 29 May 1874, quoted in Davis, p. 65.

19 *New York Times*, 24 November 1876.

20 Michael Oriard, *Reading Football: How the Popular Press Created an American Spectacle* (Chapel Hill: University of North Carolina Press, 1993), pp. 90–1.

21 Whitney, p. 164.

22 Camp, *Football Facts and Figures*, p. 47.

23 Robert W. Peterson, *Pigskin: The Early Years of Pro Football* (New York: Oxford University Press, 1997).

24 For a discussion on early American soccer, see Brian Bunk, 'The Rise and Fall of Professional Soccer in Holyoke Massachusetts, USA', *Sport in History*, vol. 31, no. 3 (2011), pp. 283–06.

25 Andrei S. Markovits and Steven L. Hellerman, *Offside: Soccer and American: Exceptionalism* (Princeton: Princeton University Press, 2001).

26 *The Field*, 12 January 1884.

27 There is a vast literature on the subject. Some of the most recent prominent examples include Deborah L. Madsen, *American Exceptionalism* (Edinburgh: Edinburgh University Press, 1998), Godfrey Hodgson, *The Myth of American Exceptionalism* (Yale: Yale University Press, 2009), Byron E. Shafer (ed.), *Is America Different?: A New Look at American Exceptionalism* (Oxford: Clarendon Press, 1991), Seymour Martin Lipset, *American Exceptionalism: A Double-edged Sword* (New York: W.W. Norton, 1998), Charles Lockhart, *The Roots of American Exceptionalism* (London: Palgrave, 2003), and Donald E. Pease, *The New American Exceptionalism* (Minnesota: University of Minnesota, 2009). For a sports' perspective of the debate see Markovits and Hellerman, *Offside: Soccer and American Exceptionalism*.

28 David Riesman and Reuel Denney, 'Football in America: A Study in Cultural Diffusion', *American Quarterly*, vol. 3, no. 3 (1951), 309–25. See also Allen Guttmann, 'Civilized Mayhem: Origins and Early Development of American Football', *Sport in Society*, vol. 9, no. 4 (2006), pp. 535–7.

29 Julie Des Jardins, *Walter Camp: Football and the Modern Man* (New York: Oxford University Press, 2015).

30 Walter Camp, 'The Game and Laws of American Football', *Outing* (October 1886), pp. 69–76.

31 *Walter Camp's Book of College Sports* (New York, 1893), pp. 88–9.

32 Proceedings of the Convention of the Intercollegiate Football Association, 23 November 1876, reprinted in Davis, *Football*, pp. 461–7. It is worth pointing out that the chronicler of American football rules, David M. Nelson, noted that twenty-three of these rules were still in the NFL rulebook in 1991, in his *The Anatomy of the Game: Football, the Rules and the Men Who Made the Game* (New Jersey: University of Delaware Press, 1994), p. 40.

33 A Yale Player, 'The Development of Football', *Outing*, vol. 15, no. 2 (1889), p. 145.

34 Robert Christison, captain of York F.C. interviewed in the *Yorkshire Evening Post*, 22 February 1901.

35 Camp, *Outing*, 1886, p. 72.

36 The phrase is from William Baker, *Sports in the Western World* (Lanham, MD: Rowman & Littlefield, 1988), p. 129.

16

CANADIAN FOOTBALL

Between scrum and snapback

As a game scientifically considered, the United States is the better . . . [but] from a spectacular and players' standpoint however, the Canadian game must be given the preference. . . . The Canadian players have more real sport than their US cousins because, although the game is rough enough to suit the most hardy, it cannot be called dangerous, and on this account the element of pleasure is more pronounced.

—George W. Orton, 1897[1]

Organised football had been played in Canada from at least 1861, when students from the University of Toronto in Ontario arranged a match among themselves. Further north, in Quebec, the first recorded match appears to have taken place in 1862 with a twelve-a-side match between teams of the Grenadier Guards and the Scots Fusiliers stationed in Montreal, which the Grenadiers won by two goals and three rouges to nil.[2] Over the next few years the British model was followed and football clubs were established in Hamilton (1869), Montreal (1872), Toronto (1873) and Ottawa (1876), all playing the rugby version of football and each comprising young men from Canada's English-speaking elite. As with the game in the rest of the Anglophone world at this time, football in Canada was a sport for gentleman.

Canada was a nation that defined itself by its position in the British Empire and its proximity to the United States. It had been created in 1867 when confederation brought together the previously autonomous British colonies north of the United States, which themselves had occupied the lands of native Canadians. With the exception of the French-speaking Quebec nation that was ceded by the French to the British in 1763, the

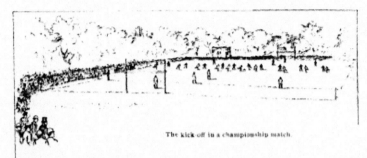

The kick off in a championship match.

When the ball is kicked off the field of play into touch by a player on one side it is considered dead and belongs to the other side, one of whose players throws it in at right angles to the touch line, and this throw in gives opportunity for a number of good plays. One trick is to throw to a forward, who passes quickly to the quarter-back, and he punts the ball down the field into touch again, with a gain of, perhaps, 20 yards; the ball, however, then belongs to the opposite side.

goes over the cross-bar no goal is scored; but if the ball goes fairly between the goal posts and above the cross-bar two points are scored, making six points in all.

When the ball is touched down by a player behind his own goal line a rouge is scored against him (one point); and if he runs or kicks behind his own goal line, and has to touch it down, a safety touch (two points) is scored against him.

When a ball goes into touch in goal it is considered dead, and one point is scored.

This picture shows a throw-out from touch. The man with arms raised is to receive the ball and pass it to the quarter-back who stands some distance behind the line. The last man in white will, however, break through and tackle him if not stopped by the tall player in black jersey.

When the ball is carried over the goal line and an opponent touches it down, a "touch down" is scored (4 points), and a "try" for goal is allowed. The ball is brought out at right angles from the goal line to a convenient distance and placed by one man, who lies down with the ball in his hands, for another of his side to kick. The defending side, who are lined up on the goal line, may charge as soon as the ball touches the ground. If any of the defending side touch the ball before it

A majority of points wins a match.

This system of scoring has been found to give every stisfaction, and there is little likelihood of it being materially changed.

A player is not allowed to hold an opponent when running for the ball, nor is he allowed to run in front of any player of his own side who has the ball.

If the ball is knocked forward with the hand or passed forward, it is brought back and scrimmaged where the foul occurred; or for a repeated foul of this kind a free

PLATE 11   An 1892 guide to Canadian football (*The Dominion Illustrated Monthly,* February 1892)

impetus towards Canadian nationhood came from the northern exodus of the self-described British-Americans who stayed loyal to George III after the American war of independence. The victory of the north in the American Civil War in 1865 made both English- and French-speaking Canadians so fearful of U.S. ambitions for continental north America that they rushed to secure themselves through confederation.[3]

Football in Canada was defined by loyalty to British sporting values and an ever-present suspicion that the grass of the American football field was greener. At just 300 miles from New England, Montreal was as close to the football-playing American colleges as it was to Toronto. But initially it was the Canadians who spurred the development of the game in North America. Barely a year after the 1874 Harvard-McGill matches, Canadian players engaged in discussions about rugby reform, reflecting debates in British rugby that led to teams being cut from twenty to fifteen players and obliged tackled players to release the ball. On 16 October 1875 a 'football convention' was held at Rossin House Hotel in Toronto at which representatives of nine clubs discussed adopting a common set of rules for the game in Ontario and Quebec, the two most populous provinces of Canada. The meeting decided to adopt RFU rules but three delegates, including those from McGill and University College Toronto, voted against, ensuring that the debate on football rules would continue. Much of their opposition was based on a dislike of the scrum, which a sympathetic correspondent of the *Toronto Daily Globe* described as 'an exhibition of brute force by thirty men crushing and jamming in a surging mass'.[4]

This debate continued vigorously in the press over the next few weeks, with supporters of association and rugby rules contributing. Most significantly, the McGill delegate to the convention described scrums as

> monotonous, uninteresting and dangerous. . . . The majority of disinterested spectators will probably include that it is far more interesting and more scientific practice for members of a team to kick or play into each other's hands, than for both sides to engage in a melee where no advantage results from precision, agility or experience.[5]

Moreover, it was claimed by a Toronto player, some clubs in Ontario simply refused to take part in scrums. Indeed, it would appear that both McGill and University College Toronto were by now playing a form of rugby without conventional scrums – which became known as the 'open formation' because the forwards spread out across the pitch facing each other – that predated Walter Camp's 1880 proposal to introduce the snapback into college football.

However, two of the early but short-lived attempts at forming a governing body for football, the Foot Ball Association of Canada (formed in 1873) and the Canadian Rugby Football Union (1880), adopted the orthodox RFU definition of the scrum.[6] To what extent this was practised when matches were being played is unclear. Given the paucity of primary sources and the disregard with which early football players often treated formal rules, it is difficult to assess how closely the game on the pitch resembled the rules written on the page. In 1880 a football lover complained about the open formation 'lately introduced in Canada from the United States' but by the mid-1880s it appears that most Canadian clubs were playing some form of 'open formation' rugby.[7] However, perhaps reflecting the tension between loyalty to its Mother Country and the attraction of its southern neighbour, Canadian rugby tried to combine the open formation and the scrum. Thus a tackled player would put the ball down in front of them and form a type of mini-scrum with a forward on each side, and then heel the ball back to the quarterback. Emphasising the global nature of the evolution of the rugby codes, the 'scrim', as it was known, seems to have anticipated rugby league's 'play-the-ball' by two decades.

The 'scrim' was composed of three, but sometimes five, players, which meant that the player heeling the ball back was supported by a player, or two, on either side. This ambiguity in the rules was confusing, and reflected the state of Canadian rugby. Rivalry for organisational supremacy between the Ontario and Quebec rugby unions resulted in them often playing different sets of rules or switching between rules in different seasons. Quebec in general favoured traditional scrummaging whereas Ontario usually favoured the 'open formation'. By 1901 Canadian football was being played under four different sets of rules, resulting in the 1905 national championship game between the Ontario and Quebec champions being played with each half under the differing rules of the two provinces.[8]

Confusion over the rules and administrative rivalry were not the only problems facing Canadian football. With one or two exceptions, until the 1910s it largely remained a sport of elite educational institutions.[9] It did not have the mass appeal of ice hockey, which had become a professional mass spectator sport by the mid-1900s in large part due to the popularity of competitions like the Stanley Cup, which began in 1893.[10] Baseball, not least because of the regular contests it offered with American sides, and even lacrosse were also more popular than football.[11] In the far west, Vancouver and the surrounding territory remained loyal to orthodox rugby union. In comparison to other sports, crowds were sparse. Only 3,500 attended the Canadian Rugby Union championship decider in 1893, a meagre figure when compared to the tens of thousands who attended big matches south of the border. But, as with many in the English RFU, some in Canadian football did not want to see it become a mass spectator sport. The game's leadership was resolutely amateur. Writing in 1891, the educationalist and physician Robert Tait McKenzie argued that

> it will be the class of people who will attend the matches that will have the greatest influence in moulding the game. If the game caters to the rougher element it will soon become rough and brutal, but if the class of spectators is of the best, players will be ashamed to disgrace themselves by ungentlemanly or foul play, and the whole tone of the game will be elevated.[12]

In October 1897, citing concerns over violence and suspicions of professionalism, Queen's University in Ontario barred non-students from playing for their senior football team. A month later it came together with other universities to create the Canadian Intercollegiate Rugby Football Union, dedicated to amateurism and social exclusivity.

MacKenzie was also a critic of those who wanted to bring the Canadian game closer to American football. 'The American style of play is in no way superior to our own Rugby game', he argued. 'The game is a much more confined and close sort of football, admitting of little of the fine punting, nice passing, fleet running, or, in fact, any of the pretty plays that go to make Canadian football what it is'.[13] The quest for a uniquely Canadian game was part of British-Canadians' late-nineteenth-century search for a distinctive identity within the British Empire.[14] But geography's gravitational pull also meant that American football could not be ignored. Four years later, two Canadians writing in *Outing* magazine noted that American-style team uniforms, protective padding and training methods were increasingly the norm in Canada. Questioning the value of rugby's scrum, they hoped that 'experts in the game, on both sides of the line, may soon see their way to modify the rules, so that international contests may take place'.[15]

In 1899, moves in this direction gathered pace when a former captain of the University of Toronto team and a scion of one of Toronto's leading families, John Thrift Burnside, proposed eight changes to the rules of the game. The most important were the complete abolition of the scrum and the introduction of the snapback, reduction of teams from fifteen to twelve players, and the legalisation of blocking with the body.[16] As much as this was an endorsement of the American style of football, it was also a rejection of the British style. The Irish national rugby union team had toured Canada in 1899, winning all but one of their matches, but although they gained many admirers, the tourists did little to popularise the traditional rugby union game.

The Burnside rules, as they became known, soon found supporters in Ontario and were tested in the Mulock Cup, Toronto University's intramural competition. In 1905 the new rules were adopted by the Ontario RFU, converting rugby into a variation of the gridiron game, albeit with twelve players per side instead of eleven, and three downs for a team to make ten yards. But the rest of Canadian rugby stayed loyal to their version of rugby rules. Isolated, the Ontarians rescinded their decision the following season and reached a compromise with the clubs of the Canadian RFU to play a fourteen-a-side game using the old-style scrimmage. But this did little to settle the issue, and the sport was consumed by battles not only about rules but also over amateurism, resulting in expulsions and splits. Over the next decade the Canadian game would remain caught between its fealty to the sporting values of its Mother Country and the lure of its American cousins.

Transatlantic problems, transatlantic solutions

It took the Canadians almost four decades to excise the scrum finally from their game, but the Americans struck it out in little more than six years. The rapidity of this change was a direct outcome of another, earlier reform in the game: Yale's insistence that football should be played by teams of eleven. Yale's commitment to eleven-a-side football derived from its victory against the former Eton College pupils in late 1873. Harvard had also originally favoured fewer players than rugby's then customary twenty-a-side, its original 1872 rules specifying that a team should consist of 'not less than ten nor more than fifteen players'.[17] At its first meeting in 1876, the Intercollegiate Football Association decided that teams should comprise fifteen players. Yale disagreed and argued for eleven-a-side. In 1877 it suggested to Harvard playing thirteen-a-side but was rebuffed.[18] It was not until October 1880 that the IFA accepted the reduction of teams to eleven.[19] This move to eleven-a-side opened the door for all future innovations in American football because it inadvertently changed the very nature of the scrum.

Up until the 1880s the rugby scrum served precisely the opposite purpose to that of today.[20] The aim was not to heel the ball back and out of the scrum, but to drive the ball forward and scatter the opposing pack. As described by RFU secretary Arthur Guillemard in 1877, as soon as a player carrying the ball was stopped by a tackle:

> the forwards of each side hurry up and a scrummage is instantly formed, each ten facing their opponents' goal, packed round the ball, shoulder to shoulder, leg to leg, as tight as they can stand, the twenty

thus forming a round compact mass with the ball in the middle. Directly the holder of the ball has succeeded in forcing it down to the ground, he shouts 'Down' and business may be commenced at once.[21]

Just as in America, many British rugby followers sought to move the game away from what *Bell's Life* described as the 'monotonous shoving matches' of endless scrums.[22] This pressure to reform the sport meant that by 1877 games were played fifteen-a-side. Ten fewer forwards on the field meant that scrums no longer lasted for minutes, because it was easier for the ball to come out of the scrum. Forwards began to break away from the scrum and dribble the ball downfield with their feet. The ball also began to be passed from the scrum-half to the other backs to start attacks. This led to teams deliberately heeling the ball backwards out of the scrum, to the horror of traditionalists. In 1878 the rules were further amended so that a tack-led player, who would previously hold the ball until the forwards gathered around to form a scrum, was forced to release the ball immediately the tackle was completed.[23] The game became faster and more open.

But the change to eleven-a-side in America had even more far-reaching consequences. The removal of so many forwards from the game meant the traditional scrum was impossible. In rugby, propelling the ball forward through a thicket of fifteen or more pairs of legs and boots took considerable skill and strength. However, with only six or seven forwards on each side, the ball could not be contained in the scrum for any length of time. Kicking the ball forward resulted in it quickly emerging out on the opponents' side, giving them the ball. Conventional scrummaging became wholly counter-productive. Yale and the other sides playing eleven-a-side rugby therefore began to position their forwards in a single line, the 'open formation', with the intention of transferring the ball to their backs as quickly as possible.

Yale quickly grasped the implications of the move to eleven-a-side. At the IFA meeting that approved eleven-a-side teams in 1880, a resolution was also passed that redefined – and renamed as the 'scrimmage' – the scrum:[24]

> A scrimmage takes place when the holder of the ball, being in the field of play, puts it down on the ground in front of him and puts it in play while on side, first, by kicking the ball; second, by snapping it back with his foot. The man who first receives the ball from the snap-back shall be called the quarter-back, and shall not then rush forward with the ball under penalty of foul.[25]

The debates about the RFU's rules were therefore part of wider trans-national debate across the rugby-playing world. Many of the American solutions also had their roots in early British rugby. Interference, defined by Camp as 'the assistance given to a runner by a companion or companions who go before him and break a path for him or shoulder-off would-be tacklers', was similar to a tactic used in rugby until the 1870s.[26] Blackheath, arguably the leading club of nineteenth-century rugby, developed a tactic in the 1860s which featured, according to RFU president Arthur Guillemard, 'forwards charging down the ground as an advance guard to ward off opponents from the back who was in full run with the ball behind them'.[27] It was not until 1888 that the RFU ruled that it was 'not lawful for a player to charge against or obstruct any opponent unless such opponent is holding the ball'.[28] And in Australian Rules, obstructing opposing players has historically been a legal tactic, known as 'shepherding'. American football was therefore not so much innovating as extending a feature present in the earliest forms of rugby codes.

There were many other contemporary similarities between the American and rugby forms of football. For example, passing the ball (known as lateral passing in modern American football) initially was as common, if not more so, in the American as in the rugby game. Harvard in particular became known for their eagerness to pass the ball among players, in contrast to rugby players' then traditional reluctance to do so. Commenting on Harvard's 'almost monotonous success' against Canadian teams in 1880, one writer pointed to the fact that 'the two styles vary as to passing. The English game discountenances passing, except in rare cases, whilst the Harvards always shy the ball back when about to be tackled, that is, if it be at all possible'.[29] In fact, unlike American football today, the game in the 1880s placed a much greater premium on passing combinations between players.[30]

Even the name 'quarterback' was taken directly from early Scottish and Irish rugby. Originally in Scotland backs were arranged originally as 'quarterback', 'half-back' and 'full-back', the same terminology as in North America, rather than the English system of 'half-back, three-quarter back' and 'full-back'.[31] American football's formalisation of the role of the quarterback, whose duty initially was to pass or kick the ball but initially not to run with it, anticipated the development of the 'passing game' in British rugby.

Similarities in the football debates on both sides of the Atlantic can also be seen in English rugby's 1895 split. Walter Camp's support for the primacy of the touchdown over the goal – 'the advocates of team play were especially strong against such a premium as existed on what seemed to be but an act of individual skill [i.e. the goal]' – mirrored precisely that of rugby reformers in northern England. 'A try in the vast majority of instances is the most deserving point in the game, and calls for the greatest exertion on the part of the team as a whole', wrote one northern journalist in 1891 who also described goal-kicking as 'an individual responsibility . . . attended by none of the combined action which forms one of the chief attractions of the game'.[32]

The scrum was also a major focus of the English rugby reformers. In 1892 James Miller argued for the reduction of players from fifteen to thirteen in terms not unlike that of Camp and his co-thinkers:

> by lessening the number of forwards taking part in a game, he was convinced it would be a reform which would . . . bring the game nearer the perfected state. It was clear to him that the end of the 'pushing age' had been reached and instead of admiring the physique and pushing power of those giants which took part in the game in the early stages, at any rate in the future they would be able to admire the skilful and scientific play of the game.[33]

The Canadian football reformers held a similar attitude to the scrum, viewing the game as:

> slow and heavy. The ball was buried in a scrimmage and the heavier team kept it there or tried to, until it had plowed a passage to the enemy's goal line. There was a constant succession of muffled shouts which, to the spectators, sounded like 'Hell! Hell!' and yell seemed to fit the occasion. The cry was really 'Held! Held!' but the uninformed patron could not be expected to get the full sound when vocalist had a mouthful of dirt. This yell was the player's salvation for if he did not cry it around and often when he had the ball dead under him, his adversary was liable to tear his head from his shoulders, such was the gentle nature of the conventionalities of the game in those days.[34]

Like the American game, both rugby league and Canadian football sought to reform the scrum by introducing a more-or-less orderly resumption of play when a player was tackled with the ball. In both Canada's scrim and league's play-the-ball, the tackled player would regain their feet, place the ball on the ground and attempt to play it backward with a foot to a teammate.

But this also brought its own problems. The automatic retention of the ball by the tackled player's team meant that by not kicking or passing the ball a side could completely starve their opponents of the ball.[35] The most notorious example of what became known in America as the 'block game' was the 1881 Princeton versus Yale encounter, when each side kept possession of the ball for a complete half of the match. The IFA's solution was the restriction of possession to three 'downs' (itself an old rugby term) to advance the ball five yards or lose ten yards.[36] Again, this was not a uniquely American solution to the problem. Rugby league also suffered from similar problems of unlimited possession, a phenomenon known as the 'creeping barrage' game. After a debate that lasted from the 1920s to the 1960s, the answer was found by ruling if a side had not scored after it had been tackled four times it would forfeit possession of the ball.[37] In Canada, the problem was eventually solved by introducing a downs and yardage system similar to American football, forcing a side to gain ten yards in three downs. As if to emphasise the transnational nature of the debate on rugby rules, Canada's insistence on a team gaining ten yards, in contrast to America's five, was advocated by Walter Camp as a solution to the problems of the American game in the 1900s.[38]

Once again, we can see that concern about the problems of the RFU's rules of rugby was a transnational debate that took place across the English-speaking football world. In America, Canada, and the north of England, the rules of rugby were being questioned and reformed from the 1870s, as would happen later in Australia and New Zealand. In the 1860s, the same critical impetus had caused footballers in Melbourne to modify Rugby School rules. Although the answers to these problems differed, there was nothing uniquely national in any of the solutions adopted by the various football codes. Rather, the emergence of the snapback and similar variations, together with limited downs or tackles, in American, Canadian, and rugby league football underlined the fundamental similarity in the way in which these issues were approached across the rugby-playing world.

Notes

1 George W. Orton, 'Canadian and United States Rugby', *The Canadian Magazine,* vol. 10, no. 1 (November 1897), p. 60.
2 *Bell's Life in London and Sporting Chronicle,* 16 November, 1862. For a detailed and comprehensive history of rugby in Canada, see Doug Sturrock, *It's a Try: The History of Rugby in Canada* (Langley, British Columbia: Sturrock Consulting, 2016).
3 For an overview, see Kenneth McNaught, *The Pelican History of Canada* (Harmondsworth: Penguin, 1969).
4 *Toronto Daily Globe,* 23 October 1875.
5 *Toronto Daily Globe,* 12 November 1875.
6 *Town & Country* [Toronto], 16 June 1880.
7 *Toronto Daily Globe,* 16 November 1880.
8 For discussions on the development of the rules of Canadian football, see Robert Sproule, 'Snap-Back versus Scrimmage', *From Scrimmage to SnapBack. Journal of the Canadian Football Historical Association,* vol. 1, no. 1 (Fall 2003), pp. 6–8, and

Ian Speers, 'The Development of the American Scrimmage System', *The Coffin Corner*, vol. 24, no. 2 (2002).

9 See Alan Matcalfe, *Canada Learns to Play: The Emergence of Organised Sport 1807–1914* (Toronto: McLelland & Stewart, 1987), pp. 56–7.

10 Daniel S. Mason, 'The International Hockey League and the Professionalization of Ice Hockey, 1904–1907', *Journal of Sport History*, vol. 25, no. 1 (Spring 1998), pp. 1–17.

11 See Charles Anthony Joyce, *From Left Field: Sport and Class in Toronto 1845–1886* (Unpublished PhD thesis, Queen's University, Kingston, ON, 1997). For baseball's popularity among the working class, see Bryan Palmer, 'In Street and Field and Hall: The Culture of Hamilton Workingmen, 1860–1914' in his *Marxism and Historical Practice*, vol. 2 (Leiden: Brill, 2015), pp. 133–7.

12 Robert Tait MacKenzie, 'Rugby Football in Canada', *The Dominion Illustrated Monthly* (Feb 1892), vol. 1, no. 1, p. 19. See Orton, 'Canadian and United States Rugby', pp. 56–60.

13 Tait MacKenzie, 'Rugby Football', p. 12.

14 See Phillip Buckner, 'The Creation of the Dominion of Canada, 1860–1901', in Phillip Buckner (ed.) *Canada and the British Empire* (Oxford: Oxford University Press, 2010), pp. 79–82.

15 A.C. Kingstone and C.A.S. Boddy, 'The Characteristics of Canadian Football', *Outing*, vol. 27, no. 3 (December 1895), p. 251.

16 *The Varsity* [University of Toronto], vol. 19, no. 11, 17 January 1900, p. 140.

17 Davis, *Football*, pp. 24 and 62. Yale's original football rules of 1872 are on p. 54, Harvard's on p. 53 and the two matches reported on pp. 251–4.

18 *Boston Daily Globe*, 25 November 1877, reprinted in Greg Gubi (ed.) *The Lost Century of American Football*, 2011, p. 60.

19 Proceedings of the Convention of the Intercollegiate Football Association, 12 October 1880, reprinted in Davis, *Football*, p. 468.

20 For example, see John Sayle Watterson, *College Football: History: Spectacle: Controversy* (Baltimore: Johns Hopkins University Press, 2003), pp. 19, or Baker, *Sports in the Western World*, p. 129.

21 A.G. Guillemard, 'The Rugby Union Game With Hints to Players', in Thomas P. Power (ed.) *The Footballer* (Melbourne: Henriques & Co., 1877), p. 11.

22 *Bell's Life*, 16 October 1875.

23 Rev. Frank Marshall (ed.), *Football. The Rugby Union Game* (London: Cassell, 1892), p. 120.

24 See for example the use of 'scrimmage' in the *Manchester Guardian,* 20 September 1906. Camp's claim is in *Outing*, October 1886, p. 73.

25 Proceedings of the Convention of the Intercollegiate Football Association, 12 October 1880, reprinted in Davis, *Football*, p. 468.

26 Camp, *American Football* (New York, 1891), p 15.

27 A.G. Guillemard, 'Foundation and progress of the Rugby Football Union' in Marshall, *Football. The Rugby Union Game*, p. 71.

28 Percy Royds, *The History of the Laws of Rugby Football* (Twickenham: Rugby Football Union, 1949), p. 149.

29 *Montreal Gazette*, 2 November 1880.

30 See, for example, reports in the *Ottawa Citizen*, 10 November 1884. "The American Game of Foot-ball", *The Century Magazine*, October 1887, p. 890.

31 R.J. Philips, *The Story of Scottish Rugby* (Edinburgh: Foulis, 1925), p. 13. See also Marshall, *Football: The Rugby Union Game*, p. 172.
32 Walter Camp, 'Football in America' in *Frank Leslie's Popular Monthly*, vol. 57, no. 1 (November 1898), 61. *The Yorkshireman*, 4 April 1893.
33 *Yorkshire Post*, 9 October 1892.
34 *The Daily Colonist* [Victoria, British Columbia], 6 October 1920.
35 The 'Block Game' is described in Camp, *American Football*, p. 19.
36 Proceedings of the Convention of the IFA, 14 October 1882, reprinted in Davis, *Football*, p. 468.
37 See Tony Collins, *Rugby League in Twentieth Century Britain* (Abingdon: Routledge, 2006), pp. 112–13. It was later increased to six tackles.
38 Camp had favoured ten yards since at least 1891; see *The Canadian Magazine*, vol. 10, no. 1 (November 1897), p. 59.

17

RUGBY LEAGUE FOOTBALL

From people's game to proletarian sport

I say with Mark Twain's bold bad boy that we glory in the sentence of outlawry pronounced on us, as freeing us from the tyrannical bondage of the English [Rugby] Union, and we breath pure air in being freed from the stifling atmosphere of deceit in which we previously existed.

—'A member of a Northern Union club', 1895[1]

The twenty-two clubs that broke away from the Rugby Football Union in August 1895 to create the Northern Union set themselves the task of making rugby a sport for the modern age of the masses. The underlying cause of the split was summed up by the first Northern Union (NU) president Harry Waller: 'where there was a preponderance of working class players [rugby] could not be honestly carried out under the existing by-laws of the English Union'.[2] The new organisation immediately legalised 'broken-time' payments to players and began to reform the rules of the game. Over the next decade the NU accepted full professionalism, changed the rules of rugby dramatically by reducing teams to thirteen–a–side to make the game more attractive, and expanded to the working-class rugby strongholds of Australia and New Zealand. Rugby league, as it became known, embodied the three elements that had come to dominate the handling codes of football: class, commercialism and how to play the game. The 1895 schism was a harbinger of the turmoil that would consume much of the football's oval world in the first decade of the twentieth century.

The split had been a long time coming. English rugby had been engulfed by civil war ever since the RFU had declared it an amateur sport in

October 1886 and embarked on a campaign to root out all forms of professionalism. In contrast to soccer, the decade-long struggle in rugby allowed the underlying class tensions to be fully drawn out. Not only was the discussion marked by overt social snobbery, as reflected in the comments of one RFU die-hard:

> if the working man cannot afford to play, he must do as other people have to do who want things they cannot afford – do without. . . . [T]he said working man, by the way, being too often a man whom a thoughtless crowd has spoiled for the dry drudgery of everyday life

but it also highlighted the relationship between class and the development of commercial sport.[3]

Unlike the northern soccer clubs that forced the FA to accept professionalism by threatening to form a rival British Football Association (BFA) in 1884, the northern rugby clubs did not consider a split until 1895, by which time they had effectively been left with no choice by the RFU's new draconian amateur regulations. This reluctance was partly due to the northern rugby clubs' greater integration into the RFU's structures – they provided four of the thirteen presidents of the RFU before 1895 – but also because the rebels believed, on the basis of soccer's experience, that professionalism in one form or another was inevitable. The simple arithmetic of the growing number of rugby clubs in the north, they surmised, would eventually win a majority in the RFU and rugby would then join soccer on the road to becoming a modern, professional mass spectator sport.

They had not reckoned with the intransigency of the leaders of the RFU. The impact of professionalism in soccer had led RFU officials to fear for their future in the game if working-class players were able to compete on equal terms. This over-rode all other considerations. 'If blind enthusiasts of working men's clubs insist on introducing professionalism, there can be but one result – disunion', explained Arthur Budd in 1892.[4] The northern clubs' campaign to be allowed to legalise broken-time payments was decisively defeated at the RFU's 1893 annual general meeting. It was a gathering that, noted the weekly *Yorkshireman*

> laid bare the position assumed by those who oppose the payment of out-of-pocket expenses to the working men. We have at last been boldly told the truth . . . if a man cannot afford to play he has no right to; that Rugby football is a game for the classes and, in effect, that the masses are neither more nor less than intruders.[5]

By the time the split finally took place in 1895, the debate about pro-fessionalism was being conducted entirely on the terrain of class and the rights of the 'working-man player'. One side sought to defend the rights of those who had learnt the game at public school to control the game, while their opponents believed 'it was their duty to place the working man on the same level with the other classes'.[6] The overt hostility to working-class players and spectators expressed in the debate meant class became embed-ded into the identity of both rugby codes and would define the culture of both. Union viewed itself predominately as the game for those educated in the British public school tradition, while league saw itself as a sport of the working class.

Sociologically, rugby league's players and spectators were overwhelmingly drawn from the industrial working classes. The RFU had responded to the 'northern declension', as those of its supporters who remembered their Latin grammar sometimes called it, by banning from rugby union all those who played rugby league, whether amateur or professional, officiated in the sport or signed any forms relating to the new organisation. This had the effect of sealing-off rugby league not only from members of rugby union clubs but also from a significant portion of 'respectable' middle-class society, for whom the threat of social ostracism could not be ignored. Although members of the northern industrial bourgeois classes played the central role in founding the first rugby clubs across the north in the 1860s, the number involved in league a decade after the split could be counted in single figures. Unlike professional soccer clubs, which retained upper- and middle-class support because they were seen as a route to national recognition and status, rugby league clubs quickly became mono-class institutions, overwhelmingly working class with a small fringe of lower middle-class officials, such as publicans, shopkeepers and local government officials, who administered them. Rugby in the north of England had gone from being a game of the people before 1895 to a sport almost exclusively of the industrial proletariat in the years after.

As a result of the intensely ideological nature of the split, rugby league developed its own egalitarian culture. This reflected the perceived virtues of the industrial north of England and was originally articulated as the 'masses versus the classes', a famous phrase of Liberal prime minister Wil-liam Gladstone. A number of the leaders of the northern clubs, such as the NU's founding president Harry Waller, were prominent Liberals but in the early 1900s this worldview merged with a social-democratic outlook, in much the same way as Labourism was derived from the earlier Liberal-ism. The NU claimed its place in the nation's life by claiming to represent the democratic 'true' England of ordinary working people. This was best expressed by the common northern saying, 't' best in t' Northern Union', which implied that the best in the game was the best that existed anywhere, regardless of what the establishment thought. This democratic sensibility was overtly referred to by rugby league spokesmen. As early as 1914 John Houghton, the manager of that year's British team in Australia and New Zealand, declared rugby league was 'the people's game'. In 1926 RFL chairman Ted Osborne argued league and union should remain separate because 'I believe rugby league is the more democratic body', and from the 1940s journalist and TV broadcaster Eddie Waring would regularly promote the belief that the game was 'the most democratic in the world'.[7]

British rugby league shared many of its social and economic characteristics as soccer. Both were mass spectator sports relying predominantly on working-class players and supporters. But the NU was constrained by factors that professional soccer did not have to deal with. The first was professional soccer itself. By 1895, the seemingly irresistible rise of the soccer juggernaut meant rugby was essentially boxed into its traditional heartlands. Areas without significant traditions in any code, such as much of the south of England in the 1890s, invariably chose soccer when it came to putting themselves on the map with their own football club. There was no virgin soil into which the new rugby code could expand. Worse still, the Football League actively sought to establish professional soccer in rugby's strongholds. Manningham, the first Northern Union champions in 1896, abandoned rugby in 1903 and were admitted into the Football League's second division as Bradford City. Over the next decade Football League sides were established in the former rugby citadels of Leeds (1905), Hull (1905), Oldham (1907) and Huddersfield (1910).

Moreover, the NU was hemmed into the northern industrial powerhouse of the Victorian era – coal and textiles in Lancashire and West Yorkshire, shipbuilding in Barrow, docks in Hull, chemicals in Widnes, and glass manufacture in St Helens and the Wakefield area – at precisely the moment when many of those industries were starting their long structural decline. Rugby league's strong regional identity with the north made it difficult to promote in soccer regions of Britain, which were already part of a national competition, and in areas where rugby still retained working-class roots, such as South Wales, the hostility of the rugby union authorities was matched by their flexibility of principle when ignoring evidence of their own clubs breaching their laws against payments to players.

In 1896 Welsh rugby union captain Arthur Gould had his house paid for by a testimonial fund organised by the Welsh rugby union in violation of its amateur rules. The controversy almost split British rugby union in two and gave rise to fears that Wales would join the NU. But the RFU backed down from expelling the Welsh because, in the words of RFU secretary Rowland Hill, it was 'a matter of expediency' that Wales should not be forced out.[8] The great opportunity for the NU to challenge the RFU for the leadership of British rugby was snuffed out. For the next century a subterranean culture of 'boot money' ensured that Welsh players who did not want to 'Go North' and play rugby league would always find some remuneration available. Thus the social and geographical template of British sport was set by the mid-1900s, and there was little that either league or union could do to alter it.

Two ways to play

The divide between the two rugby codes was not confined to payments to players. The northern clubs' conception of how rugby should be played also differed from that of the RFU leadership. Those educated in the public school tradition tended to believe that rugby was a game primarily about the forwards' struggle for the ball and that the scoring of goals was its most important feature. In contrast, most northern rugby aficionados believed that 'the acme of good play is when a skilful three-quarter or half back finishes up a skilful or dashing run by dodging a full back and planting the ball over the line'.[9] Such talk was dismissed by traditionalists like RFU president Arthur Budd, who argued that

> the very fact that try-getters are plentiful while goal-droppers are scarce shows that the latter art is very much more difficult of acquirement. . . . [Why] ought the more skilful piece of play to be depreciated, while a premium is placed on mere speed of foot?

Budd even argued that heeling the ball out of the scrum should be penalised because it undermined the importance of forward play.[10]

The northerners were not alone in their conception of how rugby should be played. Much the same ideas prevailed in South Wales, where rugby had become the mass spectator sport of the region and encompassed all social classes. In 1884 Cardiff began to play with four three-quarters, in contrast to the standard three or more traditional two, reduced the number of forwards to eight and emphasised passing the ball quickly from the scrum to the backs. From the early 1880s Australia and New Zealand also placed greater value on running and passing the ball to score tries, which reached its acme with the gloriously open rugby of the 1905 All Blacks touring team.

The logic of those favouring the open game had been summed up in 1892 by James Miller, the secretary of the Yorkshire Rugby Union. Pointing to the rapid evolution of rugby since teams had been cut from twenty- to fifteen-a-side in 1875, Miller argued the forward-dominated era was over and rugby should cut teams to thirteen to encourage try-scoring rather than goal-kicking.[11] Miller was also a leading campaigner for broken-time payments. It was no accident he and Budd were on opposite sides both in the debate about the playing of the game and about paying players. This was a fault-line that ran through global rugby in the 1880–1914 period. Where the game was played primarily by elites, such as in southern England, Ireland and South Africa, the emphasis was on the scrummaging, forward game. But in those regions where rugby had become a sport of the masses, the open passing game was preferred.

Consequently the 1895 split freed the northern clubs to reform the game along the lines suggested by Miller. This was also seen as a vital step to counter the rise of soccer, the open play of which was thought to be one of its most attractive features. In 1897, to increase the importance of try-scoring, all goals were reduced to two points (under RFU rules penalty goals were three points, the same as tries, and dropped goals were four points), and the line-out was abolished to speed the game up. As the game evolved, the NU amended the rules on a trial-and-error basis. The line-out was initially replaced by a punt-out from touch in 1897 but this led to melees and penalties as players scrambled for the ball and so it in turn was replaced by a scrum in 1902.

Just weeks after the split the NU staged experimental thirteen-a-side matches but it was felt less radical changes might facilitate a more open game. In 1903 the NU clubs decided to move to twelve-a-side but the vote failed to reach the two-thirds margin required for rule changes. Professional teams remained at fifteen-a-side but amateur rugby league moved briefly to twelve-a-side. But by 1906 it had become clear that to create the free-flowing game radical surgery was required, so in the summer of 1906 the NU voted decisively to move to thirteen-a-side.

At the same time, it also sought to address the problem of what to do when a player with the ball is tackled. The Northern Union's initial solution in 1899 was simply to cut out messy rucks and mauls and go straight to a scrum after every tackle. Initially, this increased the pace of the game as forwards became adept at following the ball and rapidly packing down. But, as would be the case throughout the history of the rugby codes, a rule designed to streamline the sport became its opposite. Teams with strong scrummagers would simply hold on to the ball, taking tackle after tackle as the forwards drove the side downfield. Scrummaging once again came to dominate the game. A 1902 Halifax versus Hunslet match witnessed a soul-crushing 110 scrums in its eighty minutes.

Faced with the sport returning to the type of game it had rejected, the NU once again decided on radical reform. It did this by partially returning to rugby's pre-1878 rule and stipulating that once a tackle had been completed, the ball-carrier had to put the ball down in front of him and play it with his foot. But instead of a full-scale scrum, a sort of mini-scrum – known as the play-the-ball – took place. A member of the tacked player's own side would stand behind him as a makeshift scrum-half and an opponent was allowed to stand in front of the player with the ball. This player could also attempt to play the ball with his foot. He too would have a player behind him who could either retrieve the ball or tackle an opponent who retrieved the ball.

Although there is no evidence the NU ever discussed the North American evolution of rugby rules, the introduction of the play-the-ball rule took the sport down the same path of American and Canadian football. The importance of the scrum was undermined and the contest for the ball at the play-the-ball gradually disappeared as players and coaches developed techniques, legal and illegal, to ensure the tackled player's team retained possession. This again created the problem of teams dominating possession for long periods. It was only in 1966 that a solution was found, when the sport's International Board took a leaf from the American game and restricted each side to four tackles. This was extended to six tackles in 1972, and eventually the struggle for possession at the play-the-ball was formally abandoned and, like the snap in the North American codes, it became simply a device for restarting play after a tackle.

The break with rugby union in 1895 had freed the northern clubs to reform the sport, and the 1906 rules changes were the culmination of the debate on the rules of rugby that had begun in the 1880s. But, although the leaders of the Northern Union did not know it at the time, they had transformed their game at precisely the point at which the rugby-based football codes of the world were undergoing deep structural turmoil – a transnational crisis that would transform rugby across the world.

Notes

1 Letter published in the *Yorkshire Post*, 21 September 1895.
2 *Yorkshire Post*, 29 April 1896.
3 *Salford Reporter*, 27 October 1894.
4 Arthur Budd, 'The Past and Future of the Game', in Revd Frank Marshall (ed.) *Football – The Rugby Union Game* (London: Cassell, 1892), p. 137.
5 OPQ, 'Payment for Broken Time', *The Yorkshireman*, 27 September 1893.
6 A Londoner, 'Metropolitan Football', in Marshall, *Football*, p. 329 and *Leeds Mercury*, 23 September 1893.
7 Eddie Waring, *England to Australia and New Zealand* (Leeds: County Press 1947), p. 5.
8 *Yorkshire Post*, 17 September 1897.

9 *Yorkshire Post*, 7 January 1888.

10 Arthur Budd, 'The Northern Union', in A. Budd, C.B. Fry, B.F. Robinson and T.A. Cook (eds) *Football* (London: Lawrence and Bullen, 1897), p. 34. *Guardian*, 18 September 1896.

11 *Yorkshire Post*, 29 October 1892.

18

THE 1905–07 FOOTBALL CRISIS IN NORTH AMERICA

Are you ready to have football abolished?
—Benjamin Ide Wheeler, 28 November 1905[1]

Rugby league was not the only football code for which 1906 was a pivotal year. In the United States and Canada, football was also consumed by a crisis over commercialism and the way the game was played. By the early 1900s American football dominated winter sport in the United States, attracting five-figure crowds that often exceeded those for baseball, and commanding vast amounts of coverage in the press. College footballers had become celebrities, their exploits watched by tens of thousands and read about by millions more. The game was now the concern not only of university presidents, for whom the game provided considerable revenue, but of the U.S. president himself, Teddy Roosevelt.[2]

Football's importance to college life and the vast public that followed the game meant players were often covertly rewarded for their deeds and recruited purely for their football achievements rather than their scholarly abilities. Suspicions of professionalism, both in deed and in spirit, were legion. The desire to win at all cost had turned the game into a war of attrition. Football was dominated by mass plays, allowing the offensive team to keep possession with wave after wave of charges through their opponents' line. Tactics such as the 'flying wedge', where offensive players would link together as an arrowhead to force the ball-carrier through the defensive line, also increased the risk of serious injury and death. In 1904 alone, twenty-one players were killed on the gridiron.[3]

By 1905 these concerns reached crisis point. At the start of the year Harvard president Charles Eliot used his annual report to declare that 'the American game of football as now played is wholly unfit for colleges and schools'. It was, he believed, promoting 'great moral mischief' and should be prohibited, not least because football's rule-makers could not be trusted to reform it.[4] 'The main objection lies against the moral quality', argued Eliot, that gave it a dangerous and 'brutalizing' nature.[5]

Four months later, an article titled 'The College Athlete: How commercialism is making him a professional' by Henry Beach Needham in *McClure's Magazine*, provided the hard evidence for Eliot's concerns. The top college players, he argued, were effectively professionals and the commercial benefits of football to universities were now so great that the game could no longer claim to be an educative or moral force.[6] Football's violence was a result of its embrace of competition and commercialism. The solution, he believed, lay 'in the awakening of the spirit of true sport – fair play, and sport for sport's sake'.[7]

The depth of Needham's research made his case unimpeachable. College sport was 'honeycombed with commercialism' a former classmate of Walter Camp told him. Even more shocking for his readers was that he conclusively demonstrated that some of the most serious abusers of the rules were the elite Ivy League colleges. The universities of Pennsylvania, Columbia, Princeton and Yale were all indicted by Needham using first-hand evidence from athletes and alumni. Pennsylvania was accused of recruiting Penn State full-back Andrew Smith in violation of the eligibility rules. Demonstrating the social snobbery underlying amateurism, Needham denounced Smith as a 'tramp athlete' for playing for more than one team. Harvard, in an embarrassing confirmation of Charles Eliot's concerns, was singled out under the heading 'Harvard's Self-Righteous Contentment'. Needham pinned the blame for this corruption firmly on the college authorities and warned that 'a growth of commercialism in college sport is a trend from amateurism to professionalism'.[8]

In the same month Needham's exposé appeared, the critics of football gained a powerful ally when President Teddy Roosevelt used his commencement speech at Harvard to denounce 'sensationalism and professionalism' in college sports. Roosevelt felt the issue personally. Not only had he publicly lauded *Tom Brown's Schooldays* but his two sons, one of whom was at Harvard, were keen footballers. Indeed, it was the headmaster of his younger son's school, Endicott Peabody of Groton, itself modelled on Rugby School, who asked Roosevelt to call a 'football summit' to tackle the crisis.[9] In October 1905, Roosevelt met with football administrators from Harvard, Yale and Princeton, and told them to find ways to return football to the 'spirit' of the game. There it may have remained were it not for the tumultuous season that was unfolding around them.

Although historians have emphasised the growing number of deaths on the field as the cause of the 1905 crisis, this was not the only concern of Roosevelt or most of the other football critics. Their focus was on what they saw as football's departure from the Muscular Christian ethos of sport. Violent play was a consequence of the sport's abandonment of honesty and transparency. 'Deaths and injuries are not the strongest arguments against football', wrote Eliot. 'That cheating and brutality are profitable is the main evil'.[10] Indeed, Roosevelt had called his summit before the violent toll of the 1905 season began to mount.

And mount it did. Brawls broke out at Columbia versus Wesleyan and also at Penn versus Harvard. Harvard freshman Francis Burr was knocked senseless fielding a fair catch against Yale. Roosevelt's son Teddy suffered a broken nose in the Harvard-Yale freshman match. But the nadir came in Union College versus New York University game on 25 November, when Union College end Harold Moore sustained a fatal head injury while making a tackle. According to the *Chicago Tribune*, this was just one of the eighteen fatalities and 159 'serious' injuries that took place during the season.[11] In response, Union College and Columbia abandoned the game completely.

That same month, *Collier's* magazine published another exposé of the rampant commercialism of football titled 'Buying Football Victories'. Underpinning much of its concern was the fact the young men committing these acts of violence and violations of the amateur code were the scions of the WASP upper classes, who were supposedly being educated to set an example to America's masses. Their moral and social superiority was being thrown into doubt by the corruption of the sport. No-one could deny that football faced a grave existential threat.

At the start of December 1905 colleges outside the Harvard-Yale-Princeton-Penn 'Big Four' called a conference to campaign for the reform of the game. Under fire, the Big Four-dominated Intercollegiate Rules Committee met to discuss rule changes. Paul Dashiell, the umpire held responsible by many for the violence at the Harvard-Yale match, proposed legalising the forward pass. Walter Camp suggested increasing the distance to be gained in three downs from five yards to ten as in Canada, but the meeting broke up without making a decision.

In response, sixty-eight smaller football-playing colleges gathered in New York on 28 December and created the Intercollegiate Athletic Association (which became today's NCAA in 1910).[12] It set as its first goal the re-assertion of amateur values and the ending of quasi-professionalism. In an open challenge to the Big Four, the ICAA established its own rules committee. Threatened with losing control of the game, the Big Four agreed to a merger in January 1906. In six meetings over three months the new body agreed to the most far-reaching football reforms since the early 1880s. The most important was the legalisation of the forward pass and the increase in yardage required for a first down to ten yards in three downs. Another ten reforms were introduced dealing with tackling, holding, fouls, and the line of scrimmage.[13]

Although these were radical changes, once the dust had settled the old mass formation plays re-entered the sport. With them came another rising toll of injuries and deaths. Twenty-six players were killed in 1909 and the clamour for reform began to sound once again.[14] This time the game's rule-makers were more responsive. In 1910 mass plays were effectively abolished by a rule that insisted on seven players being on the line of scrimmage (thus stopping a mass play gaining momentum in the backfield before the snap) and banning the ball-carrier being pushed or pulled by teammates. The game was further opened up in 1912 with the increase to four downs to gain ten yards and the removal of many of the restrictions of the forward pass. In half a decade of painful reform, the modern game of American football had emerged.

But it was too late for some. On the West Coast, the presidents of the universities of California and Stanford declared themselves in agreement with Charles Eliot's belief that football had lost its moral compass. But they had even less faith than Eliot in the ability of the game's leaders to rescue the game. Football occupied the same position in elite WASP society on the West Coast as it did in the East. The 'Big Game' between Cal and Stanford was one of the sporting and social highlights of the year. But the sheer distance between the Pacific Coast universities and the football powers of the Mid-West and the East Coast encouraged an independent approach to the football crisis.

In January 1906 the president of the University of California, Benjamin Ide Wheeler, published an article which declared that 'American intercollegiate football is a spectacle and not a sport. If the element of gate-money were removed, the whole thing would vanish away'. He called for football to be replaced by 'the Association game for the light men and runners, indeed for the average man, and the restored Rugby, perhaps with its Canadian or Australian modifications, for the heavier and more vigorous men'.[15] He was supported by his Stanford counterpart, David Starr Jordan, and in the same month that Wheeler's article appeared, a joint committee of the two universities decided to abandon football in favour of the game of rugby 'as played in England and New Zealand'.[16]

Crisis in Canada

Wheeler's suggestion that football 'with Canadian modifications' should be considered by college football programs suggested that he was not especially well-informed about football. By 1906 Canadian football was also being riven apart over the issue of professionalism. The catalyst was the Montreal Amateur Athletic Association's employment of professional players in their ice hockey and lacrosse teams. Hockey had become a mass spectator sport and was generating significant amounts of revenue, while lacrosse could still command large crowds for major matches. The Canadian Amateur Athletic Union (CAAU), the de facto governing body of sport in Canada, refused to countenance professionalism, so in February 1907 those clubs supporting the Montreal stance on professionalism broke away to form the Amateur Athletic Federation of Canada. Payments to players had long been a simmering issue in football. In 1900 Chaucer Elliott, the captain of Kingston's Queen's University team, had been suspended due to doubts about his status. In 1902 Toronto Argonauts' William Grant had been charged with professionalism after being accused of being paid to coach Toronto University in the late 1890s. The situation had become such a concern for the football authorities that in 1901 the Ontario Rugby Football Union, based in Toronto, insisted that all its players had to sign declarations that they were amateurs.[17]

Although lacking the popular appeal of hockey, football was quickly engulfed by the crisis. The Quebec Rugby Football Union, with close links to the Montreal AAA, quickly joined the new organisation, and matters came to a head in October 1907 when Montreal played the CAAU-affiliated Toronto Argonauts. The Montreal team included the Montreal Wanderers hockey club's star professional player Ernie Russell. According to the CAAU rules anyone who played against professionals like Russell would be banned from all sports controlled by the CAAU. Despite this threat, the Toronto players voted to play and the CAAU promptly banned everyone who played in the game.[18] The CAAU's 1908 annual report listed seventy-nine footballers who had been investigated for alleged professionalism.[19] But the CAAU's rigidly British conception of amateurism was difficult to enforce without accusations of unfairness and hypocrisy. Canada's own 'Big Four' football clubs – Montreal, Toronto, Hamilton Tigers and the Ottawa Rough Riders – formed their own organisation, the Interprovincial Union, and, although football remained a nominally amateur sport, the amateur influence waned over the next two decades, not least due to the gradual integration of American coaches and players into Canadian football.[20]

But the growing popularity of Canadian football also increased the pressure to reform its rules. From the mid-1900s, five-figure crowds regularly attended major matches and, to capitalise on the game's increasing appeal, the University of Toronto began building a 12,000-seat football stadium in 1911. In Ontario the solution to the difficulties facing the Canadian game was thought to lay in the Burnside rules, with its twelve-a-side game and a snapback instead of the old-style Canadian 'scrim'. But provincial rivalries stymied national acceptance of the new rules and an unsatisfactory compromise was reached. It was only when the governor general of Canada, Earl Grey, presented a trophy to be presented to the national football champions (although he had originally intended it for hockey) in 1909 that the sport gained a national focus that would eventually bring together teams and rival federations.

Even so, it would not be until 1921 that the whole game finally agreed on a common set of rules that finally introduced the snapback and reduced teams to twelve players. In 1929 American influence reached its tipping point when the forward pass was introduced on an experimental basis at different levels of the game. Two years later in 1931 the forward pass was legalised throughout Canadian football. Symbolically, this final break with British rugby rules came in same year that Canada was granted legal autonomy from Britain. Despite the fact its governing body anachronistically continued to be known as the Canadian Rugby Union until 1967, football in Canada was now truly Canadian.[21]

Notes

1 Benjamin Ide Wheeler to James B. Angell, 28 November 1905 in James B. Angell Papers, Bentley Historical Library, University of Michigan: Correspondence 1851–1916: Folder: November 1905.
2 For Roosevelt's involvement in football, see John J. Miller, *The Big Scrum: How Teddy Roosevelt Saved Football* (New York: Harper Collins, 2011).
3 Wiley Lee Umphett, *Creating the Big Game: John W. Heisman and the Invention of American Football* (Westport, CT: Greenwood, 1992), p. 86.
4 Harvard University, *Reports of the President and the Treasurer of Harvard College 1904–1905* (Cambridge: Harvard University, 1906), pp. 52–3.
5 *The Outlook*, 11 February 1905, p. 363.
6 *McClure's Magazine*, June 1905, pp. 115–28. The second part is in the July 1905 issue, pp. 260–73.
7 *McClure's Magazine*, July 1905, pp. 272.
8 *McClure's Magazine*, June 1905, p. 117.
9 John Sayle Watterson, *College Football: History: Spectacle: Controversy* (Baltimore: Johns Hopkins University Press, 2000), pp. 68–9. See also Michael Oriard, 'Rough, Manly Sport and the American Way: Theodore Roosevelt and College Football, 1905', in Stephen Wagg (ed.) *Myths and Milestones in the History of Sport* (London: Palgrave Macmillan, 2011), pp. 80–105, and Brian Ingrassia, *The Rise*

of the Gridiron University: Higher Education's Uneasy Alliance with Big-time Football (Lawrence, KS: University Press of Kansas, 2012).

10 Quoted in Ronald A. Smith, *Sports and Freedom: The Rise of Big-Time College Athletics* (New York: Oxford University Press, 1988), p. 199.

11 Quoted in David A. Nelson, *The Anatomy of a Game* (Newark: University of Delaware Press, 1994), p. 97.

12 Smith, *Sports and Freedom*, p. 202.

13 Nelson, *Anatomy of a Game*, pp. 123–26.

14 John Sayle Watterson, 'The Gridiron Crisis of 1905: Was It Really a Crisis?', *Journal of Sports History*, vol. 27, no. 2 (Summer 2000), 294. Nelson in *Anatomy of a Game*, quotes a figure of thirty-three from Alonzo Stagg (p. 141).

15 'Shall Football Be Ended or Mended?', *American Monthly Review of Reviews* (January 1906), pp. 72–3.

16 See Ingrassia, *Rise of the Gridiron University*, pp. 62–7 and Roberta J. Park, 'From Football to Rugby – and Back, 1906–1919: The University of California-Stanford University Response to the "Football Crisis of 1905"', *Journal of Sport History*, vol. 11, no. 3 (1984), pp. 5–40. The quote is from p. 19.

17 Kevin G. Jones, 'Developments in Amateurism and Professionalism in Early 20th Century Canadian Sport', *Journal of Sport History*, vol. 2, no. 1 (1975), pp. 29–40.

18 Alan Matcalfe, *Canada Learns to Play: The Emergence of Organised Sport 1807–1914* (Toronto: McLelland & Stewart, 1987), pp. 58–9.

19 Jones, 'Developments in Amateurism and Professionalism . . . ', pp. 38–9.

20 Consentino, *Canadian Football: The Grey Cup Years,* chapter 4.

21 Frank Consentino, *Canadian Football: The Grey Cup Years* (Don Mills, ON: Musson Book Publishing, 1969).

19

THE 1905–07 FOOTBALL CRISIS IN WORLD RUGBY

These men – Smith, MacGregor, Johnson and Mackrell – by coming into the limelight as professionals, were doing what any honest man should do.

—Jim Gleason, 1907[1]

The depth of the football crisis in the United States meant that many Americans looked abroad for solutions. Michigan University president James B. Angell was, according to David Starr Jordan, in favour of a return to rugby rules, Walter Camp's advocacy of the ten yards in three downs rule was borrowed from Canada, and Cal's Benjamin Ide Wheeler corresponded with Victorian Football League secretary Col Hickey. Although Wheeler may have been overly optimistic about the state of football in Canada, it was no accident that the California and Stanford joint committee bracketed England and New Zealand together when suggesting rugby as an alternative to football. England was viewed as the source of sporting wisdom but the 1905 All Blacks had a revolutionary impact on the international football world.[2]

Shortly after Stanford's decision to switch to rugby in January 1906, a student in its engineering faculty, Taranaki-born Norman Halcombe, wrote to the New Zealand RFU requesting copies of the rugby rulebook. Although neither Stanford nor Cal's athletic department had any experience of rugby, there did exist an expatriate community on the West Coast that was familiar with the game, including the captain of the inaugural 1899 British rugby tour to Australia, Matthew Mullineaux. It was one of these exiles, New Zealander Alf Cameron, who suggested that the All Blacks, still on tour in Europe, might be persuaded to play an exhibition match on their way home to New Zealand.[3] On 29 January 1906 the New Zealand tour manager George Dixon cabled the Canada's British Columbia Rugby Union asking them to arrange a match in San Francisco.[4] The timing could not have been more fortuitous and barely three weeks after Cal and Stanford abandoned football, the All Blacks played two games in San Francisco against British Columbia. Rugby had suddenly become the coming game on the West Coast.

The turmoil in America had also come to the attention of the RFU in England. In the summer of 1906 the RFU visited the American embassy in London to discuss the football crisis and the opportunity it presented to develop 'one game of football in which all English speaking races might meet periodically'.[5] Naturally, the RFU felt that its rules were best suited for the task and sent a circular enclosing a copy of the RFU rulebook to every major American college. No replies, if there were any, have survived in the RFU archives. At the same time, an Eastern Rugby Union was formed in New York which announced that it was going to invite a joint Oxford and Cambridge University side to tour America in 1907.[6] This also did not eventuate and the Eastern Rugby Union quickly disappeared.

There were also attempts to influence developments in America outside of official channels. In March 1906 a rugby-playing accounts clerk in the New Zealand Postal Department in Wellington, Albert Baskerville, wrote to Walter Camp asking for a copy of the rules of football as background for his book *Modern Rugby Football*. He also suggested to Camp that, although he believed rugby was the future of football in America, a rugby team trained using American methods 'could win anywhere'. Camp replied non-committedly and Baskerville then suggested to him that a suitably coached Yale rugby side (for which Baskerville offered his services) could tour England with similar success to the 1905 All Blacks. He also pointed out that New Zealand had pioneered the seven-forward scrum, making it similar to football's seven linemen.[7] Camp showed no further interest, but Baskerville's study of American football led him to contact David Starr Jordan, the president of the now rugby-playing Stanford University.[8] Echoing his earlier letters to Camp, he suggested that Stanford send a team to Australia and New Zealand, and proposed himself as the coach. Jordan does not appear to have replied, possibly because discussions were already taking place with the New Zealand RFU about an American universities tour in 1907.[9]

Baskerville had misjudged the nature of the debate in America. Inspired by the success of the All Blacks' tour, he had effusively told Camp and Jordan how much money could be made by touring football sides. But both men were opposed to professionalism and Jordan in particular wanted football to return to its prelapsarian origins. Camp was also well aware of the rules of rugby, telling Baskerville he was familiar with all forms of football. Undeterred, the New Zealander turned his entrepreneurial enthusiasm to another project: a professional rugby league tour to Britain.

Northern Union, southern hemisphere

The Northern Union's radical reforms of 1906 had not gone unnoticed in those parts of the British Empire where rugby was the dominant football code. As early as November 1895 Sydney's leading sports weekly, *The Referee*, discussed the NU's rule changes and, given the ease with which newspaper reports circulated around the English-speaking world, Australian and New Zealand rugby followers were probably no less informed about the new rugby developments than many in Britain itself.[10]

Moreover, for some Antipodeans who had witnessed rugby league in England, it was apparent that it shared much with rugby as played down under. In 1904 George Stephenson, a New Zealand theatre impresario who had played for Manningham in Bradford under both RFU and NU rules, wrote that 'New Zealand football is very similar to that of the North of England ... and resembles the present system of the professional game under the Northern Union'.[11] A London correspondent favourably compared the NU to the RFU during the 1905 All Blacks' tour and suggested 'the question for the rulers of rugby in Australia to consider is whether they are to be tied body and soul (as they have been in the past) to an organisation that has lost the confidence of the people of England, and, like the dying swan, is singing its requiem'.[12]

There were also social tensions causing fissures in southern hemisphere rugby. As in the rest of the world, the game began in Australia and New Zealand as a sport for the privately educated elite. Inured against the appeal of Melbourne's Australian Rules code by inter-city rivalry and its more conservative Britishness, Sydney saw its first rugby club founded in 1865. By 1874 there were ten clubs in the state of New South Wales and they created the 'Southern Rugby Football Union' as the sport's governing body. The Australian game showed an early preference for open rugby and four years before the RFU, fifteen-a-side teams were the norm by 1873.[13]

Rugby was also taken up in Brisbane, the capital of Queensland, and it slowly emerged as the most popular football code in Australia's eastern states. Its dominance was eventually assured in 1882 by the start of regular matches between New South Wales and Queensland. The importance of the game rose further in the mid-1880s with regular tours to and from New Zealand, providing the sport with a national profile. Rugby's popularity grew exponentially over the next decade, bringing with it new players and spectators from Australia's rapidly expanding industrial proletariat. Just as in Britain, this was also an era of trade union militancy and growing working-class self-confidence.

Rumours of payments and other incentives to players soon became commonplace. As early as 1898 the rugby union authorities investigated claims of money paid to NSW representative players. But RFU-style amateurism did not sit easily with those Australians who believed in a 'fair go' (at least for white citizens) and calls for players to be properly compensated grew louder. By the early 1900s crowds of 20,000 were not uncommon for major matches, and the game was awash with money. The simmering discontent came to a head in 1907, when the rugby authorities closed the game's medical insurance scheme, forcing players to pay their own premiums. At the same time, Sydney's Metropolitan Rugby Union raised its secretary's salary to an annual £250, approximately double the average wage.[14] The tension had reached breaking point.

The catalyst for change came from New Zealand. Organised rugby was first played there in 1870, when an eighteen-a-side match under rugby rules was played between the town of Nelson and the prestigious Nelson College. It slowly spread across New Zealand's two islands as part of their economic and cultural unification in the 1870s. Rugby flowed through the new transport and communication networks, linking the islands' disparate parts and bringing a sense of unity to an isolated nation. It was also a live cultural link with Britain, for some its most important quality. By 1892, when the New Zealand RFU was formed, it was estimated there were around 700 sides playing the game.[15] When the New Zealanders once again toured Australia in 1897, the three 'test' matches were watched by 72,000 people. Rugby was now not merely vastly popular, it was also hugely profitable.

This much had been demonstrated in 1888 when a predominantly Maori 'Native New Zealand' side toured Britain. Consisting of seventy-eight matches, the tour was watched by large crowds and had proved more than a match for their British opponents. The appetite for trans-hemispheric tours had been whetted, and following a British tour to Australia and New Zealand in 1904, plans were laid for an official New Zealand national tour of Britain in 1905. No-one, neither in Britain nor New Zealand, expected what happened next.

The All Blacks, as they were dubbed by the press on their arrival in England, swept through British rugby union like a whirlwind. They scored 830 points against a mere 39. Only the Welsh national side remained unconquered, holding out for a controversial 3–0 win at Cardiff Arms Park. The All Blacks' impact on the sport was as much about the style of their victories

PLATE 12 A 1909 Australian amateur view of the threat of professionalism in rugby, with anti-Semitic overtones (Rugby Football League Archive, Huddersfield)

as it was their scale. In an era when rugby union sides focused on scoring goals and the penalty goal was increasingly influential in deciding matches, the All Blacks scored 205 tries but kicked only four penalty goals and a mere two dropped goals.[16] British rugby union was thrown into a turmoil of self-doubt and confusion. Another rugby revolution was in the making.

But it was not only British rugby that was in crisis. Although the All Blacks returned home to New Zealand in March 1906 to be greeted as national heroes, the reverberations of the tour sent shockwaves throughout the game. Many of the tourists found themselves out of pocket, despite the fact that the tour had made a mammoth £8,908 profit. Other than three shillings per day to cover the expenses of the tour, the players did not receive a penny thanks to rugby union's amateur regulations. As one former player explained 'the All Blacks could scarcely raise £10 in the whole team on their return passage home. . . . [I]t was generally admitted that the team were not well treated. Several were men of means, and could well afford the loss of time, but the majority were working men'.[17] The fact that 'working men' players were paid to play rugby in the Northern Union had not gone unnoticed by the tourists.

It was Albert Baskerville who became the public face of the New Zealand players' discontent. It seems probable that at least one All Black, winger and champion sprinter George Smith, met with the Northern Union while on the 1905 tour to discuss the potential for professional rugby in New Zealand.[18] He also met like-minded Australian rugby players in Sydney on his way home from the tour. A plan was soon developed and in January 1907 Baskerville wrote to the Northern Union informing them a touring team was being assembled and proposing financial terms for a tour in the 1907–08 season. The NU quickly agreed his terms and in March 1907 it was announced that a professional All Blacks team was to tour Britain.

Worse was to follow for rugby union. In August 1907, shortly before the rebel All Blacks docked at Sydney en route to Britain, fifty people met in Sydney to form the New South Wales Rugby Football League (NSWRFL) and organise a team to play the New Zealanders. Within days, 138 players had signed with the NSWRFL, including Australian rugby's biggest star, three-quarter Dally Messenger. A few days later 20,000 people flocked to see the first openly professional rugby match in the southern hemisphere. Brimming with confidence, Baskerville invited Messenger to join the tour, and the Australian rebels announced that a rugby league competition would kick off at the start of the new season. Both the 1907 tour and the NSWRFL were successes, and rugby league quickly embedded itself in the sporting cultures of the two countries. The rugby world had split in two.

The Australasian rugby crisis of 1907–08 was very different from America's football crisis. It was as much a social revolt as it was a sporting rebellion. Rugby league in Australia was, as in England, predominantly based in the industrial working classes and intimately connected to the labour movement. Harry Hoyle, the first president of the NSWRFL, was a leader in the railway workers' union and an Australian Labor Party (ALP) election candidate. Ted Larkin, the league's first full-time secretary, was an ALP member of the New South Wales Legislative Assembly. John Storey, a future Labor Party prime minister of NSW in 1920, was a founder of the Balmain club. In New Zealand, the game had similar connections to the labour movement.[19]

Wherever it was played, rugby league saw itself, and was seen by others, as a sport of the working class. This was not necessarily a socialist belief but a more general feeling, animated by the dispute with rugby union, that the world was divided into 'us and them'. Rugby league wanted to be treated equally with the other classes in society. Horrie Miller, the secretary of the NSWRL, summed this up in 1920 when he said that 'it is essential that every class in a community should understand and appreciate the worth of every other class'.[20] In the 1920s the sport was regularly referred to in Australia as the 'people's code'.[21] Sydney's *Rugby League News* proclaimed in 1946 that 'rugby league, with justifiable pride, always emphasises the fact that it is the most democratic of sports', just as it saw itself in Britain.[22]

While rugby league sank deep roots into the industrial working classes of Australia and New Zealand, it failed to establish a significant presence in South Wales, the only other region where rugby had mass working-class support. Yet Wales was not immune from the global rugby crisis. Shortly after the announcement of the 1907 New Zealand rugby league tour, moves to establish league clubs in Wales began. By 1909 there were six professional sides playing in Wales, but a combination of institutional hostility in Wales and the indifference of the rugby league authorities led to the Welsh clubs all folding by 1912. Nevertheless, many working-class Welsh rugby players simply voted with their feet to split from rugby union and went to play rugby league in such great numbers that they created a parallel Welsh nation in northern exile.

Rugby union was even less successful in fulfilling the needs of America's middle-class supporters of amateurism. Initially, the Californian universities' move to rugby seemed to be paying off. The annual Stanford versus Cal game showed no diminution in importance and tours by the 1908–09 Wallabies, who played three matches on their way home from Europe, and the New South Wales Waratahs in 1912, were well-attended and sufficiently competitive that the Waratahs incurred two defeats. Yet tensions emerged over the playing of the game. The Waratahs believed American rugby players were too violent and did not play in the right spirit. The Americans were unhappy with the game's constant scrummaging and proposed switching to fourteen-a-side teams in 1913.[23] Walter Camp rubbed salt in the wound in *Outing*, dismissing West Coast rugby as 'mediocre play' and that in comparison 'the Northern Union game, especially in Lancashire and Yorkshire, would be a revelation to many'.[24] When the long-awaited All Blacks tour of North America took place in 1913, it offered nothing but humiliating defeats for the American sides, whose only scores were two penalty goals in thirteen matches. Rugby union could not offer meaningful international competition, it had isolated Stanford and Cal from the prestige of domestic football, and it had not been adopted by any other significant college. In 1915 Cal called time on the experiment and in 1919 Stanford followed suit.

The crisis of 1905–06 in America had been partially solved by radical reform of football's rules, which removed its deadlier aspects, but more importantly by the tacit acceptance that its commercialism could not be stopped. The supporters of amateur purity had been defeated by the exigencies of mass spectator sport. Methods of recruiting and retaining players that violated the sport's amateur code were not stopped but, rather like the Victorian attitude to prostitution, accepted as an unspoken necessary evil that every so often would be subject to a fit of moral outrage and then left alone to carry on as before. Although the sport rejected the playing rules of rugby union, college football accepted the underlying hypocrisy of rugby union's amateur ethos. Lacking a rival professional competition nor challenged by significant working-class involvement, college football was not threatened by schism or a viable alternative leadership. And as the next century would prove, organised hypocrisy was no barrier to becoming even more popular or ever richer.

Notes

1 Jim Gleason, '1907 New Zealand Rugby League Tourist', *Yorkshire Post*, 2 October 1907. George Smith, Duncan MacGregor, 'Massa' Johnson and Bill Mackrell were all 1905 Rugby Union All Blacks who were also 1907 New Zealand rugby league tourists.

2 For Camp, see *The Canadian Magazine*, vol. 10, no. 1 (November 1897), 59. For Angell and Hickey, see Roberta J. Park, 'From Football to Rugby – and Back, 1906–1919: The University of California-Stanford University Response to the "Football Crisis of 1905"', *Journal of Sport History*, vol. 11, no. 3, p. 17.

3 Park, 'From Football to Rugby – and Back, 1906–1919', p. 18.

4 Sturrock, *It's A Try*, pp. 121–3.

5 Letter from G. Rowland Hill (RFU president) dated July 1906. Box 21, Folder 599. Walter Chauncey Camp Papers. Manuscripts and Archives, Yale University Library.

6 *New York Times*, 15 April 1906.

7 Baskerville-Camp correspondence March-October 1906. Box 3, Folder 64. Walter Chauncey Camp Papers. Manuscripts and Archives, Yale University Library.

8 Baskerville to Jordan, 10 December 1906. David Starr Jordan Collection, Reel, 52, Frames, 482–5, Stanford University Archives.

9 Greg Ryan, 'Brawn against Brains: Australia, New Zealand and the American "Football Crisis", 1906–13', *Sporting Traditions*, vol. 20, no. 2 (May 2004), 26.

10 *The Referee*, 27 November 1895.

11 *The Referee*, 13 July 1904.

12 *The Referee*, 6 December 1905.

13 Thomas V. Hickie, *They Ran With The Ball. How Rugby Football Began in Australia* (Melbourne: Longman Cheshire, 1993), p. 111.

14 Sean Fagan, *Rugby Rebellion* (Sydney: Fagan, 2005), p. 126.

15 Alan Turley, *Rugby – The Pioneer Years* (Auckland: Harper Collins, 2009), p. 105.

16 Greg Ryan, *The Contest for Rugby Supremacy: Accounting for the 1905 All Blacks* (Christchurch: Canterbury University Press, 2005).

17 'Rugby Football in the Colonies' by 'An Original All Black' in *Yorkshire Post* 13 November 1908.

18 J.F. O'Loghlen (ed.), *Rugby League Annual & Souvenir 1928* (Sydney: NSWRFL, 1928), p. 23. Sean Fagan, *Rugby Rebellion* (Sydney: Fagan, 2005), pp. 100–1.

19 Andrew Moore, 'Opera of the Proletariat: Rugby League, the Labour Movement and Working-Class Culture in New South Wales and Queensland', *Labour History*, 79 (November 2000), 57–70. Ryan Bodman, 'Rugby League and the New Zealand Trade Union Movement', *Labour History Project Bulletin* 64 (2015), pp. 15–16.

20 The Cynic, *Football Annual 1920* (Sydney: *The Referee* newspaper, 1920), p. 56. This article was reprinted in World War Two in the *Rugby League News* (Sydney), 7 June 1941.

21 Undated press clipping (c. July 1914) in JC Davis collection, box 51, item 4, Mitchell Library, Sydney. For Australian usage of 'the people's game' see, for example, *Rugby League News* (Sydney), 29 May 1926 and many subsequent references.

22 *Rugby League News* (Sydney), 4 May 1946.

23 Greg Ryan, 'Brawn against Brains: Australia, New Zealand and the American "Football Crisis", 1906–13', pp. 19–38.

24 Walter Camp, 'Rugby Football in America', *Outing Magazine*, vol. 57 (March 1911), p. 710.

20

SOCCER

The modern game for the modern world

Each week, it brings together millions of young people, of all nationalities, under the banner of joyful sporting camaraderie; . . . I believe that football is destined to be at the forefront of the work undertaken by organisations with the same goal: that is, to hasten the day where reason and understanding replace suspicion and rivalries that pit people against each other.

—Jules Rimet[1]

On 24 July 1898 São Paulo Athletic Club played a match against São Paulo Railway Club. Founded ten years earlier by British expatriates, the Athletic Club won a fiercely contested game, with one of their three tries created by their left centre-threequarter Charles Miller, who was also praised for his sterling efforts in defence.[2] It was the first organised rugby match to take place in Brazil, but despite his contribution to the birth of the oval ball game, Miller would subsequently be remembered as the father of Brazilian soccer.

Just as with the founding of the football codes in the English-speaking world, the expansion of soccer beyond its British roots also had its own creation myths and invented traditions. Like Alexander Watson Hutton in Argentina and William Leslie Poole in Uruguay, Miller was one of a number of British soccer players who became known as 'the father of football' in their respective countries. These three men personified the common origin story of the emergence of soccer in Europe and Latin America, in which the game was brought to each country by the British, whereupon it was taken up with enthusiasm by the local population. The success of these countries in their adopted sport led to the observation, often heard during World Cup tournaments, that 'Britain gave football to the world and has been trying to get it back ever since'.

Indeed, it is true that very often the first football games and clubs in numerous countries were initiated by British young men, either as teachers at English-speaking schools or as visiting businessmen or technicians. Thus it was British mining engineers who took the sport to Bilbao and the Basque country, railway engineers who started football in Latin America, and seamen and merchants who first played the sport in port cities such as Le Havre, Marseilles and Naples.[3] Famous Italian clubs like Genoa and Milan adopted anglicised names because they were formed by British expatriates in the 1890s.

However, this emphasis on soccer's 'firsts' and 'fathers' (the deep-going male chauvinism of sport means that there are never 'mothers of football') does not explain how or why the game spread far beyond its expatriate founders and became, in the words of the pioneering football historian Tony Mason, the 'passion of the people' in dozens of nations far beyond the cultural reach of the British Empire. Nor does it explain why in many countries soccer was abandoned for rugby union by the expatriate British communities that had founded it.

Nowhere can this be seen more clearly than in Argentina. Argentinian soccer history is portrayed as a seamless story of upward progression after its introduction to the country by the British. But soccer became a mass spectator sport in Argentina only when it slipped out of the control of the local British community, which then embraced rugby as its premier sport. In 1882 Alexander Watson Hutton introduced football into South America's oldest English school, St Andrew's Scots School in Buenos Aires. By the 1890s, rugby and soccer were of equal status and popularity in Argentina. Its first soccer league began in 1891, and its championship was won seven times in the first decade by clubs that also played rugby. In 1899 two of those clubs, Lomas and Belgrano Athletic Club, were founding members of the River Plate Rugby Union (which became the Argentinian Rugby Union in 1951), along with Buenos Aires FC, Flores Athletic Club and Rosaria AC. Most of these clubs were multi-sport institutions in which soccer and rugby, along with sports such as cricket and tennis, were played.[4]

But the catalyst for the rapid expansion of soccer across all sections of Argentine society did not come from the English-speaking community but was a result of the 1898 Argentinian Ministry of Justice and Public Instruction decree that all schools, public or private, had to teach physical education and establish sports clubs for past and present pupils. Argentina at this time was also experiencing massive waves of immigration from Europe, especially from Italy but also Jews from Eastern Europe. Spurred by government support for sports clubs, many new teams were formed in the first decade of the new century. Boca Juniors was founded by working-class Italian immigrants in 1905 and Atlanta, established a year previously, found much of its support in the Jewish community. Almost all of these new clubs came from outside of the English-speaking enclaves.

Moreover, as the rail network extended its reach across the nation, railway companies set up recreation clubs for their employees, not least because there was little else for workers to do after they had finished long shifts building or operating the railway. The vast majority of these workers were Argentinians or recent immigrants. Rosario Central FC was founded in 1889 as the Central Argentine Railway Athletic Club, one of dozens of clubs created this way.[5] The influx of new, non-English speaking players into the game from schools, local clubs and workplaces revolutionised the face of Argentinian soccer. When it played its first official international match, against Uruguay in 1902, ten of the Argentina eleven had British surnames. A decade later against the same opponents, the position was the exact opposite.[6]

However, despite its status and high profile in Argentina, rugby did not become a mass spectator sport. As working-class Argentinians and other non-British immigrants took up soccer, English-speaking sports clubs that played both games abandoned soccer for rugby's amateur exclusivity. Alexander Watson Hutton's son, Arnaldo, became an international rugby player as well as playing his father's sport. When Buenos Aires' first non-British rugby club was formed in 1904 it was established by upper-class Argentinian engineering students. Rugby became a haven for those who wished to stay aloof from popular sport. This difference between rugby and soccer was illustrated by the governance of the two codes. After 1914, Argentinian soccer never had a British-born president. In contrast, Argentinian rugby had twenty presidents in its first fifty years of existence, of whom only six were not British.

The same process of rugby consciously choosing exclusivity over popularity can also be seen in Brazil. Soccer had been introduced into schools in 1896 and football clubs had been established in textile factories in the São Paulo area in 1902, providing the base for the game's popularity.[7] But rugby confined itself to the social elite even more than in Argentina. Its major stronghold was the São Paulo Athletic Club, the multi-sport club that had Charles Miller among its members. As in Argentina, the popularity of soccer among the masses proved to be unpalatable for the British-educated elite that ran the club and, despite winning São Paulo's soccer championship in the first three years of its existence, the club severed its soccer link in 1912 to focus on rugby.[8]

The experience of Argentina and Brazil highlights how, although football was introduced to South America by the British, they were not responsible for popularising it.[9] Indeed, they had no desire to see it become a mass spectator sport, hence their retreat into rugby in the years immediately before World War One. Those who took the game to the masses and established soccer as the national sport of their respective countries were not the British but the young men of the professional middle classes who were attracted to the modernity and openness of soccer.[10]

Beyond Muscular Christianity

In one sense, soccer's route to the masses in Europe and South America was little different to the one it followed in Britain, with schools and workplace teams providing the opportunities for those outside of the middle classes to take up the game. But soccer also quickly became a means of expressing national identity for people who had not been educated in the traditions of Muscular Christianity, much less read *Tom Brown's Schooldays*. Even those who opposed the British Empire and its cultural influence could embrace soccer and invest it with their own nationalist or anti-imperialist politics.[11]

Many of the young men who led soccer outside of Britain in the early twentieth century were drawn from the local technical and managerial middle classes.[12] Indeed, the driving force behind the creation of FIFA, Robert Guérin, was an engineer and a journalist.[13] Soccer was attractive to men like Guérin because it was seen to embody a modernity based on 'commerce and aspirational lifestyles'. Their promotion of the game was not based on a relationship with Britain but, as Christiane Eisenberg has pointed out in Germany, was due to it being 'an indicator of their receptiveness to new things, in particular to economic modernity'.[14]

Many of these new leaders of the game were educated at British schools or in schools established by English educators. Walter Bensemann, who founded the club that eventually became FV Karlsruhe in 1888, spent part of his career teaching languages at private schools in England.[15] In Germany, soccer found its most important constituency among 'technicians, engineers, salesmen, teachers and journalists, who had previously found their personal and professional advancement blocked for lack of the right certificate or university examination'.[16] Protestants and Jews were especially prominent in the formation of clubs in German-speaking countries such as Germany, Austria and Switzerland. This desire for a 'career open to talent' was precisely what soccer's meritocratic structure offered, in contrast to amateur sports such as rugby.[17]

This desire to escape the restrictions of a hierarchical society also explains why Germans and German-speaking Swiss played an important role in establishing the sport beyond their own countries. Hans Gamper, a Swiss evangelical Protestant, arrived in Barcelona to work as an accountant and founded FC Barcelona in late 1899, and thus helped soccer become a central part of the new culture of the rising Catalan urban middle classes.[18] Swiss educators established the first clubs in Bulgaria and, 10,000 kilometres away, Medellin's Sporting FC was founded by Swiss merchants working in Colombia.[19] In Brazil, the Anglo-Swiss Oscar Cox returned from college in Lausanne to his home in Rio de Janeiro and founded Fluminense FC in 1902. In São Paulo, Hamburg-born Hans Nobiling founded two soccer clubs in 1899, one of which was SC Germania that went on to win the local championship twice.[20]

The extensive involvement of Germans and German speakers in the expansion of the game underlines the extent to which soccer was now seen as a universal, cosmopolitan sport. Up until the 1900s, physical recreation in German-speaking nations was dominated by the *Turnverein* movement. The Turners combined nationalist politics and gymnastic exercises, and rejected team sport as a British invention that was unsuitable for the German character. Football in particular was opposed because it was seen as unpatriotic. As the German empire spread around the world, so too did Turner gymnastics follow in its wake.[21] In propagating soccer, German pioneers of the game were consciously rejecting their own national physical culture. But they had not abandoned conservative German traditions to become British, but to promote a sport that reflected their own cosmopolitan modernity.

Indeed, almost all of those who founded soccer clubs outside of the English-speaking world had Anglophile sympathies, were often educated in English-speaking schools, or had business links with Britain. But in contrast to the socially conservative Anglophilia of the Muscular Christianity, as expressed by Pierre de Coubertin, their Anglophilia was part of a wider cosmopolitanism, as Pierre Lanfranchi has noted.[22] They admired what they believed was the liberal, modern capitalist values of the British legal and political system. Thus English names were commonly used as the names of clubs even where there was no or little British involvement, such as Grasshoppers of Zurich or Young Boys of Bern. English technical terms and rules were used, for example the founding constitution of Rio de Janeiro's Liga Metropolitana de Football of 1905 stated that only English terms should be used for the game, a practice also insisted upon by the footballers of Chilean port Valparaiso.[23] Although the English language indicated high social status, its use as a *lingua franca* among non-British soccer enthusiasts also underlined the cosmopolitan modernity that soccer was seen as representing. This was a modern game for the modern middle classes of the world.

A game open to talent

What allowed soccer to eclipse rugby and become capable of offering multiple social and cultural meanings to the liberal middle classes of Europe and Latin America, many of whom would not regard themselves as supporters of the British Empire? Most explanations focus on soccer's intrinsic qualities as the 'beautiful game'. David Goldblatt has argued eloquently that soccer 'offers a game in which individual brilliance and collective organisation are equally featured. . . . The game's balance of physicality and artistry, of instantaneous reaction and complex considered tactics, is also rare'.[24] But supporters of other codes of football offer similar arguments for their own game. Discussions about sporting aesthetics largely consist of supporters selecting their sport's attractive features and constructing an argument to support their desired conclusion. And, of course, in significant parts of the world, rugby-derived football remains more popular than soccer. Like beauty, the aesthetics of sport must always be in the eye of the beholder.[25]

Nor did soccer become more popular because kicking a ball is simpler and more natural than handling the ball. The game appears to be natural only because it is so ubiquitous today. Its kicking game is due as much to the preferences of nineteenth-century British men as is rugby's handling.[26] What's more, soccer's insistence on using only the feet was often viewed as a novelty when it was first seen. When the Russian writer Yuri Olesha explained soccer to his father in the early 1900s he was incredulous: 'They play with their feet. With their feet? How can that be?'[27] Soccer's very 'unnaturalness' may have been one of its most appealing features to those seeking to escape into modernity from traditional culture.

Nor was soccer considered less dangerous to play than the rugby-based codes. In 1894, the *Lancet*, the British Medical Association journal, compared soccer and rugby injuries. It concluded that

> Association, at first sight a tame game compared with the other, is possibly more perilous than Rugby Union . . . its modern developments, though in many ways so similar, are more certainly towards danger than are the developments in the tactics of the older branch.

It revisited the issue in 1907 and drew exactly the same conclusion: 'everything seems to show that the degree of danger incurred by players is greater in the dribbling than in the carrying game'.[28]

The explanation for soccer's rise to globalism is not to be found in how the game was played but in how it was administered. Its transformation into a world game was made possible because of its acceptance of professionalism in 1885. The decision opened the way for league competitions to be created and, together, professionalism and the league system gave the game the appearance of a meritocracy. It could now claim to be – and more importantly, was perceived as being – a 'career open to talent', regardless of a player's social or educational background. Leagues also meant that teams could be assessed objectively by their playing record rather than their social status. Soccer had become a system of continuous competition, legal regulation and the supplanting of personal relationships by the exigencies of the commercial market. Rugby in the 1880s had no league structures, was governed largely by unelected elites, and amateurism allowed the RFU arbitrary control over the sport at home and abroad.

The increasing use of the term 'science' in soccer symbolically underlined the difference between its gentlemanly origins and its global future. It not only described the playing style of professional sides but also indicated the social stratum of the men who promoted professionalism and league football. William Sudell, the manager of Preston North End, was a factory manager and accountant. John Lewis, the founder of Blackburn Rovers, built coaches for railway engines. William MacGregor, the chairman of Aston Villa and the prime mover behind the creation of the Football League, was a shopkeeper. John Bentley, the secretary of Bolton Wanderers and president of the Football League, was a journalist.

These men saw themselves as bringing modern principles of science and technology to the way that football was organised, as much as they had done in their businesses. Their enthusiasm for cup and league competition reflected their belief that sport should be free from arbitrary social restrictions imposed from above.[29] This conception of sport as an expression of the modern industrial meritocratic world where advancement was based on talent and skill would be critical in making soccer so appealing beyond Britain and its empire.

This was very different from the beliefs of the privately educated men who still controlled rugby. Largely from the upper middle classes, they were members of professions such as medicine, the law, the church and the higher civil service. In the mid-nineteenth century this social layer consolidated their status and established legally recognised associations, such as the British Medical Association, which allowed them to regulate entry into their professions and exclude those they saw as undesirable. They believed in competition but only to the extent that it did not threaten their own position in the social hierarchy. Their imposition of amateurism in sport in the 1880s was an attempt to stem working-class encroachment on 'their' pastimes, and keep tight control of rugby.

The leaders of the RFU also had little interest in seeing rugby develop beyond the middle classes of the British Empire. Indeed, it was not until 1978 that France was admitted as a full member of the International Rugby

Board (IRB), the sport's world governing body. Even Australia, New Zealand and South Africa were not made full members of the IRB until 1948. Rugby was a symbol of Britishness almost everywhere it was played. And in the few places where it wasn't, it was played because of its relationship to the British. So, in France, it was the desire to emulate the success of the British Empire that led to rugby's adoption, and in Afrikaans-speaking white South Africa, it offered the opportunity to avenge the iniquities of the Boer War.

The men who led professional soccer were no less patriotic or parochial than the men who ran rugby or any other British sport. Football League president Charles Sutcliffe's declaration that 'I don't know the name of a club or a single individual on the continent', was typical of the game's lack of interest in anything beyond the immediate success of their highly successful domestic league.[30] The English national side did not play against a non-British nation until 1908 and played just six more similar matches before World War One.[31] Moreover, the booming success of English and Scottish soccer meant that soccer's leaders were largely indifferent to the international expansion of their game and therefore uninterested in the formation of FIFA.

But there was one major difference between soccer and rugby. The leaders of British soccer no longer had arbitrary or unconditional control of the game. Its transformation by professionalism laid the basis for it to become independent from its British administrators. Professionalism necessitated an external, objective set of rules for the governance of the game. British soccer was still led by the same people, but professionalism eroded their direct control over the game. Soccer was no longer based on social status and networks, but ultimately controlled by rules that were independent of whoever led the sport. Unlike rugby, there was now no inherent reason why soccer could not be led by those who owed no allegiance to Britain or the British Empire. Soccer's relationship to Britain had become a conditional one.

FIFA and soccer beyond Britain

Thus the men representing the seven European soccer nations who met in Paris in May 1904 to establish the Fédération Internationale de Football Association (FIFA) did not need the imprimatur of British football for their legitimacy (although they did invite the British football associations to join it). Because soccer now existed independently of its British administrators, British officials could do nothing to prevent FIFA's formation even if they had wanted to. As FIFA's founding president Robert Guérin explained, the European footballers simply ignored the British and took matters into their own hands: 'Tiring of the struggle [with the FA], and recognising that the Englishmen, true to tradition, wanted to watch and wait, I undertook to unite delegates from various nations myself'.[32]

Men like Guérin had fallen in love with soccer not simply for what it is, but also for what it represented. In Europe, the decade before World War One saw soccer become identified with a new sense of cosmopolitan modernity, that feeling that the world was entering a new era of speed, technology and urban life that was unlike anything experienced before. This link between football and modernity was expressed by modernist works of art such as Kasimir Malevich's *Painterly Realism of A Football Player. Colour Masses in the Fourth Dimension* (1915), Robert Delaunay's *Football* (1917), Picasso's *Footballers on the Beach* (1928), Willi Baumeister's *Fussballspieler* (1929) and Christopher Nevinson's *Any Wintry Afternoon in England* (1930). In the hands of these and other artists, soccer became a symbol of a rapidly changing world, in which new and exciting opportunities were opening up, not least for the liberal middle classes. The cosmopolitan, liberal ideals of the early pioneers of international soccer can be seen in FIFA's self-consciously universalist philosophy. As Jules Rimet, FIFA president from 1921 to 1954, would later write, they believed that football 'draws men together and makes them equal'.[33]

The meritocratic culture of soccer also undermined the appeal of ama-teurism. Although most of soccer's early national federations paid lip-service to the principle of amateurism, their practice differed qualitatively from its British adherents. Unlike in Britain, where amateurs refused to allow leagues because they saw them as a step towards professionalism, league tournaments were quickly set up in every country where soccer was established. Moreo-ver, British professional clubs regularly toured Europe and Latin America in the decade or so before World War One, attracting huge crowds and helping to popularise soccer beyond its original elite and middle-class constituency. For the growing number of clubs that competed at the highest levels of these new leagues, professional British managers became essential in their quest for success. Scottish international Jake Madden coached Slavia Praha from 1905, Bolton's Jimmy Hogan was appointed manager of the Nether-lands in 1910 and Arsenal's Willie Garbutt was appointed coach of Genoa in 1912. Such was the importance of these British coaches to the development of the sport that the English word 'Mister' became the informal term for the team coach in Italy, Portugal and Spain.[34]

Even then European soccer's definition of amateurism differed mark-edly from the British. Most federations allowed 'broken-time' compensa-tion to be paid to players who lost wages to play the game, precisely the issue over which English rugby had split bitterly in 1895. This version of amateurism, upheld by many European sports associations at that time, was not viewed as true amateurism by its British sports administrators, as the FA noted in 1923.

> Practices which are forbidden to English amateur clubs and players are permitted by some continental nations, and the effect is that English amateur teams meet opponents which, while regarded as amateurs in their respective countries, would be classed as professionals if under English jurisdiction.[35]

There was widespread suspicion in Britain that the Olympic Games were not a truly amateur venture, and this distrust helped stimulate the creation of the British Empire Games in 1930.[36] Indeed, the British football associations' opposition to broken-time payments being classed as amateurism was the ostensible reason for their resignation from FIFA for a second time in 1928.

Amateurism still retained its attraction for some members of the European middle classes who saw football as a social recreation for well-to-do young men. In 1913 the Dutch football federation, the NVB, turned down a motion from clubs that believed that the social status of teams should not play role in the organisation of tournaments, and the NVB ensured that Dutch soccer remained a formally amateur sport until 1954.[37] The desire to preserve soccer's respectability, especially in countries where its rivals were strong – such as rugby in France and Argentina, or the *Turnverein* and similar gymnastics movements in Germany and central Europe – was also a factor in the attachment to amateurism of some football federations. In Germany, the official acceptance of professionalism did not take place until 1963, although it was an open secret that players had received monetary and other benefits since the 1920s. Indeed, professionalism might have emerged in Germany in the 1930s but for Hitler's coming to power in 1933 that saw the Nazi regime impose a strict amateur code on all sports.[38]

But in general, as soccer became a commercial mass spectator sport in Europe and Latin America, amateurism dissolved. Professionalism was allowed in Italian football in 1926 and in Argentina in 1931, although covert payments and the provision of easy jobs was commonplace long before this.[39] Uruguay followed suit in 1933. And even those national federations that remained nominally amateur did not carry out systematic campaigns against professionals in the same way as Anglo-Saxon amateur sports' administrators.[40] The elaborate systems of discipline and punishment that some British sports erected to defend amateur principles were not repeated outside of the British world. Conversely, where British amateur ideology remained strong, soccer struggled. In Canada, the grassroots popularity of soccer (and its ability to compete with football and hockey) was undermined by a split over whether to support the Amateur Athletic Union of Canada's draconian anti-professional regulations.[41]

The incompatibility of amateurism with soccer's growing popularity around the world eventually led to FIFA's decision to organise its own world cup in 1930. The amateurism of the Olympic Games, which in the 1920s was briefly the stage for soccer's most important international tournament, excluded a growing number of soccer-playing nations that had embraced professionalism, leading FIFA secretary Henri Delauney to declare in 1926 that 'today international football can no longer be held within the confines of the Olympics'.[42] This final break with amateurism meant that soccer could now become the modern game for the modern world.

Notes

1 Jules Rimet, *Le football et le rapprochement des peuples* (Genève: Éditions René Kister, 1954), p. 47.

2 Match report in *The Rio News*, 2 August 1898, p. 7, available at https://archive. org/stream/1898therionews31/189808-Vol.24N.312agoTheRioNews#page/ n5/mode/2up.

3 For an excellent summary of the expansion of soccer, see Matthew Taylor, 'The Global Spread of Football', in Robert Edelman and Wayne Wilson (eds) *The Oxford Handbook of Sports History* (New York: Oxford University Press, 2017), pp. 183–95.

4 For English language histories of football in Argentina, see Tony Mason, *Passion of the People* (London: Verso, 1995), Jonathan Wilson, *Angels With Dirty Faces: The Footballing History of Argentina* (London: Orion, 2016) and Raanan Rein, *Fútbol, Jews and the Making of Argentina* (Stanford: Stanford University Press, 2015).

5 The first football established in Bolivia was set up for its workers by the Antofagasta & Bolivia Railway Company, while Uruguay's Penarol began life as the football section of the Central Uruguay Railway Cricket Club.

6 For line-ups, see www.11v11.com.

7 Paulo Fontes and Bernardo Borges Buarque de Hollando (eds), *The Country of Football: Politics, Popular Culture and the Beautiful Game in Brazil* (London: C Hurst & Co., 2014), pp. 18 and 23–5.

8 For the origins of Brazilian rugby, see Victor Sá Ramalho Antonio, *Passe para trás! Os primeiros anos do rúgbi em São Paulo (1891–1933)* (Masters thesis, University of São Paulo, 2017).

9 For a similar thesis, see Matthew Brown, 'The British Informal Empire and the Origins of Association Football in South America', *Soccer & Society,* vol. 16, nos. 2–3 (2015), 169–82, and his *From Frontiers to Football, An Alternative History of Latin America Since 1800* (London: Reaction, 2014). For a complementary viewpoint, see Brenda Elsey, *Citizens and Sportsmen: Futbol and Politics in Twentieth-century Chile* (Austin: University of Texas Press, 2011).

10 Mason, *Passion of the People*, pp. 10–13.

11 The greatest modern example of this is Eduardo Galeano's *Soccer in Sun and Shadow* (London: Verso, 1998).

12 For an outline of the expansion of soccer beyond Britain, see, Christiane Eisenberg, Pierre Lanfranchi, Tony Mason and Alfred Wahl, *One Hundred Years of Football* (London: Weidenfield & Nicholson, 2004), ch. 2 and 3.

13 Bill Murray, *Football: A History of the World Game* (Aldershot: Scolar Press, 1994), pp. 68–9.

14 P. Lanfranchi, T. Mason, C. Eisenberg and A. Wahl, *100 Years of Football* (London: Weidenfeld & Nicolson, 2004), p. 49.

15 Ulrich Hesse-Lichtenberger, *Tor! The Story of German Football* (London: WSC, 2003), p. 23.

16 Kay Schiller and Chris Young, 'The History and Historiography of Sport in Germany: Social, Cultural and Political Perspectives', *German History*, vol. 27, no. 3 (2009), p. 321.

17 'For a broader discussion of this, see Eisenberg's '"Not Cricket!": Sport in Germany, or How the British Model Fell into Oblivion', in Arnd Bauerkamper and Christiane Eisenberg (eds) *Britain as a Model of Modern Society? German Views* (Augsburg: Wissner-Verlag, 2006), pp. 242–56.

18 Andrew McFarland, 'Founders, Foundations and Early Identities: Football's Early Growth in Barcelona', *Soccer & Society*, vol. 14, no. 1 (2013), pp. 93–107.

19 Taylor, 'The Global Spread of Football', p. 187. Matthew Brown, 'British Informal Empire and the Origins of Association Football in South America', *Soccer and Society*, vol. 16, nos. 2–3 (2015), p. 177.

20 David Goldblatt, *Futebol Nation: A Footballing History of Brazil* (Harmondsworth: Penguin, 2014), pp. 8–10.

21 Heikki Lempa, *Beyond the Gymnasium: Educating the Middle-class Bodies in Classical Germany* (Lexington, 2007), pp. 67–111. Gertrud Pfister, 'Colonialism and the Enactment of German National Identity', *Journal of Sport History*, vol. 33, no. 1 (2006), pp. 59–83.

22 See his 'Exporting Football: Notes on the Development of Football in Europe', in Richard Giulianotti and John Williams (eds) *Game Without Frontiers: Football, Identity and Modernity* (Aldershot: Arena, 1994), pp. 23–45.

23 Gregg Bocketti, *Invention of the Beautiful Game: Football and the Making of Modern Brazil* (Gainesville: University Press of Florida, 2016), pp. 75–6. Brenda Elsey, *Citizens and Sportsmen: Futbol and Politics in Twentieth-century Chile*, p. 27.

24 David Goldblatt, *The Ball is Round* (London, Viking, 2006), p. 178. See also Graham Curry and Eric Dunning, *Association Football: A Study in Figurational Sociology* (Abingdon: Routledge, 2015), p. 188.

25 See 'The Aesthetics of Sport: Responses to Hans Ulrich Gumbrecht's "In Praise of Beauty"', a special issue of *Sport in History*, vol. 28, no. 1 (2008).

26 Montague Shearman, *Athletics and Football* (London: Longmans, Green, 1887), p. 260.

27 Quoted in Goldblatt, p. 188.

28 *Lancet*, 24 March 1894, p. 765 & 16 November 1907, p. 1402.

29 For a comprehensive examination of the backgrounds of soccer's early administrators, see Simon Inglis, *League Football and the Men Who Made It* (London: Harper Collins Willow, 1988).

30 *Topical Times*, 2 July 1927, quoted in Matthew Taylor, 'Football's Engineers? British Football Coaches, Migration and Intercultural Transfer, c.1910–c.1950s', *Sport in History*, vol. 30, no. 1 (March 2010), p. 161.

31 The seven matches were against Austria, Hungary and Bohemia. This position runs counter to that in Stefan Szymanski and Andrew Zimbalist's *National Pastime: How Americans Play Baseball and the Rest of the World Plays Soccer* (Washington: Brookings Institute, 2005), pp. 52–4.

32 Quoted in Pierre Lanfranchi, Christiane Eisenberg, Tony Mason and Alfred Wahl, *100 Years of Football: The FIFA Centennial Book* (London: Weidenfeld & Nicolson, 2004), p. 99.

33 Rimet, *Le football et le rapprochement des peuples,* p. 47.

34 Pierre Lanfranchi, 'Mister Garbutt: The First European Manager', *The Sports Historian*, vol. 22, no. 1 (2002), pp. 44–59.

35 *Football Association Statement on the British Olympic Committee*, 27 April 1923, National Football Museum, Manchester. See also Matthew Taylor, *The Association Game: A History of British Football* (London: Pearson, 2008), p. 163.

36 Daniel Gorman, 'Amateurism, Imperialism, Internationalism and the First British Empire Games', *International Journal of the History of Sport*, vol. 27, no. 4 (2010), pp. 611–34.

37 Nicholas Piercey, *Four Early Histories About Dutch Football 1910–20* (London: UCL Press, 2016), p. 48 and pp. 121–2.

38 Hesse-Lichtenberger, *Tor! The Story of German Football*, pp. 46–8.

39 John Foot, *Calcio: A History of Italian Football* (London: Fourth Estate, 2010), p. 36. Joel Horowitz, 'Soccer Clubs and Civic Associations in the Political World of Buenos Aires Prior to 1943', *Soccer & Society*, vol. 18, nos. 2–3 (2017), p. 274.

40 Joel Horowitz, 'Soccer Clubs and Civic Associations in the Political World of Buenos Aires Prior to 1943', 270–85. Nicholas Piercey, *Four Early Histories About Dutch Football 1910–20*, pp. 121–2. Ulrich Hesse-Lichtenberger, *Tor! The Story of German Football* (London: WSC, 2003), pp. 46–8.

41 See Alan Metcalfe, *Canada Learns to Play: The Emergence of Organised Sport 1807–1914* (Toronto: McLelland & Stewart, 1987), pp. 78–80.

42 Quoted in Tony Mason, *Passion of the People: Football in Latin America* (London: Verso, 1995), p. 38.

21

THE GLOBAL GAME

> By it [soccer] the mark of England may well remain in the world when the rest of her influence has vanished.
>
> —A.J.P. Taylor, 1965[1]

In February 1868, the Football Association held its annual meeting at the Freemason's Tavern in London. Only four delegates turned up and of the twenty-eight clubs in membership, only six had paid their annual membership fee. Two months later, in Shibden, an industrial West Yorkshire village between Halifax and Bradford, John Sutcliffe was born to a working-class family. At the age of 18 he made his debut as a centre-three-quarter for Bradford FC, one of England's leading rugby clubs. In February 1889, he played for England against the Native New Zealand tourists, the first football side of any code to tour Britain.

Six months later he was investigated by the rugby union authorities about his transfer from Bradford to the nearby Heckmondwike club. They found him guilty of violating rugby's amateur rules by receiving ten shillings per match. Unwilling to submit to the sentence of suspension that was handed down, Sutcliffe switched codes and signed for Bolton Wanderers to play as a goalkeeper. Less than four years later, he made his debut for the England soccer side. The following year he made the first of four appearances in an FA Cup Final in a career that would see him play for five other clubs, including a stint as captain of Manchester United. When he retired from playing in 1914, he moved to Europe to coach the Dutch side Vitesse

Arnhem, a member of the first wave of British soccer coaches that would transform the continental game.[2]

Sutcliffe died at the age of 79 in 1947, having lived a life that reflected football's journey since the 1860s. He was born into a world where there were fewer than a hundred football clubs in Britain, started his playing career when rugby was the dominant football code, fell victim to the RFU's amateur purge that destroyed rugby's leadership of the football codes, and switched to soccer at precisely the point that it was becoming the most popular sport the world had ever seen. He then moved to the Netherlands just as the game was on the cusp of seizing hold of the imaginations of millions of Europeans.

Football, like the railway, the mass media and the modern city, was one of the most successful products of the great expansion of industrial capitalism in the second half of the nineteenth century. Sutcliffe began life in a village that specialised in woollen production and, like millions of others, would find his way to a major city in search of work as the factory era superseded small-scale manufacture. His skills as a footballer would make him a celebrity thanks to the popular press's obsession with the game, and then soccer's increasing international popularity would enable him to work in Europe.

In the course of his life, the tiny football world of 1868 had fragmented into seven different codes, soccer had gone from having no national cup competitions to staging a regular world cup, and there were now more nation-states playing the game then there had been local clubs in existence when Sutcliffe was born. In the course of one man's lifetime, football had expanded from a recreational interest of a handful of young middle-class British men to become the passion of millions of men and women across the entire planet. Yet, of all the sets of rules created to provide a satisfying way to propel a ball towards a goal, only one would become a truly global game.

This would have come as a surprise to the young Sutcliffe and his contemporaries. When he made his debut for the England rugby side in 1889, the dominant international code was rugby. It was played across the colonial-settler states of the British Empire, and its variants were established winter sports in Australia, Canada and the United States. Governing bodies existed wherever rugby was played, each of which was either affiliated to the English RFU or accepted its authority. Tours by representative national rugby sides had begun to take place in the 1880s, making it a vehicle for expressing national pride. In 1882 a team representing New South Wales toured New Zealand, thus initiating one of sport's oldest international rivalries. In 1888 an unofficial British side undertook an epic tour of Australia and New Zealand, and later that year the predominantly Maori Native

New Zealand team – against whom Sutcliffe would make his international debut – embarked on an even more extensive tour of the British Isles. At the same time, discussions began about a British rugby tour to South Africa, which eventually took place in 1891. The following year regular visits by British sides to the fledgling rugby clubs of France started. Rugby union's international footprint had been largely established by 1895.

In contrast, international soccer beyond England and Scotland was still in its embryonic stages. In Ireland and Wales, soccer played second fiddle to rugby, and would only begin to challenge its popularity until the 1900s. Outside of the British Isles, only Denmark and the Netherlands had created national governing bodies for soccer before 1890, and its regional organisations remained weak and lacked authority. FIFA was founded by just seven nations in 1904. But by the eve of World War One, the game had advanced so rapidly in Europe that men like Sutcliffe could be handsomely rewarded for coaching local teams. And within the next decade the unprecedented popularity that the game had experienced in England and Scotland would be replicated across Europe and Latin America.

Much of soccer's growth in the decade after 1914 was due to the tumultuous social impact of World War One. The war introduced the game to millions of young men in the military across Europe. The new, mass war of the trenches meant that in between intense periods of unimaginable carnage soldiers had considerable time on their hands, and the military authorities quickly realised that soccer helped to fill up time while also maintaining fitness. Moreover, by organising teams as part of the existing military structures, regimental, national and other loyalties could be strengthened.[3] Initial fears that soccer would be a distraction to the troops or, on the home front, would undermine recruitment soon passed, and by the end of the war most of the major belligerents had organised soccer tournaments behind their front lines.[4] Those who had played or watched the sport while on military service more often than not returned home with a passion for the game.

That enthusiasm was often complemented by a new post-war sense of national identity. The old world had been destroyed by war and revolutions that swept across Europe from 1917. From the ashes of Tsarism and the Austro-Hungarian Empire, new nation-states emerged across Central and Eastern Europe. For mass-circulation daily newspapers and new media technology like radio, football offered a simple and understandable way of creating a patriotism that they hoped could unite classes, an important asset for the rulers of countries confronted by the threat of class struggle inspired by the Bolshevik revolution in Russia. It was therefore no accident that Austria, Hungary, Czechoslovakia and Yugoslavia, all former components of the Hapsburg Empire, were among the nations at the heart of European soccer in the inter-war years, playing prominent roles in establishing international competitions such as the Mitropa Cup and the Central European Cup for national sides.[5] Mussolini's fascist regime, and later Hitler's, also recognised the importance of soccer in building national unity, and government backing for the sport was a major reason for Italy's dominance of the World Cup in the 1930s. A similar pattern could be seen under Brazil's Vargas government in 1930s and Juan Peron's Argentina in the 1940s and 1950s. Especially for right-wing authoritarian regimes, soccer became an important part of nation-building among the masses.

Yet, despite the use of the game by nationalist and fascist governments in the inter-war years, soccer had also emerged from World War One as a symbol of peace. The image of informal kickabouts between British and German troops in No Man's Land during the unofficial truces of Christmas 1914 had a deep resonance among the war-weary European masses. Its message of international fraternisation – heartily endorsed by Bolshevik leader V.I. Lenin – stood in sharp contrast to the militarism of other codes such as rugby union or American football.[6]

Although these trench matches broke out spontaneously and had nothing to do with organised soccer, they became part of FIFA's promotion of its game as a universalist and cosmopolitan sport. Five weeks before the outbreak of World War One, FIFA's annual congress had pledged to 'support any action aiming to bring nations closer to each other and to substitute arbitration for violence in the settlement of any conflicts which might arise between them'. In 1929 Jules Rimet praised the game as an alternative to war, arguing that soccer turned war-like emotions 'into peaceful jousting in stadiums where their original violence is subject to the discipline of the game, fair and honest, where the benefits of victory are limited to the exhilaration of winning'. Indeed, Rimet would refer to FIFA as a more successful version of the League of Nations.[7] Once again, this sharply conflicted with prevailing attitudes to sport in Britain, whose soccer organisations left FIFA in 1920 in protest against matches with sides from central European nations defeated in World War One.[8] To underline the extent to which soccer was now far beyond the control of its inventors, the British absence had no impact whatsoever on the growth of either the game or FIFA.

Soccer's rise to globalism was not, as it might seem from the perspective of today, inevitable or automatic. Its ascension to become the world's most popular sport was not an unimpeded arc of progress. Its success was based on the defeat of its rugby rival and the eclipse of its British leaders by European and South American administrators – and neither would have been possible without soccer's adoption of professionalism in 1885. This provided the basis for the meritocratic and modern outlook that would free the sport from the suffocating grip of British Muscular Christianity and abandon the Anglo-Saxon attitudes upon which soccer had been founded. Indeed, soccer's increasing popularity across the globe grew in an inverse ratio to the declining influence of the British Empire, especially in the second half of the twentieth century, leading to A.J.P Taylor, among others, suggesting that soccer might well come to be viewed as Britain's most enduring cultural legacy.

To explain soccer's expansion around the world as a manifestation of its cosmopolitan, meritocratic ideology is also to understand why other football codes could not match its global reach. Rugby union, as we have seen, was too closely associated with British, Muscular Christian nationalism to appeal to the non-Anglophone world, with the partial exception of a France seeking a model after its defeat in the 1870 Franco-Prussian war and the spectre of the 1871 Paris Commune. Wherever rugby threatened to become a commercial mass spectator sport, the RFU used its amateur ideology to block its development into a modern game. Rugby league had little international presence beyond the industrial working-class rugby players of England, Australia and New Zealand. And of the nationally named rugby derivatives in America, Australia, Canada and Ireland, only the Irish game developed anything of an international profile due to its cultural importance for the Irish diaspora. The much later attempts by America's NFL to establish its own European league between 1991 and 2007 failed because it was ultimately unable to offer meaningful cultural resonance beyond its own aficionados, while the Canadian Football League's expansion into the United States in the 1990s foundered on the very fact that it was Canadian and could not provide an outlet for the American nationalism that college and NFL football prided themselves on. No football code other than soccer has qualitatively expanded beyond its 1914 national boundaries. And soccer still continues to increase in popularity. Today FIFA claims, with little reason to doubt it, that one in every twenty-five people on the planet plays soccer in some form.

There is no record that John Sutcliffe was ever asked what he thought about the dramatic changes to football that had taken place during the course of his life, or whether he could have imagined what soccer would become. If he had, one likes to think that as a plain-speaking son of the Victorian industrial working class, he would have perhaps anticipated the words of another son of the industrial proletariat who would be born into the football cauldron of twentieth-century Glasgow a few years before Sutcliffe died:

'Football. Bloody Hell!'[9]

Notes

1 A.J.P. Taylor, *English History 1914–1945* (Harmondsworth: Penguin, 1975), p. 274.
2 *Yorkshire Post*, 20 and 28 September 1889.
3 See, for example, Tony Mason and Eliza Reidi, *Sport and the Military* (Cambridge: Cambridge University Press, 2010).
4 See, for example, Arnaud Waquet and Thierry Terret, 'Ballons ronds, Tommies et tranchées: l'impact de la présence britannique dans la diffusion du football-association au sein des villes de garnison de la Somme et du Pas-de-Calais (1915–1918)', *Modern & Contemporary France*, vol. 14, no. 4 (2006), pp. 449–64, and Arnaud Waquet and Joris Vincent, 'Wartime Rugby and Football: Sports Elites, French Military Teams and International Meets During the First World War', *International Journal of the History of Sport*, vol. 28, nos. 3–4 (2011), pp. 372–92.
5 Matthias Marschik, 'Between Manipulation and Resistance: Viennese Football in the Nazi Era', *Journal of Contemporary History*, vol. 34, no. 2 (1999), pp. 215–29.
6 V.I. Lenin, 'The Slogan of Civil War Illustrated', *Collected Works, vol. 21* (Moscow: Progress Publishers, 1974), pp. 181–2.
7 Quoted in Paul Dietschy, 'Did a "Europe of Football" Exist in the 1930s?' *Sport in History,* vol. 35, no. 4 (2015), p. 517.
8 Football Association, Minutes of the International Selection Committee, 22 April 1921, National Football Museum, Manchester. Paul Dietschy, 'Making Football Global? FIFA, Europe, and the Non-European Football World, 1912–74', *Journal of Global History*, vol. 8, no. 2 (2013), pp. 279–98.
9 The famous words of Manchester United manager Alex Ferguson after his side won the 1999 European Champions League final with two goals in the final two minutes against Bayern Munich.

BIBLIOGRAPHY

Folk football

Books and theses

Birley, Derek, *Sport and the Making of Britain* (Manchester: Manchester University Press, 1993).

Carew, Richard, *Survey of Cornwall* (1710) (London: Faulder edition, 1811).

Falvey, Heather, *Custom, Resistance and Politics: Local Experiences of Improvement in Early Modern England* (unpublished PhD thesis, University of Warwick, 2007).

Hornby, Hugh, *Uppies and Downies: The Extraordinary Football Games of Britain* (London: English Heritage, 2008).

Malcolmson, Robert, *Popular Recreations in English Society 1700–1850* (Oxford: Oxford University Press, 1973).

Moor, Edward, *Suffolk Words and Phrases: or, An Attempt to Collect the Lingual Localisms of that County* (London: Woodbridge, 1823).

Robertson, John D. M., *The Kirkwall Ba'. Between the Water and the Wall* (Edinburgh: Dunedin Academic Press, 2005).

Strutt, Joseph, *The Sports and Pastimes of the People of England* (1801) (London: Methuen edition, 1903).

Articles and book chapters

Dymond, David, 'A Lost Social Institution: The Camping Close', *Rural History*, vol. 1, no. 2 (October 1990).

Magoun, Francis P., 'Football in Medieval England and in Middle-English Literature', *American Historical Review*, vol. 35, no. 1 (October 1929).

Thompson, E. P., 'The Moral Economy of the English Crowd in the Eighteenth Century', *Past & Present*, vol. 50, no. 1 (1971).

Newspapers and magazines

Bolton Chronicle.
Daily Journal.
Leicester Chronicle.
Mist's Weekly Journal.
Nottingham Review.
Severall Proceedings in Parliament.

Association football

Books and theses

Alcock, C.W. (ed.), *John Lilywhite's Football Annual* (London: Lilywhite, 1868).

Alcock, C.W., *Football: The Association Game* (London: George Bell, 1906).

Bennett, Arnold, *The Card* (London: Methuen, 1911).

Bilsborough, Peter, *The Development of Sport in Glasgow, 1850–1914* (MLitt thesis, University of Glasgow, 1983).

Bocketti, Gregg, *Invention of the Beautiful Game: Football and the Making of Modern Brazil* (Gainesville: University Press of Florida, 2016).

Booth, Keith, *The Father of Modern Sport: The Life and Times of Charles W. Alcock* (Manchester: Parrs Wood Press, 2002).

Brown, Matthew, *From Frontiers to Football, An Alternative History of Latin America since 1800* (London: Reaction, 2014).

Brown, Tony, *The Football Association 1863–83: A Source Book* (Nottingham: Soccerdata, 2011).

Budd, Catherine, *Sport in Urban England: Middlesbrough, 1870–1914* (Lanham, MD: Lexington, 2017).

Carter, Neil, *The Football Manager* (Abingdon: Routledge, 2006).

Curry, Graham and Dunning, Eric, *Association Football: A Study in Figurational Sociology* (Abingdon: Routledge, 2015).

Dawes, Andrew, *The Development of Football in Nottinghamshire c.1860–1915* (PhD thesis, De Montfort University, 2017).

Eisenberg, Christiane, Lanfranchi, Pierre, Mason, Tony and Wahl, Alfred, *One Hundred Years of Football* (London: Weidenfeld & Nicolson, 2004).

Elsey, Brenda, *Citizens and Sportsmen: Futbol and Politics in Twentieth-century Chile* (Austin: University of Texas Press, 2011).

Fontes, Paulo, de Hollando, Buarque and Borges, Bernardo, Bernardo (eds), *The Country of Football: Politics, Popular Culture and the Beautiful Game in Brazil* (London: C. Hurst & Co., 2014).

Foot, John, *Calcio: A History of Italian Football* (London: Fourth Estate, 2010).

Galeano, Eduardo, *Soccer in Sun and Shadow* (London: Verso, 1998).

Goldblatt, David, *The Ball is Round* (London, Viking, 2006).

Goldblatt, David, *Futebol Nation: A Footballing History of Brazil* (Harmondsworth: Penguin, 2014).

Goulstone, John, *Football's Secret History* (Catford: 3–2 Books, 2001).

Harvey, Adrian, *Football: The First Hundred Years* (Abingdon: Routledge, 2006).

Hesse-Lichtenberger, Ulrich, *Tor! The Story of German Football* (London: WSC, 2003).

Inglis, Simon, *League Football and the Men Who Made It* (London: Harper Collins Willow, 1988).

Lee, James F., *The Lady Footballers: Struggling to Play in Victorian Britain* (Abingdon: Routledge, 2008).

Lempa, Heikki, *Beyond the Gymnasium: Educating the Middle-class Bodies in Classical Germany* (Lanham, MD: Lexington, 2007).

Macbeth, Jessica, *Women's Football in Scotland: An Interpretive Analysis* (PhD thesis, University of Stirling, 2004).

Martin, Simon, *Sport Italia: The Italian Love Affair with Sport* (London: I.B. Taurus, 2011).

Mason, Tony, *Association Football and English Society 1863–1915* (Brighton: Harvester, 1981).

Mason, Tony, *Passion of the People* (London: Verso, 1995).

Mason, Tony and Riedi, Eliza, *Sport and the Military* (Cambridge: Cambridge University Press, 2010).

McDowell, Matthew L., *A Cultural History of Football in Scotland* (New York: Edwin Mellen Press, 2013).

Melling, Alethea, *"Ladies' Football": Gender and the Socialization of Women Football Players in Lancashire 1916–1960* (PhD thesis, University of Central Lancashire, 2000).

Mitchell, Andy, *First Elevens: The Birth of International Football* (Edinburgh: CreateSpace, 2012).

Murphy, Brendan, *From Sheffield With Love* (Sheffield: Sports Books, 2007).

Murray, Bill, *The Old Firm* (Edinburgh: John Donald Publishers, 1984).

Murray, Bill, *Football: A History of the World Game* (Aldershot: Scolar Press, 1994).

Piercey, Nicholas, *Four Early Histories About Dutch Football 1910–20* (London: UCL Press, 2016).

Rein, Raanan, *Fútbol, Jews and the Making of Argentina* (Stanford: Stanford University Press, 2015).

Rimet, Jules, *Le football et le rapprochement des peuples* (Genève: Éditions René Kister, 1954).

The Rules of Association Football 1863 (Oxford: Bodleian Library, 2006).

Russell, Dave, *Football and the English* (Preston: Carnegie, 1997).

Sanders, Richard, *Beastly Fury: The Strange Birth of British Football* (London: Bantam, 2010).

Steen, Rob, *Floodlights and Touchlines: A History of Spectator Sport* (London: Bloomsbury, 2014).

Sutcliffe, C.E. and Hargreaves, F., *History of the Lancashire Football Association 1878–1928* (Blackburn: Toulmin & Sons, 1928).

Szymanski, Stefan and Zimbalist, Andrew, *National Pastime: How Americans Play Baseball and the Rest of the World Plays Soccer* (Washington: Brookings Institution, 2005).

Taylor, Matthew, *The Leaguers: The Making of Professional Football in England, 1900–1939* (Liverpool: Liverpool University Press, 2005).

Taylor, Matthew, *The Association Game: A History of British Football* (London: Pearson, 2008).

Tischler, Stephen, *Footballers and Businessmen: The Origins of Professional Soccer in England* (New York: Holmes & Meier, 1981).

Walvin, James, *The People's Game: The History of Football Revisited* (Edinburgh: Mainstream, 2000).

Williams, Jean, *A Game for Rough Girls?* (London: Routledge, 2003).

Wilson, Jonathan, *Angels With Dirty Faces: The Footballing History of Argentina* (London: Orion, 2016).

Articles and book chapters

Brown, Matthew, 'The British Informal Empire and the Origins of Association Football in South America', *Soccer & Society*, vol. 16, no. 2–3 (2015).

Connell, R. M., 'The Association Game in Scotland', *The Book of Football* (London: Amalgamated Press, 1906).

Cooke, Martyn Dean and James, Gary, 'Myths, Truths and Pioneers: The Early Development of Association Football in the Potteries', *Soccer and Society*, vol. 19, no. 1 (2018).

Curry, Graham, 'The Trinity Connection: An Analysis of the Role of Members of Cambridge University in the Development of Football in the Mid-Nineteenth Century', *The Sports Historian*, vol. 22, no. 2 (2002).

Curry, Graham, 'The Contribution of John Dyer Cartwright to the Football Rules Debate', *Soccer and Society*, vol. 4, no. 1 (2003).

Curry, Graham, 'The Origins of Football Debate: Comments on Adrian Harvey's Historiography', *International Journal of the History of Sport*, vol. 31, no. 17 (2014).

Curry, Graham and Eric Dunning, Eric, 'The "origins of football debate" and the Early Development of the Game in Nottinghamshire', *Soccer and Society*, vol. 18, no. 7 (2015).

Dietschy, Paul, 'Making Football Global? FIFA, Europe, and the Non-European Football World, 1912–74', *Journal of Global History*, vol. 8, no. 2 (2013).

Dietschy, Paul, 'Did a "Europe of Football" Exist in the 1930s?' *Sport in History*, vol. 35, no. 4 (2015).

Eisenberg, Christiane, '"Not Cricket!": Sport in Germany, or How the British Model Fell into Oblivion', in Arnd Bauerkamper and Christiane Eisenberg (eds) *Britain as a Model of Modern Society? German Views* (Augsburg: Wissner-Verlag, 2006).

Gorman, Daniel, 'Amateurism, Imperialism, Internationalism and the First British Empire Games', *International Journal of the History of Sport*, vol. 27, no. 4 (2010).

Graham, R.H., 'The Early History of the Football Association', *Badminton Magazine*, vol. 8 (1899).

Harvey, Adrian and Swain, Peter, 'On Bosworth Field or the Playing Fields of Eton and Rugby? Who Really Invented Modern Football?' *International Journal of the History of Sport*, vol. 29, no. 10 (2012).

Hay, Roy, Harvey, Adrian and Smith, Mel, 'Football Before Codification: The Problems of Myopia', *Soccer & Society*, vol. 16, no. 2–3 (2015).

Holt, Richard, 'Football and the Urban Way of Life in Nineteenth-century Britain', in J.A. Mangan (ed.) *Pleasure, Profit and Proselytism: British Culture and Sport at Home and Abroad 1700–1914* (London: Frank Cass, 1988).

Horowitz, Joel, 'Soccer Clubs and Civic Associations in the Political World of Buenos Aires Prior to 1943', *Soccer & Society*, vol. 18, no. 2 3 (2017).

Kitching, Gavin, 'The Origins of Football: History, Ideology and the Making of "The People's Game"', *History Workshop Journal*, vol. 79, no. 1 (2015).

Lanfranchi, Pierre, 'Exporting Football: Notes on the Development of Football in Europe', in Richard Giulianotti and John Williams (eds) *Game Without Frontiers: Football, Identity and Modernity* (Aldershot: Arena, 1994).

Lanfranchi, Pierre, 'Mister Garbutt: The First European Manager', *The Sports Historian*, vol. 22, no. 1 (2002).

Lewis, Robert, '"Our Lady Specialists at Pikes Lane": Female Spectators in Early English Professional Football, 1880–1914', *International Journal of the History of Sport*, vol. 26, no. 15 (2009).

Marschik, Matthias, 'Between Manipulation and Resistance: Viennese Football in the Nazi Era', *Journal of Contemporary History*, vol. 34, no. 2 (1999).

McFarland, Andrew, 'Founders, Foundations and Early Identities: Football's Early Growth in Barcelona', *Soccer & Society*, vol. 14, no. 1 (2013).

Michallat, Wendy, 'Terrain de lutte: Women's Football and Feminism in "Les anneés folles"', *French Cultural Studies*, vol. 18, no. 3 (2007).

Pfister, Gertrud, 'Colonialism and the Enactment of German National Identity', *Journal of Sport History*, vol. 33, no. 1 (2006).

Porter, Dilwyn, 'Revenge of the Crouch End Vampires: The AFA, the FA and English Football's "Great Split", 1907–1914', *Sport in History*, vol. 26, no. 3 (2006).

Russell, Dave, 'From Evil to Expedient: The Legalization of Professionalism in English Football, 1884–85', in Stephen Wagg (ed.) *Myths and Milestones in the History of Sport* (Basingstoke: Palgrave, 2011).

Schiller, Kay and Young, Chris, 'The History and Historiography of Sport in Germany: Social, Cultural and Political Perspectives', *German History*, vol. 27, no. 3 (2009).

Swain, Peter, 'The Origins of Football Debate: Football and Cultural Continuity, 1857–1859', *International Journal of the History of Sport*, vol. 35, no. 5 (2015).

Taylor, Matthew, 'Football's Engineers? British Football Coaches, Migration and Intercultural Transfer, c.1910–c.1950s', *Sport in History*, vol. 30, no. 1 (2010).

Taylor, Matthew, 'The Global Spread of Football', in Robert Edelman and Wayne Wilson (eds) *The Oxford Handbook of Sports History* (New York: Oxford University Press, 2017).

Waquet, Arnaud and Terret, Thierry, 'Ballons ronds, Tommies et tranchées: l'impact de la présence britannique dans la diffusion du football-association au sein des villes de garnison de la Somme et du Pas-de-Calais (1915–1918)', *Modern & Contemporary France*, vol. 14, no. 4 (2006).

Waquet, Arnaud and Vincent, Joris, 'Wartime Rugby and Football: Sports Elites, French Military Teams and International Meets during the First World War', *International Journal of the History of Sport*, vol. 28, no. 3–4 (2011).

Newspapers and magazines

Athletic News.
Bath Chronicle.
Blackburn Standard.
Bell's Life in London.
Football Field.
The Goal.
Lancashire Daily Post.
Maidenhead Advertiser.
Morning Post.
North-Eastern Daily Gazette.
Nottingham Daily Express.
Nottinghamshire Guardian.
Preston Guardian.
Rio News.
Saturday Night [Birmingham].
Sheffield & Rotherham Independent.
Sporting Gazette.
Sporting Life.
The Times.

Websites

www.scottishsporthistory.com.
www.donmouth.co.uk/womens_football/womens_football.html.

Archival sources

Football Association minute books, National Football Museum.
Moses Heap, *My Life & Times*, typescript in Rawtenstall Library, RC942 ROS.
Sheffield FC, Minutes and list of members, letterbooks, results and misc papers, Sheffield City Archives.

Rugby Union

Books and theses

Bodis, Jean-Pierre, *Histoire mondiale du rugby* (Toulouse: Bibliothèque historique Privat, 1987).

Bodis, Jean-Pierre, *Le rugby d'Irlande: Identité, territorialité* (Bordeaux: Maison des sciences de l'Homme d'Aquitaine, 1993).

Collins, Tony, *Rugby's Great Split* (London: Frank Cass, 1998).

Collins, Tony, *A Social History of English Rugby Union* (Abingdon: Routledge, 2009).

Collins, Tony, *The Oval World: A Global History of Rugby* (London: Bloomsbury, 2015).

Darbon, Sébastien, *Une brève histoire du rugby* (Paris: Editions Jean-Claude Béhar, 2007).

Dine, Philip, *French Rugby Football: A Cultural History* (Oxford: Berg, 2001).

Dunning, Eric and Sheard, Kenneth, *Barbarians, Gentlemen and Players* (Abingdon: Routledge, 2005, Second Edition).

Football Rules (Rugby School, 1845).

Grundlingh, Albert, *Potent Pastimes: Sport and Leisure Practices in Modern Afrikaner History* (Pretoria: Protea Book House, 2015).

Grundlingh, Albert, Odendaal, Andre and Spies, Burridge (eds), *Beyond the Tryline: Rugby and South African Society* (Randburg: Ravan Press, 1995).

Hickie, Thomas V., *They Ran With The Ball: How Rugby Football Began in Australia* (Melbourne: Longman Cheshire, 1993).

Macrory, Jennifer, *Running With the Ball* (London: Collins, 1991).

Marshall, Rev. Frank (ed.), *Football: The Rugby Union Game* (London: Cassell, 1892).

O'Callaghan, Liam, *Rugby in Munster* (Cork: Cork University Press, 2011).

Owen, O.L., *The History of the Rugby Football Union* (London: Welbecson Press, 1955).

Philips, R.J., *The Story of Scottish Rugby* (Edinburgh: Foulis, 1925).

Prescott, Gwyn, *The Birth of Rugby in Cardiff and Wales: 'This Rugby Spellbound People'* (Cardiff: Ashley Drake Publishing Ltd, 2011).

Richards, Huw, *A Game for Hooligans: The History of Rugby Union* (Edinburgh: Mainstream, 2011).

Royds, Percy, *The History of the Laws of Rugby Football* (Twickenham: Rugby Football Union, 1949).

Ryan, Greg (ed.), *Tackling Rugby Myths* (Dunedin: Otago University Press, 2005).

Ryan, Greg, *The Contest for Rugby Supremacy: Accounting for the 1905 All Blacks* (Christchurch: Canterbury University Press, 2005).

Sá Ramalho Antonio, Victor, *Passe para trás! Os primeiros anos do rúgbi em São Paulo (1891–1933)* (Masters thesis, University of Sao Paulo, 2017).

Smith, David and Williams, Gareth, *Fields of Praise: The Official History of the Welsh Rugby Union 1881–1981* (Cardiff: University of Wales Press, 1980).

Titley, U.A. and McWhirter, R., *Centenary History of the Rugby Football Union* (London: Rugby Football Union, 1970).

Turley, Alan, *Rugby – The Pioneer Years* (Auckland: Harper Collins, 2009).

Williams, Gareth, *1905 and All That* (Llandysul: Gomer, 1991).

Wood, Desmond, *New Zealand Rugby Country* (Auckland: Bateman, 2017).

Articles and book chapters

Almond, H.H., 'Athletics and Education', *Macmillan's Magazine*, vol. 43 (November 1880–April 1881).

An Old Player, 'The Rugby Union Game', in *The Football Annual 1888–89* (London: George Bell & Sons, 1890).

Baker, William, 'William Webb Ellis and the Origins of Rugby Football', *Albion*, vol. 13, no. 2 (1981).

Budd, Arthur, 'The Rugby Union Game', in *The Football Annual* (London: Lilywhite, 1886).

Collins, Tony, 'English Rugby Union and the First World War', *The Historical Journal*, vol. 45, no. 4 (2002).

Cox, Barbara, 'The Rise and Fall of "The Girl Footballer" in New Zealand in 1921', *International Journal of the History of Sport*, vol. 29, no. 3 (2012).

Curtin, Jennifer, 'More than Male-Gazing: Reflections of Female Fans of Rugby Union in New Zealand, 1870–1920', *International Journal of the History of Sport*, vol. 32, no. 18 (2015).

Curtin, Jennifer, 'Before the "Black Ferns": Tracing the Beginnings of Women's Rugby in New Zealand', *International Journal of the History of Sport*, vol. 33, no. 17 (2016).

Free Critic, 'The Past and the Future', *Athletic News Football Annual, 1892–93* (Manchester: Athletic News, 1892).

Mitchell, Frank, 'A Crisis in Rugby Football', *St James's Gazette*, 24 September 1897.

Ryan, Greg, 'Brawn against Brains: Australia, New Zealand and the American "Football Crisis"', 1906–13', *Sporting Traditions*, vol. 20, no. 2 (2004).

Newspapers and magazines

The Athlete.
Cardiff Times.
Clarion.
The Field.
The Lantern (St Helens).
Leeds Mercury.
Manchester Guardian.
The New Rugbeian.
Otago Daily Times.
The Sportsman.
Yorkshire Evening Post.
Yorkshire Post.
The Yorkshireman.

Archival sources

Australian Rugby Union archives, Sydney.
RFU committee minutes, World Rugby Museum, Twickenham.

Australian Rules

Books and theses

Blainey, Geoffrey, *A Game of Our Own: The Origins of Australian Football* (Melbourne: Information Australia, 1990).
Broome, Richard, *Aboriginal Victorians: A History Since 1800* (Sydney: Allen & Unwin, 2005).
Cashman, Richard, O'Hara, John and Honey, Andrew (eds), *Sport, Federation, Nation* (Sydney: Walla Walla Press, 2001).
Davidson, Graham, *The Rise and Fall of Marvellous Melbourne* (Melbourne: Melbourne University Press, 1978).
Dawson, James, *Australian Aborigines: The Language and Customs of Several Tribes of Aborigines in the Western District of Victoria, Australia* (Melbourne: George Robertson, 1881).
de Moore, Gregory, *Tom Wills: His Spectacular Rise and Tragic Fall* (Sydney: Allen & Unwin, 2008).
Frost, Lionel, *Australian Cities in Comparative View* (Melbourne: Penguin, 1990).
Harrison, H.C.A., *The Story of An Athlete* (Melbourne: Alexander McCubbin, 1924).
Hess, Rob and Bob Stewart, Bob (eds), *More Than a Game: An Unauthorised History of Australian Rules Football* (Carlton: Melbourne University Press, 1998).
Hogan, Tim, *Reading the Game: An Annotated Guide to the Literature and Films of Australian Rules Football* (Melbourne: Australian Society for Sports History, 2005).
McDevitt, Patrick F., *'May the Best Man Win' Sport, Masculinity and Nationalism in Great Britain and the Empire, 1880–1935* (Basingstoke: Palgrave Macmillan, 2004).
Mullen, C.C., *History of Australian Rules Football From 1858 to 1958* (Carlton: Horticultural Press, 1958).
Pascoe, Rob, *The Winter Game* (Melbourne: Text Publishing, 1996).
Power, Thomas P. (ed.), *The Footballer* (Melbourne: Henriques & Co., 1877).
Read, Peter, *Charles Perkins, A Biography* (Melbourne: Penguin, 2001).
Sandercock, Leonie and Turner, Ian, *Up Where Cazaly? The great Australian Game* (Sydney: Granada, 1981).
Slattery, Geoff (ed.), *The Australian Game of Football* (Melbourne: Australian Football League, 2008).
Williamson, John, *Football's Forgotten Tour* (Perth: Applecross, 2003).

Articles and book chapters

'Bramham College Football Rules, October 1864', *The Bramham College Magazine* (November 1864).
Burke, Peter, 'Harry and the Galahs', *ASSH Bulletin*, no. 29 (1998).

Burke, Peter, 'Patriot Games: Women's Football During the First World War in Australia', *Football Studies*, vol. 8, no. 2 (2005).

Collins, Tony, 'National Myths, Imperial Pasts and the Origins of Australian Rules Football', in Stephen Wagg (ed.) *Myths and Milestones in Sports History* (Basingstoke: Palgrave Macmillan, 2011).

Collins, Tony, 'The Invention of Sporting Tradition: National Myths, Imperial Pasts and the Origins of Australian Rules Football', in Stephen Wagg (ed.) *Myths and Milestones in the History of Sport* (Basingstoke: Palgrave Macmillan, 2011).

Flanagan, Martin, 'Football Ebbs and Flow with Tide of Society', *The Age* (Melbourne), 9 August 2008.

Grow, Robin, 'From Gum Trees to Goal Posts, 1858–76', in Rob Hess and Bob Stewart (eds) *More Than A Game* (Carlton: Melbourne University Press, 1998).

Hess, Rob, 'Playing with "Patriotic Fire": Women and Football in the Antipodes During the Great War', *International Journal of the History of Sport*, vol. 28, no. 10 (2011).

Hess, Rob, 'Missing in Action? New Perspectives on the Origins and Diffusion of Women's Football in Australia during the Great War', *International Journal of the History of Sport*, vol. 31, no. 18 (2014).

Hess, Rob, Hogan, Tim, Nicholson, Matthew, Wedgewood, Nikki and Ian, Warren, 'Women and Australian Rules Football: An Annotated Bibliography', *Football Studies*, vol. 8, no. 2 (2005).

Hibbins, Gillian, 'The Cambridge Connection: The English Origins of Australian Rules Football', in J.A. Mangan (ed.) *The Cultural Bond* (London: Frank Cass 1993).

Mandle, W.F., 'Games People Played: Cricket and Football in England and Victoria in the Late-nineteenth Century', *Historical Studies*, vol. 15, no. 60 (1973).

McConville, Chris and Hess, Rob, 'Forging Imperial and Australasian Identities: Australian Rules Football in New Zealand During the Nineteenth Century', *International Journal of the History of Sport*, vol. 29, no. 17 (2012).

O'Dwyer, Barry, 'The Shaping of Victorian Rules Football', *Victorian Historical Journal*, vol. 60, no. 1 (1992).

Pill, Shane and Frost, Lionel, 'R.E.N. Twopeny and the Establishment of Australian Football in Adelaide', *International Journal of the History of Sport*, vol. 33, no. 8 (2016).

Syson, Ian, 'The "Chimera" of Origins: Association Football in Australia before 1880', *International Journal of the History of Sport*, vol. 30, no. 5 (2013).

Newspapers and magazines

The Age.
The Argus.
The Australasian.
Australia Junior.
Bell's Life in Victoria.
Sydney Mail.

Sydney Morning Herald.
The Tasmanian.

Gaelic football

Books and theses

Bracken, Patrick, *The Growth and Development of Sport in County Tipperary 1840–1880* (PhD Thesis, De Montfort University, 2014).

Corry, Eoghan, *The History of Gaelic Football* (Dublin: Gill & Macmillan, 2010).

Cronin, Mike, Murphy, William and Rouse, Paul (eds), *The Gaelic Athletic Association 1884–2009* (Dublin: Irish Academic Press, 2009).

Curran, Connor, *The Development of Sport in Donegal 1880–1935* (Cork: Cork University Press, 2015).

de Burca, Marcus, *The GAA: A History* (Dublin: GAA, 1980).

de Burca, Marcus, *Michael Cusack and the Gaelic Athletic Association* (Dublin: Anvil Books, 1989).

Fitzgerald, Dick, *How to Play Gaelic Football* (Cork: Guy & Co., 1914).

Garnham, Neal, *The Origins and Development of Football in Ireland* (Belfast: Ulster Historical Association, 1999).

Garnham, Neal, *Association Football and Society in Pre-Partition Ireland* (Belfast: Ulster Historical Association, 2004).

Grimes, Seamus and O Tuathaigh, Gearoid, *The Irish Australian Connection* (Galway: UC Galway, 1988).

Hunt, Tom, *Sport and Society in Victorian Ireland: The Case of Westmeath* (Cork: Cork University Press, 2007).

Kelly, James, *Sport in Ireland, 1600–1840* (Dublin: Four Courts Press, 2014).

Lennon, Joe, *The Playing Rules of Football and Hurling 1884–1995* (Gormanstown: Northern Recreation Consultants, 1997).

Mandle, William, *The Gaelic Athletic Association and Irish Nationalist Politics. 1884–1924* (London: Gill and Macmillan, 1987).

McElligott, Richard, *Forging a Kingdom: The GAA in Kerry 1884–1934* (Cork: Collins Press, 2013).

Rouse, Paul, *Sport and Ireland: A History* (Oxford: Oxford University Press, 2015).

Articles and book chapters

Bracken, Patrick, 'The Emergence of Hurling in Australia 1877–1917', *Sport in Society*, vol. 19, no. 1 (2016).

Connolly, John and Dolan, Paddy, 'The Amplification and De-Amplification of Amateurism and Professionalism in the Gaelic Athletic Association', *The International Journal of the History of Sport*, vol. 30, no. 8 (2013).

Cronin, Mike, 'Fighting for Ireland, Playing for England? The Nationalist history of the Gaelic Athletic Association and the English Influence on Irish Sport', *The International Journal of the History of Sport*, vol. 15, no. 3 (1998).

Gleason, A.B., 'Hurling in Medieval Ireland', in Mike Cronin, William Murphy and Paul Rouse (eds) *The Gaelic Athletic Association 1884–2009* (Dublin: Irish Academic Press, 2009).

Hassan, David, 'The Gaelic Athletic Association, Rule 21, and Police Reform in Northern Ireland', *Journal of Sport & Social Issues*, vol. 29, no. 1 (2005).

Kinsella, Eoin, 'Riotous Proceedings and the Cricket of Savages: Football and Hurling in Early Modern Hurling Ireland', in Mike Cronin, William Murphy and Paul Rouse (eds) *The Gaelic Athletic Association 1884–2009* (Dublin: Irish Academic Press, 2009).

McAnallen, Donal, '"The Greatest Amateur Association in the World"? The GAA and Amateurism', in Mike Cronin, William Murphy and Paul Rouse (eds) *The Gaelic Athletic Association 1884–2009* (Dublin: Irish Academic Press, 2009).

Moore, Martin, 'The Origins of Association Football in Ireland, 1875–1880: A Reappraisal', *Sport in History*, vol. 37, no. 4 (2017).

Newspapers and magazines

Celtic Times.
Daily Journal.
Freeman's Journal.
Freeman's Journal (Sydney).
The Irishman.
London Gazette.
United Ireland.

American football

Books and theses

Baker, William, *Sports in the Western World* (Lanham, MD: Rowman & Littlefield, 1988).

Camp, Walter, *Walter Camp's Book of College Sports* (New York: The Century Company, 1893).

Camp, Walter, *Football Facts and Figures* (New York: Harper & Bros, 1894). Davis, Parke H., *Football: The American Intercollegiate Game* (New York: Charles Scribner, 1911).

Des Jardins, Julie, *Walter Camp: Football and the Modern Man* (New York: Oxford University Press, 2015).

Elliott Gorn, Elliot, *The Manly Art* (Cornell: Cornell University Press, 1986).

Gubi, Greg (ed.), *The Lost Century of American Football* (BookSurge Publishing, 2011).

Hodgson, Godfrey, *The Myth of American Exceptionalism* (Yale: Yale University Press, 2009).

Hutner, Gordon (ed.), *Selected Speeches and Writings of Theodore Roosevelt* (New York: Vintage 2014).

Ingrassia, Brian, *The Rise of the Gridiron University: Higher Education's Uneasy Alliance with Big-Time Football* (Kansas: University Press of Kansas, 2012).

Lipset, Seymour Martin, *American Exceptionalism: A Double-Edged Sword* (New York: W.W. Norton, 1998).

Lockhart, Charles, *The Roots of American Exceptionalism* (London: Palgrave, 2003).

Madsen, Deborah L., *American Exceptionalism* (Edinburgh: Edinburgh University Press, 1998).

Markovits, Andrei S. and Hellerman, Steven L., *Offside: Soccer and American. Exceptionalism* (Princeton: Princeton University Press, 2001).

Matthews, William, *Getting on in the World* (Toronto: S.C. Griggs, 1876).

Miller, John J., *The Big Scrum: How Teddy Roosevelt Saved Football* (New York: Harper Collins, 2011).

Nelson, David M., *The Anatomy of the Game: Football, the Rules and the Men Who Made the Game* (New Jersey: University of Delaware Press, 1994).

Oriard, Michael, *Reading Football: How the Popular Press Created an American Spectacle* (Chapel Hill: University of North Carolina Press, 1993).

Pease, Donald E., *The New American Exceptionalism* (Minnesota: University of Minnesota, 2009).

Peterson, Robert W., *Pigskin: The Early Years of Pro Football* (New York: Oxford University Press, 1997).

Shafer, Byron E. (ed.), *Is America Different?: A New Look at American Exceptionalism* (Oxford: Clarendon Press, 1991).

Smith, Ronald, *Sports and Freedom: The Rise of Big-Time College Athletics* (New York: Oxford University Press, 1991).

Umphett, Wiley Lee, *Creating the Big Game: John W. Heisman and the Invention of American Football* (Westport, CT: Greenwood, 1992).

Watterson, John Sayle, *College Football: History: Spectacle: Controversy* (Baltimore: Johns Hopkins University Press, 2003).

Yost, Fielding, *Football for Player and Spectator* (Ann Arbor: University Publishing, 1905).

Articles and book chapters

A Yale Player, 'The Development of Football', *Outing*, vol. 15, no. 2 (1889).

Bunk Brian D., 'The Rise and Fall of Professional Soccer in Holyoke Massachusetts, USA', *Sport in History*, vol. 31, no. 3 (2011).

Camp, Walter, 'The Game and Laws of American Football', *Outing*, October 1886.

Collins, Tony, 'Unexceptional Exceptionalism: The Transnational Origins of American Football', *Journal of Global History*, vol. 8, no. 2 (2013).

Guttmann, Allen, 'Civilized Mayhem: Origins and Early Development of American Football', *Sport in Society*, vol. 9, no. 4 (2006).

Henderson, W. J., 'College Football Twenty-Five Years Ago', *Outing*, vol. 37, no. 1 (October 1899).

Oriard, Michael, 'Rough, Manly Sport and the American Way: Theodore Roosevelt and College Football, 1905', in Stephen Wagg (ed.) *Myths and Milestones in the History of Sport* (London: Palgrave Macmillan, 2011).

Park, Roberta J., 'From Football to Rugby – and Back, 1906–1919: The University of California-Stanford University Response to the "Football Crisis of 1905"', *Journal of Sport History*, vol. 11, no. 3 (1984).

Park, Roberta J., 'Sport, Gender and Society in a Transatlantic Victorian Perspective', *The International Journal of the History of Sport*, vol. 24, no. 12 (2007).

Riesman, David and Denney, Reuel, 'Football in America: A Study in Cultural Diffusion', *American Quarterly*, vol. 3, no. 3 (1951).

Smith, Ronald, 'American Football Becomes the Dominant Intercollegiate National Pastime', *International Journal of the History of Sport*, vol. 31, no. 1–2 (2014).

Walter Camp, 'Football in America', *Frank Leslie's Popular Monthly*, vol. 57, no. 1 (1898).

Walter Camp, 'Rugby Football in America', *Outing Magazine*, vol. 57 (March 1911).

Watterson, John Sayle, 'The Gridiron Crisis of 1905: Was It Really a Crisis?', *Journal of Sports History*, vol. 27, no. 2 (2000).

Newspapers and magazines

American Monthly Review of Reviews.
Boston Daily Globe.
Harvard Advocate.
McClure's Magazine.
New York World.
New York Times.
Outing.
The Outlook.
San Francisco Call.

Websites

Meacham, Scott, *Old Division Football, the Indigenous Mob Soccer of Dartmouth College*, Dartmo (2006), at www.dartmo.com/football.pdf (viewed 12 August 2017).

Scudder, Winthrop S., *An Historical Sketch of the Oneida Football Club of Boston, 1862–1865* (1926) at https://babel.hathitrust.org/cgi/pt?id=wu.89098742 257;view=1up;seq=3.

Archival sources

David Starr Jordan Collection, Reel 52, Frames 482–5, Stanford University Archives.

Harvard University, *Reports of the President and the Treasurer of Harvard College 1904–1905*.

James B. Angell Papers, Bentley Historical Library, University of Michigan.

Walter Chauncey Camp Papers, Manuscripts and Archives, Yale University Library.

Canadian football

Books and theses

Consentino, Frank, *Canadian Football: The Grey Cup Years* (Don Mills, ON: Musson Book Publishing, 1969).

Howell, Colin, *Blood, Sweat and Cheers: Sport and the Making of Modern Canada* (Toronto: University of Toronto Press, 2001).

Joyce, Charles Anthony, *From Left Field: Sport and Class in Toronto 1845–1886* (PhD Thesis, Queen's University, Kingston, ON, 1997).

Kidd, Bruce, *The Struggle for Canadian Sport* (Toronto: University of Toronto Press, 1996).

McNaught, Kenneth, *The Pelican History of Canada* (Harmondsworth: Penguin, 1969).

Metcalfe, Alan, *Canada Learns to Play: The Emergence of Organised Sport 1807–1914* (Toronto: McLelland & Stewart, 1987).

Sturrock, Doug, *It's A Try. The History of Rugby in Canada* (Langley, BC: Sturrock Consulting, 2016).

Articles and book chapters

Buckner, Philip, 'The Creation of the Dominion of Canada, 1860–1901', in Philip Buckner (ed.) *Canada and the British Empire* (Oxford: Oxford University Press, 2010).

Jones, Kevin G., 'Developments in Amateurism and Professionalism in Early 20th Century Canadian Sport', *Journal of Sport History*, vol. 2, no. 1 (1975).

Kingstone, A.C. and Boddy, C.A.S., 'The Characteristics of Canadian Football', *Outing*, vol. 27, no. 3 (1895).

MacKenzie, Robert Tait, 'Rugby Football in Canada', *The Dominion Illustrated Monthly*, vol. 1, no. 1 (1892).

Mason, Daniel S., 'The International Hockey League and the Professionalization of Ice Hockey, 1904–1907', *Journal of Sport History*, vol. 25, no. 1 (1998).

Orton, George W., 'Canadian and United States Rugby', *The Canadian Magazine*, vol. 10, no. 1 (1897).

Palmer, Bryan, 'In Street and Field and Hall: The Culture of Hamilton Working-men, 1860–1914', in *Marxism and Historical Practice*, vol. 2 (Leiden: Brill, 2015).

Speers, Ian, 'The Development of the American Scrimmage System', *The Coffin Corner*, vol. 24, no. 2 (2002).

Sproule, Robert, 'Snap-Back versus Scrimmage', *From Scrimmage to SnapBack: Journal of the Canadian Football Historical Association*, vol.1, no. 1 (2003).

Newspapers and magazines

The Canadian Magazine.
Century Magazine.
The Daily Colonist [Victoria, British Columbia].
Montreal Gazette.
Ottawa Citizen.
Toronto Daily Globe.
Town & Country [Toronto].
The Varsity [University of Toronto].

Rugby league

Books and theses

Bodman, Ryan, 'Rugby League and the New Zealand Trade Union Movement', *Labour History Project Bulletin*, vol. 64 (2015).

Collins, Tony, *Rugby League in Twentieth Century Britain* (Abingdon: Routledge, 2006).

Collins, Tony, *1895 and All That* (Leeds: Scratching Shed, 2009).

Dawson, Victoria S., *Women and Rugby League: Gender, Class and Community in the North of England, 1880–1970* (PhD thesis, De Montfort University, 2017).

Fagan, Sean, *Rugby Rebellion* (Sydney: Fagan, 2005).

Football Annual 1920 (Sydney: *The Referee* newspaper, 1920).

Greenwood, Bill, *Class, Conflict and the Clash of Codes: The Introduction of Rugby League to New Zealand, 1908–1920* (PhD thesis, Massey University, 2008).

Haynes, John, *From All Blacks to All Golds* (Christchurch: Ryan and Haynes, 1996).

Moore, Andrew, *The Mighty Bears! A Social History of North Sydney Rugby League* (Sydney: Macmillan, 1996).

O'Loghlen, J. F. (ed.), *Rugby League Annual & Souvenir 1928* (Sydney: NSWRFL, 1928).

Rylance, Mike, *The Forbidden Game* (Brighouse: League Publications, 1999).

Waring, Eddie, *England to Australia and New Zealand* (Leeds: County Press, 1947).

Articles and book chapters

Budd, Arthur, 'The Northern Union', in A. Budd, C.B. Fry, B.F. Robinson and T.A. Cook (eds), *Football* (London: Lawrence and Bullen, 1897).

Falcous, Mark, 'Rugby League in the National Imaginary of New Zealand Aotearoa', *Sport in History*, vol. 27, no. 3 (2007).

Fassolette, Robert, 'Rugby League Football in France 1934–54: The Decisive Years and their Long-term Consequences', *Sport in History*, vol. 27, no. 3 (2007).

Greenwood, Bill, '1908: The Year Rugby League Came to New Zealand', *Sport in History*, vol. 27, no. 3 (2007).

Haines, Katherine, 'The 1921 Peak and Turning Point in Women's Football History: An Australasian, Cross-Code Perspective', *International Journal of the History of Sport*, vol. 33, no. 8 (2016).

Little, Charles, '"What a Freak-Show They Made!": Women's Rugby League in 1920s Sydney', *Football Studies*, vol. 4, no. 2 (2000).

Moore, Andrew, 'Opera of the Proletariat: Rugby League, the Labour Movement and Working-Class Culture in New South Wales and Queensland', *Labour History*, vol. 79 (2000).

Newspapers and magazines

Hull Daily Mail.
Rugby League News (Sydney).
The Referee (Sydney).
Salford Reporter.
Toby, The Yorkshire Tyke.
Wigan Observer.
Yorkshire Owl.

Archival sources

JC Davis Collection, Mitchell Library, Sydney.
Rugby Football League Archives, Heritage Quay, University of Huddersfield.

General

Books and theses

Angus, J. Keith, *The Sportsman's Year Book* (London: Cassell, 1880).
Briggs, Asa, *Victorian Cities* (London: Odhams, 1964).
Collins, Tony, *Sport in Capitalist Society* (Abingdon: Routledge, 2013).
Collins, Tony and Vamplew, Wray, *Mud, Sweat and Beers: A Cultural History of Sport and Alcohol* (Oxford: Berg 2002).
Hobsbawm, E.J., *Industry and Empire* (London: Weidenfeld & Nicolson, 1968).
Hobsbawm, E.J., *Worlds of Labour* (London: Weidenfeld & Nicolson, 1984).
Hobsbawm, E.J., *The Age of Empire* (London: Weidenfeld & Nicolson, 1987).
Hobsbawm, E.J., *Nations and Nationalism Since 1870* (Cambridge: Cambridge University Press, 1990).
Hobsbawm, E.J. and Ranger, Terence (eds), *The Invention of Tradition* (Cambridge: Cambridge University Press, 1983).
Holt, Richard, *Sport and the British* (Oxford: Clarendon Press, 1989).
Light, Robert, *Cricket's Forgotten Past: A Social and Cultural History of the Game in the West Riding, 1820–70* (PhD thesis, De Montfort University, 2008).

Magee, Gary B. and Thompson, Andrew S., *Empire and Globalisation* (Cambridge: Cambridge University Press, 2010).

Martin-Jenkins, Christopher, *The Wisden Book of County Cricket* (London: Queen Anne Press, 1981).

Russell, Dave, *Popular Music in England, 1890–1914: A Social History* (Manchester: Manchester University Press, 1987).

Seymour, Harold, *Baseball: The Early Years* (New York: Oxford University Press, 1960).

Smith, Dennis, *Conflict and Compromise: Class Formation in English Society 1830–1914: A Comparative Study of Birmingham and Sheffield* (London: RKP, 1982).

Taylor, A.J.P., *English History 1914–1945* (Harmondsworth: Penguin, 1975).

Thompson, E.P., 'Time, Work-Discipline and Industrial Capitalism', in *Customs in Common* (Harmondsworth: Penguin, 1993).

Tranter, Neil, *Sport, Economy and Society in Britain 1750–1914* (Cambridge: Cambridge University Press, 1998).

Vamplew, Wray, *Pay Up and Play The Game* (Cambridge: Cambridge University Press, 1988).

Vlasich, James A., *A Legend for the Legendary: The Origin of the Baseball Hall of Fame* (Madison: University of Wisconsin Press, 1990).

Weber, A. F., *The Growth of Cities in the Nineteenth Century: A Study in Statistics* (London: Macmillan, 1899).

Williams, Graham, *The Code War* (Harefield: Yore Publications, 1994).

Articles and book chapters

Engels, Friedrich, 'May 4 in London', in Karl Marx and Frederick Engels, *Collected Works*, vol. 27, 61–6.

Gould, Stephen Jay, 'The Creation Myths of Cooperstown', in *Triumph and Tragedy in Mudville* (London: Jonatahn Cape, 2004).

Park, Jihang, 'Sport, Dress Reform and the Emancipation of Women in Victorian England: A Reappraisal', *International Journal of the History of Sport*, vol. 6, no. 1 (1989), 10–30.

Reid, D.A., 'The Decline of Saint Monday 1766–1876', *Past & Present*, vol. 71, no. 1 (1976), 76–101.

INDEX

Printed in Great Britain
by Amazon

15302586R00127